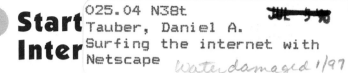

Start
Inter

1 Book 1 Disk

The Web is like thousands of TV channels, or 10,000 New York Public Libraries—it includes volumes and volumes of information. You can browse the Web, following links in an intuitive way, or you can search for what interests you. Here is a brief list of good starting places. Each of these documents lists or organizes other documents to make it easy for you to find your way to the documents you find intriguing or useful.

John December's list of Internet Resources

    http://www.rpi.edu/Internet/Guides/decemj/text.html

University of Illinois at Urbana-Champaign Index to Web Pages

    http://www.cen.uiuc.edu/~jj9544/index.html

The InterNIC (Network Information Center)

    http://www.internic.net/infoguide.html

The Virtual Reference Desk from UC Irvine

    gopher://peg.cwis.uci.edu:7000/11/gopher.welcome/peg/uci

The Clearinghouse for Subject-Oriented Internet Resource Guides

    http://http2.sils.umich.edu/~lou/chhome.html

Scott Yanoff's list of Internet Resources

    http://slacvx.slac.stanford.edu:/misc/
    internet-services.html

NCSA Mosaic World Wide Web Starting Points Document

    http://www.ncsa.uiuc.edu/SDG/Software/Mosaic/
    Starting-Points/NetworkStartingPoints.html

The NCSA Mosaic What's New Page

    http://www.ncsa.uiuc.edu/SDG/Software/Mosaic/Docs/
    whats-new.html

The Yahoo subject-oriented list of Internet Resources

    http://www.yahoo.com

FOR EVERY COMPUTER QUESTION,
THERE IS A SYBEX BOOK THAT HAS THE ANSWER

Each computer user learns in a different way. Some need thorough, methodical explanations, while others are too busy for details. At Sybex we bring nearly 20 years of experience to developing the book that's right for you. Whatever your needs, we can help you get the most from your software and hardware, at a pace that's comfortable for you.

We start beginners out right. You will learn by seeing and doing with our **Quick & Easy** series: friendly, colorful guidebooks with screen-by-screen illustrations. For hardware novices, the **Your First** series offers valuable purchasing advice and installation support.

Often recognized for excellence in national book reviews, our **Mastering** titles are designed for the intermediate to advanced user, without leaving the beginner behind. A **Mastering** book provides the most detailed reference available. Add our pocket-sized **Instant Reference** titles for a complete guidance system. Programmers will find that the new **Developer's Handbook** series provides a more advanced perspective on developing innovative and original code.

With the breathtaking advances common in computing today comes an ever increasing demand to remain technologically up-to-date. In many of our books, we provide the added value of software, on disks or CDs. Sybex remains your source for information on software development, operating systems, networking, and every kind of desktop application. We even have books for kids. Sybex can help smooth your travels on the **Internet** and provide **Strategies and Secrets** to your favorite computer games.

As you read this book, take note of its quality. Sybex publishes books written by experts—authors chosen for their extensive topical knowledge. In fact, many are professionals working in the computer software field. In addition, each manuscript is thoroughly reviewed by our technical, editorial, and production personnel for accuracy and ease-of-use before you ever see it—our guarantee that you'll buy a quality Sybex book every time.

To manage your hardware headaches and optimize your software potential, ask for a Sybex book.

FOR MORE INFORMATION, PLEASE CONTACT:

Sybex Inc.
2021 Challenger Drive
Alameda, CA 94501
Tel: (510) 523-8233 • (800) 227-2346
Fax: (510) 523-2373

SYBEX

Surfing the Internet with Netscape™

Daniel A. Tauber and Brenda Kienan

SYBEX®

San Francisco • Paris • Düsseldorf • Soest

Acquisitions Manager: Kristine Plachy
Editor: Neil Edde
Technical Editors: Samuel Faulkner and Fred Cooper
Chapter Artist: Lucka Zivny
Desktop Publisher: Thomas Goudie
Production Coordinator: Sarah Lemas
Indexer: Ted Laux
Cover Designer: Design Site
Cover Illustrator: Daniel Ziegler

SYBEX is a registered trademark of SYBEX Inc.

TRADEMARKS: SYBEX has attempted throughout this book to distinguish proprietary trademarks from descriptive terms by following the capitalization style used by the manufacturer.

Every effort has been made to supply complete and accurate information. However, SYBEX assumes no responsibility for its use, nor for any infringement of the intellectual property rights of third parties which would result from such use.

Photographs and illustrations used in this book have been downloaded from publicly accessible file archives and are used in this book for news reportage purposes only to demonstrate the variety of graphics resources available via electronic access. Text and images available over the Internet may be subject to copyright and other rights owned by third parties. Online availability of text and images does not imply that they may be reused without the permission of rights holders, although the Copyright Act does permit certain unauthorized reuse as fair use under 17 U.S.C. §107. Care should be taken to ensure that all necessary rights are cleared prior to reusing material distributed over the Internet. Information about reuse rights is available from the institutions who make their materials available over the Internet.

Library of Congress Card Number: 95-67726
ISBN: 0-7821-1740-6

Manufactured in the United States of America
10 9 8 7 6 5 4

Software Support

On the enclosed disk is a copy of NetManage's Chameleon Sampler software. This software and any offers associated with it are supported by NetManage, Inc. NetManage can be reached by calling (408) 973-7171.

Should the manufacturer cease to offer support or decline to honor the offer, SYBEX bears no responsibility.

Disk Warranty

SYBEX warrants the enclosed disk to be free of *physical defects* for a period of ninety (90) days after purchase. If you discover a defect in the disk during this warranty period, you can obtain a replacement disk at no charge by sending the defective disk, postage prepaid, with proof of purchase to:

SYBEX Inc.
Customer Service Department
2021 Challenger Drive
Alameda, CA 94501
(800) 227-2346
Fax: (510) 523-2373

After the 90-day period, you can obtain a replacement disk by sending us the defective disk, proof of purchase, and a check or money order for $10, payable to SYBEX.

Disclaimer

SYBEX makes no warranty or representation, either express or implied, with respect to this medium or its contents, its quality, performance, merchantability, or fitness for a particular purpose. In no event will SYBEX, its distributors, or dealers be liable for direct, indirect, special, incidental, or consequential damages arising out of the use of or inability to use the medium or its contents even if advised of the possibility of such damage.

The exclusion of implied warranties is not permitted by some states. Therefore, the above exclusion may not apply to you. This warranty provides you with specific legal rights; there may be other rights that you may have that vary from state to state.

Copy Protection

None of the programs on the disk is copy-protected. However, in all cases, reselling or making copies of these programs without authorization is expressly forbidden.

To L.E.M.—sister, mother, friend
and to her mother and family, with grateful thanks

Acknowledgements

The book you hold in your hands is actually the result of a collaborative effort; we are indebted to the many people who helped to make it happen.

At Sybex, our thanks go to Dr. R.S. Langer, who had the idea and brought this project to our attention; also to Neil Edde, who edited with a fine-tooth comb; and to Samuel Faulkner and Fred Cooper, who carefully checked all the URLs.

Special thanks to Sybex heroines Barbara Gordon, Chris Meredith, Kristine Plachy, Carrie Lavine, Janet Boone, and Celeste Grinage.

Thanks also to the multitalented Michael Gross, who researched and drafted Chapters 8 and 9 and Appendix A.

Many thanks are owed to the production team of Thomas Goudie and Sarah Lemas, who made this book a reality; to Lucka Zivny, who created the charming line drawings; to indexer Ted Laux, who compiled references with admirable compulsion; and to assistant editors Malcolm Faulds, Stephanie La Croix, and Emily Smith, without whom nothing would ever get into production.

Thanks to Bob Williams at NetManage for his permission to include Chameleon Sampler; and to Marc Andreessen, Jon Mittelhauser, and the folks at Netscape Communications for creating Netscape, a marvelous product. Thanks also to U.S. Robotics for the loan of high-speed modems.

Our gratitude goes as always to family and friends for their continued support and all the understanding they can muster. Special thanks to:

◆ Margaret Tauber, Ron and Frances Tauber, Jessica and Martin Grant, and the rest of the Tauber family; also to Gino Reynoso.

◆ Joani Buerhle, Sharon Crawford, Jerry Doty, Rion Dugan, Thaisa Frank, Fred Frumberg, Carol Heller, Karen Kevorkian, Xuan Mai Le, Kathleen Lattinville, the McArdle family, Amy Miller, Carolyn Miller, Lonnie Moseley, Mrs. W. Moseley and her family, Freeman Ng, Ron Nyren, Carol Piasanti, Cordell Sloan, John Undercoffer, Mary Undercoffer, the Undercoffer brothers, Savitha Varadan, Sally Borie Wilson, and Robert E. Williams III.

Contents at a Glance

Contents

Part Two: Navigating and Publishing with Netscape
51

Chapter 3:
Running Netscape
53

Chapter 4:

Good and Useful Starting Points

89

Chapter 5:
Spots on the Web You Won't Want to Miss

111

Chapter 6:

Tools and Techniques for Searching and Finding

151

Chapter 7:
You Too Can Be a Web Publisher

171

Part Three: Getting Started with Netscape
207

Chapter 8:
Laying the Groundwork for Installing Netscape

209

Chapter 9:
Getting Netscape Going

237

Chapter 10:
Getting and Installing Video Viewers and Sound Players

251

Appendix A:
What's on the Disk: The Chameleon Sampler

275

Appendix B:
Internet Service Providers

301

Glossary

307

Index

317

Introduction

Everybody wants to get in on the Internet. If you want to join the action but you don't want to learn Unix and type a lot of obscure commands to get anywhere, read on. This book, written in plain English and filled with how-to know-how, will get you started in no time exploring and using the World Wide Web, the fastest growing portion of the Internet, via Netscape. Netscape is the highly popular Web browser that includes security and other features you won't find in any other Web browser. This book covers both versions 1.0 and 1.1 of this powerful software; it also includes NetManage's Chameleon Sampler, a set of Internet tools that will get you on the Internet in no time.

Is This Book for You?

If you want to start exploring the beautiful, graphical World Wide Web using Netscape, this book is for you.

This book has been written by two Internauts with years of combined experience. It avoids jargon and explains any necessary terms clearly. It's a great place to start for beginners, but that's not all—because it includes complete information on publishing on the Internet and on getting and using special tools to enhance your Web experience, this book is a good follow-up for people who already are familiar with the Internet.

Getting and installing Netscape involves setting up an Internet connection that will "introduce" your Internet service provider to Netscape each and every time you access the Internet using Netscape. Setting up this connection can be tricky, but don't worry. This book provides you with the vital connecting software (known as SLIP/PPP) you need, and shows you clearly how to get Netscape from the Internet itself and how to set up a working, reliable connection.

What's on the Disk

On the disk that comes with this book you'll find Chameleon Sampler, a software package that includes:

◆ The vital connecting software (SLIP/PPP) you need to get Netscape and set up your Internet connection

◆ A powerful set of Internet tools (e-mail, FTP, and Ping) you can use everyday

All you need is a PC, a modem, Windows, and an account with an Internet service provider.

 Instructions for getting Netscape and setting up a connection are in Chapters 8 and 9; information on service providers is in Appendix B.

How This Book Is Organized

This book is organized into ten chapters, beginning, logically enough, with Chapter 1, a brief introduction to the Internet. Chapter 2 goes into more detail about the World Wide Web, and how Netscape can get you there. Chapter 3 tells you in basic terms how to use Netscape, Chapter 4 describes some good jumping off places for your Web travels, and Chapter 5 describes some good and useful places you might want to visit. With basic navigation skills under your belt, you might want to focus your Web travels, so Chapter 6 tells you how to use Netscape's search capabilities. Chapter 7 follows up by showing you how you, too, can be a Web publisher—it includes a primer on HTML, the mark-up language used to create Web documents, along with tips for successful Web page design and information on how to publicize your Web page. Chapter 8 shows you how to get Netscape from the Internet. Chapter 9 follows up by providing step-by- step instructions for setting up Netscape and making your connection. Chapter 10 tells you how to get and use sound and video "viewers"—special tools that will further enhance your experience of Netscape and the World Wide Web.

Internet and Web terms are defined throughout the book, but you might want to look something up as you go along, so toward the back of the book you'll find a handy Glossary. You'll also find two appendices: Appendix A describes the three Internet utilities that come with the Chameleon Sampler package—e-mail, FTP, and Ping; Appendix B is a listing of Internet service providers that will work with Netscape and Chameleon Sampler.

Conventions Used in This Book

Surfing the Internet with Netscape uses various conventions to help you find the information you need quickly and effortlessly. Tips, Notes, and Warnings, shown here, are placed strategically throughout the book, to help you hone in on important information in a snap.

Here you'll find insider tips and shortcuts—information meant to help you use Netscape (and Chameleon Sampler) more adeptly.

Here you'll find reminders, asides, and bits of important information that should be emphasized.

Here you'll find cautionary information describing trouble spots you may encounter either in using the software or in using the Internet.

A simple kind of shorthand used in this book helps to save space so more crucial matters can be discussed; in this system, directions to "pull down the File menu and select Save" will appear as "select File ➤ Save," and the phrase "press Enter" appears as "press ↵," for example—again, these conventions are described as they are introduced.

Long but important or interesting digressions are set aside as boxed text, called *sidebars*.

These Are Called "Sidebars"

In boxed text like this you'll find background information and side issues—anything that merits attention but that can be skipped in a pinch.

And throughout the book you'll find special "What's Out There" sidebars telling you exactly where on the World Wide Web you can find out more about whatever's being discussed, or where to find the home page being described.

What's Out There?

The URL for the home page of interest at the moment will appear in a different font, like `http://cuiwww.unige.ch/w3catalog`.

 # The Sybex Home Page

If you want to find out more about what Sybex has to offer in the way of Internet-related books, check out the Sybex home page at the URL:

`http://www.sybex.com.`

There you'll find access to an online version of the Sybex catalog, announcements of upcoming books, and information about special promotions.

Let's Get This Show on the Road...

Enough about what's in the book and on the disk—to start your Internet exploration using Netscape, turn to Chapter 1; to find out how to get and install the software, turn to Chapter 8.

If You Need Help

Technical Support for Chameleon Sampler is available from NetManage at (408) 973-7171. For answers to your questions about Netscape, call (800) NET-SITE or e-mail info@mcom.com.

Part One:

The Internet, the World Wide Web, and Netscape

The Big Picture

You'd have to live in a vacuum these days not to have heard of the Internet. Scarcely a day goes by without some mention of it on the nightly news or in the local paper. Internet e-mail addresses are even becoming common in advertisements. Millions of people—inspired by excited talk and armed with spanking new accounts with Internet service providers—are taking to the Internet, with visions of adventures on the "information superhighway."

Contrary to all the fashionable hype, the first time you attempt to "cruise" the Internet, you may be in for a rude awakening. Until recently, most access to the Internet was via text-based viewers that left a lot to be desired in the realm of aesthetics and ease of use. The Internet was trafficked for a long time only by academicians and almost nerdy computer enthusiasts.

In fact, with your old or low-budget Internet account a prompt that looks like this:

```
%
```

may be all you get, even if you're running the thing under Windows. Your trek into cyberspace may feel more like a bumpy ride on an old bicycle.

A Netscape View of the Internet

That's why Netscape is so great: It offers an elegant point-and-click interface to guide you through the Internet's coolest resources, all linked to a growing number of global Internet resources. Netscape is a *browser*—a program with which you can view graphically intriguing, linked documents all over the world and search and access information in a few quick mouse clicks. You don't have to type cryptic commands or deal with screens filled with plain text; all you have to do is point and click on highlighted words (or pictures) to follow the links between related information in a single, giant web of linked "pages." Figure 1.1 compares a text-based view of the Internet to a Netscape view.

Within the Internet is a special network of linked documents known as the World Wide Web. With Netscape, you can perform point-and-click online research on the Web or just follow your whims along an intuitive path of discovery. Netscape is available for all popular computers—PCs running Windows, Macintoshes, even Unix workstations. Netscape on any of these machines looks just about the same, too. (In this book, we focus mainly on Netscape for Windows, although many of the principles we discuss apply as well to the Unix and Mac versions.) There are some differences between using Netscape on a machine that's networked and a machine that stands alone, though.

To run Netscape on your stand-alone (un-networked) PC, you need a dial-up connection to the Internet via a service provider, and not just any service provider—you need one with specific capabilities. You also need software (known as SLIP or PPP) that provides a connection between Netscape and your Internet service provider. (Don't worry, this is not difficult.)

 On the disk included with this book you'll find Chameleon Sampler, software that provides a SLIP/PPP connection. Chapters 8 and 9 explain everything you need to know about how to put Chameleon Sampler together with Internet service to get Netscape from the Internet itself and then make it run.

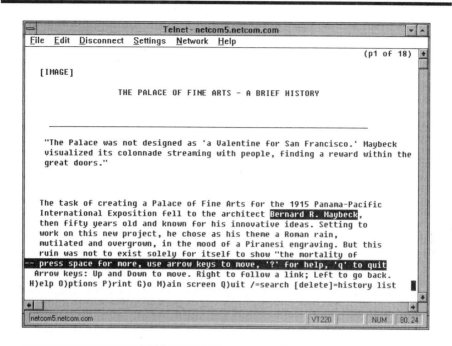

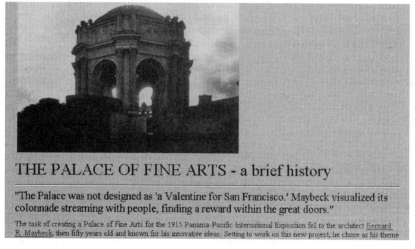

THE PALACE OF FINE ARTS - a brief history

"The Palace was not designed as 'a Valentine for San Francisco.' Maybeck visualized its colonnade streaming with people, finding a reward within the great doors."

The task of creating a Palace of Fine Arts for the 1915 Panama-Pacific International Exposition fell to the architect Bernard R. Maybeck, then fifty years old and known for his innovative ideas. Setting to work on this new project, he chose as his theme

FIGURE 1.1: Here you can see the difference between the old text-based view of the Internet (above) and the easy-to-use, graphically pleasing Netscape view of the Internet (below).

Let's take a quick look at the Internet first. Then, in the next chapter, we'll investigate how the Web fits into the Internet and just what kinds of stuff you can look at out there.

What's Out There?

As we go along, we're going to tell you what you can find using Netscape and where that stuff is located. You'll see notes like this describing an item of interest and giving you the item's *URL* (its *Uniform Resource Locator* or address on the Web). Don't worry if you don't understand this URL business yet—you will soon, and then you can look for the stuff we've described.

What the Internet Is All About

The Internet is a happening thing—interest in the Internet seems to have taken on the proportions of a new national pastime. And yet, when we're asked to define the Internet, many of us are at a loss for words. Even those who are intimately familiar with the "Net" are likely to disagree on a strict definition.

So what is this Internet thing we're hearing so much about? At its most basic level, you can think of the Internet as a vast collection of even vaster libraries of information, all available online for you to look at or retrieve and use. At another level, the Internet might be thought of as the computers that store the information and the networks that allow you to access the information on the computers. And finally (lest we forget who made the Internet what it is today), it is a collection of *people*—people who act as resources themselves, willing to share their knowledge with the world. This means, of course, that when you interact with the Internet—particularly when you make yourself a resource by sharing communications and information with others—you become a part of the vast network we call the Internet.

The idea of the "information superhighway," popularized in part by the Clinton administration, is a convenient metaphor: information flowing great distances at incredible speeds, with many on-ramps of access and many potential destinations. In the information superhighway of the future, we might expect an electronic replacement for the everyday postal system (this has already begun to happen in Germany, we're told), and integration of our TV, phone, and newspapers into online information and entertainment services.

We're not quite up to that fully integrated superhighway envisioned by futurists yet, but the Internet as it exists today delivers plenty of power. The resources and information you find on the Internet are available for use on the job, as part of personal or professional research, or for just plain fun. No matter how you view the Internet, the idea that individuals as well as corporations can access information around the world has a particular appeal that borders on the irresistible.

What's Out There?

The Electronic Frontier Foundation (EFF) is active in lobbying to ensure that the information superhighway of the future includes protections for individual rights. You can find out about the EFF, and what it is up to, with the URL http://www.eff.org. Other information about the government's initiative for building the information superhighway is available with the URL http://far.mit.edu/diig.html.

The Internet does act much like a highway system. There are high-speed data paths called *backbones* to connect the major networks; these actually do function much like an electronic version of the interstate highways. There are also lower-speed *links* through which local networks tie in to the Internet, much as city streets feed onto the highway (see Figure 1.2). The beauty of the Internet's system is that not all networks are, or even need to be, directly connected, because the Internet structure is one of *interconnection*. You can in effect hop from network to network to get where you want and what you want.

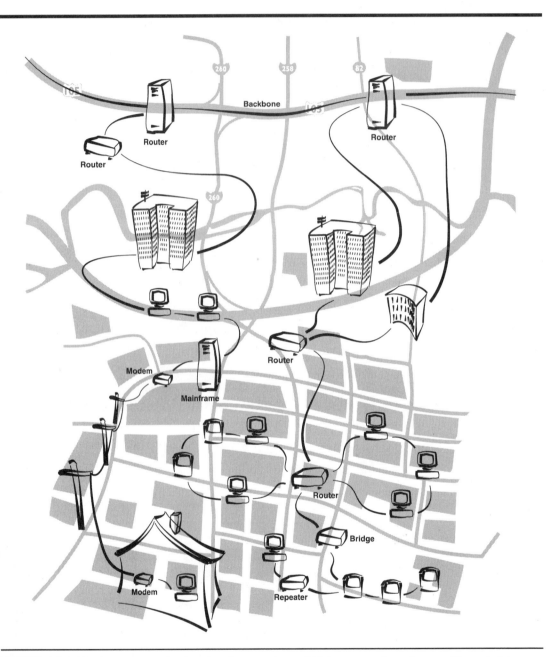

FIGURE 1.2: The Internet can be imagined as a system of highways and roadways, although it has no actual geography.

The highway metaphor begins to break down, however, when you realize that the Internet transcends geography. It's a global system, that's true, but when you use the Net you probably won't be very conscious that the material you're viewing on your screen at one moment is actually located on a machine in Switzerland, and what you see the next moment is actually on a machine in Japan. Perhaps a more accurate metaphor for the Internet would be having a global remote control at your fingertips, able to switch to just about any topic (channel if you prefer) of your choosing. And now, with user-friendly tools such as Netscape available, access is no longer limited to scholars and hackers.

Where It All Began

To understand how the Internet came into being, you'd have to go back 30 years or so, to the Cold War era. The think-tank military planners of that age were concerned not only with surviving a nuclear war, but also with communicating in its aftermath if one should occur. They envisioned a control network, linking bases and command posts from state to state, that would remain operational in spite of direct attacks. With this in mind, the U.S. Defense Department's Advanced Research Projects Agency began work on a computer network called ARPAnet during the 1960s.

The principles of the network were simple. It had to operate from the outset as if it were "unreliable"—to adjust up-front for the possibility of downed communication links. Control, therefore, would be decentralized to further minimize any single point of failure. Data would be split up and sent on the network in individual Internet Protocol (IP) *packets*. (A packet can be thought of as similar to an envelope.) Each packet of data would carry within it the address of its destination, and could reach its endpoint by the most efficient route. If part of the network became unavailable, the packets would still get to their destinations and would be reassembled with their full content intact.

Though at first this may sound inefficient, it put the burden of communicating on the computers themselves, rather than on the communications network. That was the foremost issue on the minds of the planners: that the system did not rely on a central *server* (a machine on the network that holds or processes data for the other machines on the network). This proposal linked the computers together as *peers* instead, giving each computer equal status on the network and allowing for different types of computers

to communicate, de-emphasizing the communications infrastructure. Thus, even if large pieces of the network were destroyed, the data itself could still reach its destination because it was not concerned with *how* to get there. So it was that the Department of Defense commissioned the initial implementation of ARPAnet in 1969.

Perhaps you work in a business where a lot of machines are cabled together as a LAN (local area network). Each of these networks is like a smaller version of the Internet, in that a bunch of machines are linked together; but they are not necessarily linked to other networks via phone lines. LANs also usually have a central server—a machine that holds data and processes communications between the linked machines, which is unlike the Internet in that if your LAN server goes down, your network goes down.

Throughout the '70s and early '80s, the ARPAnet continued to grow, and more developments occurred to spur interest in networking and the Internet. Other services and big networks came into being (such as Usenet and BITnet) and e-mail began to gain wide use as a communications tool. Local area networks (LANs) became increasingly common in business and academic use, until users no longer wanted to connect just select computers to the Internet but entire local networks (which might mean all the computers in the organization).

Today the original Internet, the ARPAnet, is no more, having been replaced in 1986 by a new backbone, the National Science Foundation (NSFnet) network. NSFnet forever changed the scope of the Internet in that it permitted more than just a few lucky people in the military, academia, and large corporations to conduct research and access supercomputer centers. With the good, however, came the bad as well. More people using the Internet meant more network traffic, which meant slower response, which meant better connectivity solutions would have to be implemented. Which brings us to where we are today, with demand increasing exponentially as more and more people want to connect to the Internet and discover the online riches of the '90s. (See Figure 1.3.)

Annual rate of growth for World-Wide Web traffic: 341, 634% (1st year)

◆

Annual rate of growth for Gopher traffic: 997%

◆

Number of countries reachable by electronic mail: 159 (approx.)
Number of countries not reachable by electronic mail: 77 (approx.)

◆

Average time, in minutes, during business hours, between registration of new domains: 2
Percentage increase in number of Internet hosts from October, 1994, to January 1995: 26
Percentage increase in number of registered domains from October, 1994, to January 1995: 28

◆

Estimated number of U.S. newspapers offering interactive access: 3,200

◆

Number of attendees at Internet World, December, 1994: over 10,000
Number of attendees at Internet World, January, 1992: 272

◆

Advertised network numbers in October, 1993: 16,533
Advertised network numbers in October, 1992: 7,505

◆

Date after which more than half the registered networks were commercial: August, 1991

◆

Number of financial service firms with registered domains: 398
Percentage increases in the number of financial service firms with registered domains
during 1994: 197

◆

Number of online coffeehouses in San Francisco: 18
Cost for four minutes of Internet time at those coffeehouses: $0.25

◆

Estimated number of Usenet sites, worldwide: 260,00
Estimated number of readers of the Usenet group
rec.humor.funny: 480,000

◆

Round-trip time from Digital CRL to mcmvax.mcmurdo.gov in McMurdo, Antarctica: 640
milliseconds

◆

Amount of time it takes for Supreme Court decisions to become available on the
Internet: less than one day

FIGURE 1.3:   These Internet statistics (courtesy of Win Treese) tell an amazing story.

● The Burning Questions of Control, Funding, and Use

As odd as it may sound, there is no one person with overall authority for running the Internet. In spite of this—or perhaps because of it—the Internet runs just fine. A group called the Internet Society (ISOC), composed of volunteers, directs the Internet. ISOC appoints a subcouncil, the Internet Architecture Board (IAB), and it is the members of this board who work out issues of standards, network resources, network addresses, and the like. Another volunteer group, the Internet Engineering Task Force (IETF), tackles the more day-to-day issues of Internet operations. These Internet caretakers, if you will, have proven quite ably that success does not have to depend on your typical top-down management approach.

Likewise, the Internet's funding system may seem odd. There is a common misconception that the Internet is by its very nature free, but this is certainly not the case. It costs a pretty penny to maintain a machine that can serve up stuff on the Internet, and someone has to pay those costs. Individual groups and institutions—such as the federal government (via the National Science Foundation), which runs NSFnet—do indeed pay to provide the information they serve on the Internet. At the other end, new users quickly find out that connecting to the Internet through a service provider (such as Netcom, CRL, or PSI) requires a monthly usage fee; and because it is necessary to connect through a phone line, telephone charges may also be involved. Meanwhile, in the middle, the service providers pay for leasing high-speed communication lines; they also pay to access the Commercial Internet Exchange, and they may even pay to access a regional Internet provider such as BARRNet. As you can see, the Internet is by no means free, although it is a great value.

The funding issue is directly tied to how the Internet can be used. Because NSFnet (like ARPAnet) is funded by the federal government, its use is controlled for education and research and does not really permit commercial activities. (Exact guidelines for use of NSFnet is outlined in a document called the Acceptable Use Policy (AUP), which is available—like most items these days—on the Internet.) The good news is that these restrictions are gradually being relaxed, and that with the addition of new networks such as the Commercial Internet Exchange (CIX), created specifically for commercial traffic, the Internet is experiencing a boom in use for the sake of business. The Internet, then, is becoming commercialized. To be sure, it is this entrepreneurial business spirit which is the driving force behind the expanding Internet today.

The basic concepts on which the Internet was founded have accounted for its ability to grow and handle more and more computers and users, which now happens on a daily basis. What started as a military experiment during the heyday of Cold War politics has turned into a world-wide resource, allowing millions of people to connect seamlessly to a far-flung web of computers and information. (See Figure 1.4). Who among the Internet's initial creators could have envisioned where we are today?

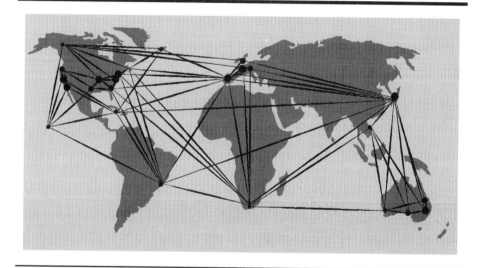

FIGURE 1.4:   The Internet is a global resource, with servers on every continent.

What You Can Do with the Internet

Once you are connected to the Internet, here are some of the things you can do:

◆ Send messages to friends and associates all over the world with *e-mail*. (Remarkably, this usually does not involve long-distance charges to you or the recipient; all you're charged for is the call to your Internet service provider and, if that's a local number, it's a *local call*.)

◆ Exchange ideas with other people in a public forum with *Usenet*. (Note that unlike e-mail, which is more or less private, Usenet is public. Everyone else using Usenet can read what you post there. Also, while Usenet is not actually part of the Internet, it is accessible through most Internet providers.)

◆ Copy files from and to computers on the Internet with *FTP*. Many giant software archives, such as the CICA Windows archive, hold literally gigabytes of files you can retrieve.

◆ Connect to other computers on the Internet with *telnet*. (In order to connect to another computer, you need permission to use the computer.)

◆ Traverse and search directories of information with *gopher*.

◆ Search far and near for information on the Internet with the services *Archie, Veronica,* and *Jughead.*

◆ View documents, browse, search for data, and traverse other resources on the Internet via the *World Wide Web.*

Many of these tools are used (either visibly or behind the scenes) in the course of using Netscape, so we'll talk about each one as it arises in later chapters.

What's Out There?

Netscape provides limited support for e-mail—you can send e-mail messages with Netscape and you can even include in your message the page you are currently viewing, but Netscape does not allow you to receive e-mail. More on this later....The Internet itself, however, provides a number of resources you can use via Netscape for finding people's e-mail addresses. You can look at the URL gopher://gopher.tc.umn.edu/11/Phone%20Books/other to search for people that have recently posted to Usenet. The URL gopher://gopher.tc.umn.edu/11/Phone%20Books includes links to many other databases of e-mail addresses.

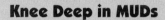

Knee Deep in MUDs

The Internet is not all business; games are a big part of what's going on. Multi-User Dungeons (MUDs) are popular these days—they're adventure games that started as Internet versions of the cult-classic Dungeons and Dragons. Some educational MUDs have also cropped up, but they all hold to the basic tenet of MUDs in that you interface with things in a world of fantasy. Unfortunately, you cannot access MUDs straight from Netscape …at least not yet.

The Internet as Medium

The Internet itself is just a medium. There's plenty of room to develop services to be used to make the most of the Internet, just as happened when the phone system was devised for simple communication and then many products and services were developed to take advantage of its potential (ranging from voicemail, pagers, and automated banking, to the 911 system and, in fact, the Internet).

The Internet's fundamental openness has been responsible for bringing forth a number of tools for use by the masses. A great example of this is, of course, Netscape. In the next chapter, we'll look at how you can access the best of the Internet—the World Wide Web—via Netscape.

Best of the Internet: The World Wide Web via Netscape

Before we leap head first into using Netscape, an appreciation of the World Wide Web is in order. Let's take a quick look at the Web, then we'll glance at a typical Netscape session and, still in this chapter, we'll talk more about what Netscape can do.

How the Web Came to Be

The World Wide Web (a.k.a. WWW, W3, or simply, *the Web*) was originally developed to help physicists at Conseil Européen pour la Recherche Nucleaire (CERN), which is the European particle physics laboratory in Geneva, Switzerland. CERN is one of the world's largest scientific labs, composed of two organizations straddling the Swiss-French border—the European Laboratory for High Energy Physics in Switzerland, and the Organisation Européen pour la Recherche Nucleaire in France. The physicists there needed a way to exchange data and research materials quickly with other scientists.

The Web technology developed at CERN by Tim Berners-Lee enabled collaboration among members of research teams scattered all over the globe. How? Through a system that allows for *hypertext* links between documents on different computers.

Unlike regular documents, with static information on every page, *hypertext* documents have links built in so that readers can jump to more information about a topic by (typically) simply clicking on the word or picture identifying the item. That's why they call it hypertext—it's not just text, it's *hyper*text. (The term hypertext was coined by computer iconoclast Ted Nelson.) Hypertext is what makes Netscape—and many multimedia tools—possible. The term *hypermedia* is sometimes used to refer to hypertext with the addition of other data formats. In addition to just text, Netscape supports graphics and, equipped with the proper external programs, can support sound and video as well.

Before going to CERN, Berners-Lee had worked on document production and text processing, and had developed for his own use a hypertext system—Enquire—in 1980. (According to some reports, he wasn't aware of the notion of hypertext at the time, but hypertext has been around since the Xanadu project in the 1960s.)

In 1992, the Web grew beyond the confines of the CERN's research community, and in just two years, its use and growth have been increasing exponentially. This was all part of the plan in a sense—the Web was meant to allow for open access—but it's hard to imagine that anyone could have expected the phenomenon that's occurred. Activity on the server at CERN doubles every four months, which is twice the rate of Internet expansion. At last count, it was estimated that there were over 2000 Web servers worldwide, although official counts are impossible to do, given the size of the Web and the magnitude of its expansion.

Protocols, HTTP, and Hypertext: What It All Means

The Web's rapid expansion can be attributed in part to its extensive use of hypertext, held together by the HyperText Transfer Protocol (HTTP). A *protocol* is an agreed upon system for passing information back and forth that allows the transaction to be efficient (HTTP is a *network protocol*, which means it's a protocol for use with networks).

On "Mosaic" and Netscape

Maybe you're a bit confused about all the different "Mosaics" and how Netscape fits into the Mosaic picture. The short version of this story is that Netscape is Mosaic-like, but it's not Mosaic…Well, not exactly.

The first version of Mosaic, which was developed by Marc Andreessen and a team of programmers at the National Center for Supercomputing Applications (NCSA), was X Mosaic for Unix workstations. Since then, versions of NCSA Mosaic have become available for Windows-based PCs and the Macintosh. NCSA Mosaic was, for a time, distributed freely via the Net itself. Anyone could download and use the software without charge.

In mid-1994, NCSA began to license the rights to version 1.*x* of the software to other (often commercial) organizations. (NCSA is still developing version 2 as of this writing.) These organizations are allowed, by virtue of their licensing agreements with NCSA, to enhance the software. They can then *distribute* the enhanced software (called a *distribution*), and they can license others to distribute the software along with whatever enhancements they've included in their distribution. All distributions of Mosaic have the word *Mosaic* in their names.

In their wisdom, the folks at Netscape got Marc Andreessen, along with some other very smart people, to create and market a *new* Web browser—one that would be faster and more reliable than Mosaic. They also wanted the new browser to be *secure*. (They wanted you to be able to conduct economic transaction, or in other words, *buy* things over the Internet without fear of someone stealing and using your credit card number.) The result of this venture was Netscape. Netscape took the World Wide Web by storm and was soon named by *Wired* magazine as one of their favorite products.

Throughout this book, we're concentrating on the Web browser called Netscape, though most of the principles and many of the features we discuss are true across all platforms and distributions of Mosaic as well.

Here's how this goes: if you (the *client*) go into a fast food place, the counter-person (the *server*) says, "May I help you?" You answer something like, "I'll have a Big Burger with cheese, fries, and a cola." Then he or she verifies your order by repeating it, tells you the cost, and concludes the transaction by trading food for cash. Basically, when you walk into any fast food place, you'll follow that same pattern and so will the person who takes your order. That's because you both know the *protocol*. The fast food protocol is part of what makes it "fast food."

In just that way, HTTP, which is the protocol that was developed as part of the Web project, enables the kinds of network conversations that need to occur quickly between computers so that leaps can be made from one document to another. You can use other protocols to do the same things HTTP does (Netscape is *open-ended*, meaning that it's designed to support other network protocols as well as HTTP), but HTTP is terrifically efficient at what it does.

Information from around the Globe

The Web, as we've mentioned, is a network of global proportions. To ensure the continued success of the Web, the W3 Organization, headed jointly by CERN and by MIT's Laboratory for Computer Science (LCS), acts as the formal policy body and guiding light for the Web. The relationship between CERN and MIT/LCS as policy directors of the Web was formalized in June 1994 when both organizations announced an "international initiative for a universal framework for the information Web." The goal of the W3 Organization is to further the development and standardization of the World Wide Web, to make the global network easier to use for research, commerce, and future applications.

Web servers are located in many countries around the world, providing information on any topic you might imagine; a typical session using the Web might lead you through several continents. For example, research in the field of psychology may start at Yale and end up at a research hospital in Brussels, all within a few mouse-clicks that lead you along a series of hypertext links from a file at one location to another somewhere else.

The caveat here is that links are forged by the people who publish the information, and they may not make the same kinds of connections you would. That's why it's important to keep an open mind as you adventure around in the Web—just as you would when browsing in a library. You never know what you'll stumble across while you're looking for something else; conversely, you might have to do a bit of looking around to find exactly what you're seeking.

Who Makes This Information Available

Much of the information published on the Web exists thanks to the interest (and kindness) of the academic and research community; almost all the available information about the Web (and the Internet) is available through the work of that community. Files are stored on computers in research centers, hospitals, universities, and so on.

 Increasingly, the Web is a forum for commercial use. Given that the telephone system did not fully develop for personal use until it was seen by commerce as a tool for business, we see commercial use of the Web as a positive development. So far, most commercial users of the Web have adhered to the Internet philosophy in that they give to the Internet as well as use it.

Anyone can become a Web publisher, as you'll see in Chapter 7. The Web software was developed at CERN on a NeXT computer, but has since been ported to many different platforms, including Macs, machines running Microsoft Windows, and others running versions of Unix and Linux. Rules about how to participate in publishing information on the Web are available from a variety of sources on the Internet, including the Web itself.

What's Out There?

Software you can use to set up a Web server on a Windows workstation is available at `ftp://ftp.ncsa.uiuc.edu/Web/httpd/Windows`. This will get you into a subdirectory from NCSA at the University of Illinois at Urbana-Champaign (UIUC); the software can be downloaded via anonymous FTP.

Web servers can be set up for strictly in-house purposes, too. For example, a large organization with massive amounts of internal documentation might publish its data for technical support staff using the HTTP service. This makes it possible to expand the idea of *in-house* to mean not just "in the building," but "company-wide." Just as members of a research team can use the Web to collaborate without having to be in the same location, so can members of a company's workgroup.

What's Out There?

You can retrieve information about creating and publicizing your Web documents from `http://www.pcweek.ziff.com/~eamonn/crash_course.html/`.

What Types of Information Exist

CERN also maintains the *Virtual Library*, a hypertext document that lists all resources by subject (see Figure 2.1). This may be a good point of entry for your first plunge into the Web if you just want to see what's out there. The hypertext page you'll see when you access the Virtual Library presents an alphabetized list of starting points for research. Topics cover standard academic research areas like Anthropology, Computer Science, and Literature; they branch out to Movies and Music; and they even include such esoterica as Fortune Telling.

What's Out There?

You can access the Virtual Library using the URL
`http://info.cern.ch/hypertext/DataSources/bySubject/Overview.html`.

 The WWW Virtual Library

This is a distributed subject catalogue. See Category Subtree, Library of Congress Classification (Experimental), Top Ten most popular Fields (Experimental), Statistics (Experimental), and Index. See also arrangement by service type , and other subject catalogues of network information .

Mail to maintainers of the specified subject or www-request@mail.w3.org to add pointers to this list, or if you would like to contribute to administration of a subject area.

See also how to put your data on the web. All items starting with ! are *NEW!* (or newly maintained). New this month:

Aboriginal Studies
　　This document keeps track of leading information facilities in the field of Australian Aboriginal studies as well as the
　　Indigenous Peoples studies.
Aeronautics and Aeronautical Engineering
African Studies
Agriculture
Animal health, wellbeing, and rights
Anthropology

FIGURE 2.1: Here you see a page from CERN's Virtual Library, a good index from which to start your exploration of the Web.

The Web has quickly moved beyond the world of academia and research, with more and more commercial applications appearing all the time. Large hardware and software vendors often publish price lists, monthly sales figures, and technical support information—for example, Dell Computer's Web service includes a "Solve Your Own Problem" section.

What's Out There?

A growing number of high tech companies are making information available on the Web. Some familiar names—Microsoft, Novell, and Sybex—all maintain a presence on the Web. You can access these companies' home pages by using the URLs:

```
http://www.microsoft.com/
http://www.novell.com/
ftp://ftp.netcom.com/pub/sybex/Sybex.html
```

Other nonacademic, consumer-oriented Web servers (see Figure 2.2) include San Francisco Bay Area Parent Magazine, which provides lots of information on the Web that is of interest to all parents. MCA Records set up a "Woodstock '94" informational Web site, (but alas, with no hyperlinks to the original event). You can take a tour of Graceland via the Web, finding photos of the "King" and listening to sound clips of Elvis music, and you can even order a pizza using a Web order form. (This last is a pilot project so far; the pizza will be delivered only if you live in Santa Cruz, California. Solamente in California, eh?) We'll show you how to explore these and many other places in Chapter 5.

What's Out There?

We accessed Woodstock '94 and Parent Magazine with the following URLs:

```
http://metaverse.com/woodstock/
http://www.internet-is.com/parent/
```

The Role of the Browser

So far we've talked mainly about the structure and content of the Web, describing some of the information and links that make up the Web. So how does one jump into this Web and start cruising? You need a tool called a *browser*.

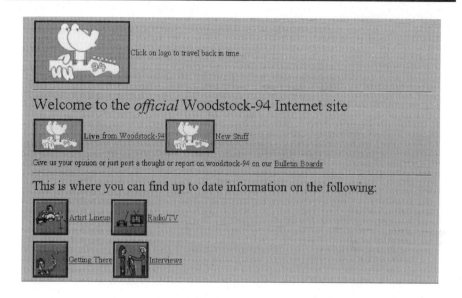

FIGURE 2.2: Many companies see the Web as a way to put their messages in front of a wide audience. The top home page was set up by MCA Records for Woodstock '94; the bottom one was set up by Parent Magazine to provide information to parents.

A Couple of Caveats Sitting around Talking

Remember that the Web is ever-changing by its very nature. In this book, we attempt to guide you toward a lot of home pages that seem stable. Some others are just so interesting or unusual we can't pass them up, though. If you don't find a site we've described, it may be that it has gone the way of all things. Not to worry; something even more remarkable will probably crop up elsewhere. Another thing is that in the growing, ever- expanding Web, many of the servers you encounter may not be complete—their links may be "under construction." You'll usually see a warning if that's the case, along with an admonition to wear a hardhat.

Now at the risk of sounding like the nerds we said you don't have to be, a browser, in technical terms, is a client process running on your computer that accesses a server process—in the case of the Web, the HTTP service—over the network. This is what's being discussed when people describe the Web as being based on client-server technology.

More simply put, the browser establishes contact with the server, reads the files—hypertext documents—made available on the HTTP server, and displays that stuff on your computer.

The document displayed by the browser is a hypertext document that contains references (or *pointers*) to other documents, which are very likely on other HTTP servers. These pointers are also called *links*. When you select a link from a hypertext page, the browser sends the request back to the new server, which then displays on your machine yet another document full of links.

In the same way, you and a waiter at a restaurant have a client-server relationship when you ask for and receive water, a browser and the Web have a client-server relationship. The browser sends requests over the network to the Web server, which then provides a screenful of information back to your computer.

Before Web browsers like Netscape were developed, all of this had to be accomplished using text-based browsers—the basic difference between them and browsers like Netscape is just like the difference between PC programs written for DOS and those written for Windows. (DOS is text-based, so using DOS requires you to type in commands to see and use text-filled screens; Windows, like Netscape, is graphical, so all you have to do is point and click on menu items and icons to see and use more graphically presented screens.) Figure 1.1 in Chapter 1 shows two views of the same information—one viewed with a text-based browser, the other with Netscape.

How Netscape Fits In

Netscape, one of the "new generation" of Web browsers, is a lot like the original and still famous Web browser called Mosaic but with considerable improvements. In fact, some of the key programmers who worked on the original Mosaic were behind the creation of Netscape.

Mosaic was developed by the Software Development Group (SDG) at the National Center for Supercomputing Applications (NCSA) at the University of Illinois at Urbana-Champaign. In early 1993, their research for developing an easy-to-use way to access the Internet led them to explore the World Wide Web and use of the HyperText Markup Language (HTML). HTML was being used for marking up documents on the Web—it's HTML that is used to *make* the document; browsers like Mosaic and Netscape simply allow you to look at it easily.

HTML, a mark-up language with which text can be made to look like a page, is the coding scheme used in hypertext documents that both handles the text formatting on screen and makes it possible to create *links* to other documents, graphics, sound, and movies. Figure 2.3 shows a Netscape document and the HTML coding that was used to create the document.

Remember, though, that Netscape is not just a way to look at visually appealing documents on the Internet. It also provides search capabilities within a hypertext document through links. We'll get into this more and more as we go along....

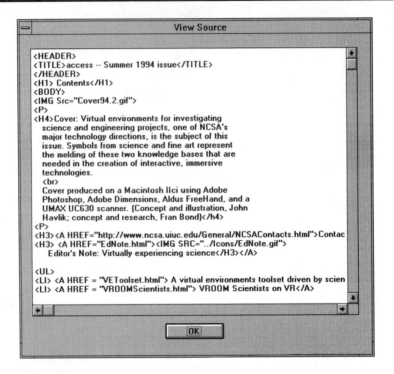

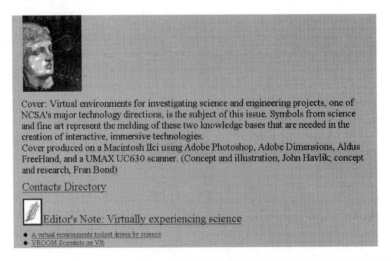

FIGURE 2.3: Here you can see the HTML coding (above) that makes this document (below) look the way it does.

Looking into HTML

If you want to see what HTML looks like, while you are viewing a document in Netscape, you can select View ➤ Source from Netscape's menu bar. A window will open showing the HTML for that document. You can't change the HTML you see, but you can copy pieces of it or even the whole thing to your Windows Clipboard (highlight what you want and press Ctrl-C) or you can save it as a text file to your local machine (see Chapter 3). Click on OK when you're done, and your view will once more be the document as it appears in Netscape.

Using Netscape to Access World Wide Web Information

Netscape lets you browse the information available on the Web just as you might browse the shelves of a large library. In fact, Netscape makes it so you can easily and quickly browse *entire rooms* of shelves, and the Web makes available literally thousands of "rooms" in "libraries" as expansive as, say, the New York Public Library. Using Netscape, you can skim material quickly, or you can stop and delve into topics as deeply as you wish. Let's take a quick look at a Netscape session in action.

A Typical Netscape Session

In our sample session, let's look for information about the Rolling Stones.

 This is a sample session; it's here to give you an idea of how things go. We'll talk in more detail in later chapters about how to accomplish various things using Netscape.

To start Netscape, we first double-click on Chameleon's Custom icon in the Windows Program Manager to start Chameleon's Custom application (that's the one that makes the SLIP/PPP connection). Then, we select Connect on

the Custom application's menu bar and click on OK to signal it to dial your Internet service provider. Having made this connection, we now double-click the Netscape icon in the Windows Program Manager. (We'll go over starting the software again in detail in Chapter 3.) The Welcome to Netscape page (Figure 2.4) appears on screen. From here we can traverse the Web by clicking on links, which appear on the home page as pictures and as underlined words in blue.

 Chapters 8 and 9 provide detailed directions for installing and setting up both Chameleon Sampler and Netscape.

Let's say in an earlier session we found the NCSA Mosaic home page. There we clicked on What's New and we got the NCSA Mosaic What's

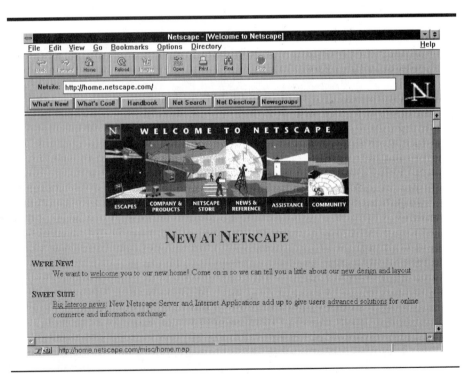

FIGURE 2.4: The Welcome to Netscape page will be your first view of the Internet via Netscape.

New document. Near the top of this document we found a link (appearing as a word in blue) that said something like "search back documents," which led us to the CUI W3 Catalog, which is actually stored on a machine at CERN, in Switzerland. The CUI W3 Catalog is a catalog of announcements of new services and information available on the Web. Its URL was shown at the top of the screen while we were viewing the catalog; we stored the URL as a bookmark (more on this in Chapter 4) so we could find it easily again when we wanted to.

What's Out There?

The CUI W3 Catalog is not the only catalog of resources on the Web, but it is one of the most useful, and is always a good place to start your search. Its URL is `http://cuiwww.unige.ch/w3catalog`.

To open the CUI W3 Catalog without retracing all of the steps we went through when we discovered the catalog, we select File ➤ Open Location. The Open Location dialog box appears.

From our previous session, we know the URL; now we can type this into the URL text box, then press ↵. After a few seconds, the document is transferred from Switzerland and displayed on screen. You can see it shown in Figure 2.5.

To go on with our research on the Rolling Stones, we type into the space next to the Submit button a term to search for, in our case "Rolling Stones." Then we click on the Submit button to activate the search. It may take a minute to search the database (it's a *big* database). Once the search is done, the results appear on screen.

The first entry we see starts, "The World's Greatest Rock 'n' Roll Band is proud to announce their very own Web server," and goes on to say that the Rolling Stones now have a Web server with information about their Voodoo Lounge tour. In that description, the phrase <u>Rolling Stones</u> is in blue—it's a link to the server's home page. We click on the link to access the Rolling Stones Web server and the Rolling Stones home page appears. You can see it in Figure 2.6.

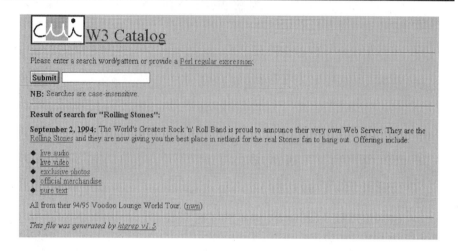

FIGURE 2.5: Searching the CUI W3 Catalog for the term <u>Rolling Stones</u> finds this entry about the Rolling Stones Web server.

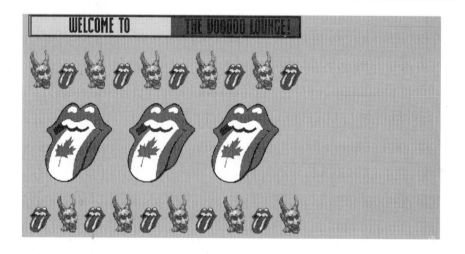

FIGURE 2.6: The Rolling Stones home page looks pretty much like you might expect it to look.

The Rolling Stones home page is our entry point to scads of information about the Voodoo Lounge tour (and perhaps by the time you read this, even more). Here we can click on links to view backstage snap shots, video clips of performances, a schedule of performance dates, and a catalog of stuff to buy.

With our curiosity about the Stones satisfied, we can exit the program directly from wherever we happen to be, by selecting File ➤ Exit from Netscape's menu bar.

Netscape Is Fast

If you worked along with this session, you probably found that Netscape displayed the pages on your machine in a jiffy. The graphics included in each page trailed the text, appearing just a moment later, however. If your access to the Web is via modem on a stand-alone PC and not from a network, you'll find that there's always *some* delay in transferring images to your screen. This is because there can be an awful lot of data involved in transferring graphics, and your 9600 or 14,400 bps modem acts as a bottleneck through which the data must squeeze. Many Web browsers halt all their other operations while they make you wait for images to appear. Netscape was designed specifically to get around this issue: instead of waiting 'til the graphics appear, Netscape goes ahead and shows you the text on the page and allows you to start working with it. You can click on links in the text, for example, and move on to the next page of interest to you, before the graphics in the original page have appeared.

Further, you can decide whether you want the graphics to appear at all. Netscape, like other Web browsers, usually shows you both the text and the graphics in a given Web page. But if you find the graphics bogging you down, you can turn the graphics off and see only the text.

To toggle off the graphics, making it so you'll see only text, select Options ➤ Auto Load Images from Netscape's menu bar. After you do this, the Web pages you view will include little markers where the graphics go. If you're viewing a page with graphics toggled off and you decide you want to see the graphics after all, just click on the Images icon on Netscape's toolbar and the page will be reloaded, this time with its graphics.

To toggle graphics back on, so you'll see them loaded a moment after the text for each page appears, select Options ➤ Auto Load Images again from the menu bar. (Note that this is a *toggle* situation, so you can go back and forth in your choice to include or exclude images again and again using the exact same process.)

How Data Travels

Usually you can't install Netscape on your Windows computer and expect it simply to work. You have to go through a little rigmarole to get things going. The interface mechanism between the client—Netscape—and the Web server (the machine dishing up the information you want to view) depends on the Internet protocol known as TCP/IP (Transmission Control Protocol/Internet Protocol). TCP/IP creates *packets* (see Figure 2.7)—which are like electronic envelopes to carry data on a network—and then places the packets on the network. It also makes it possible, of course, to receive packets.

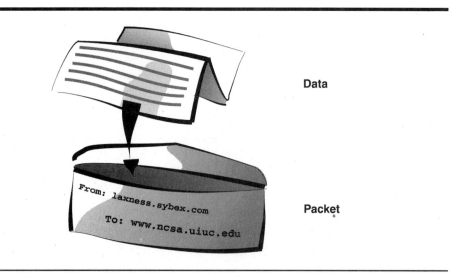

FIGURE 2.7: Data (e-mail, documents, video, whatever) travels across the Internet in <u>packets</u>.

E-Mail Addressing

Electronic mail, or e-mail, is the established form of communication on the Internet. In fact, typically this is where most of us encounter the Internet for the first time. A friend tells you his Internet e-mail address at work is `kmfez@schwartz.com`, and asks for your e-mail address, and you begin exchanging messages that magically pop up in your on-screen e-mail in-basket. Users around the country—for that matter, around the world—readily grasp e-mail as a quick, convenient means for conducting research or just for staying in touch (and for doing so without the expense associated with a long-distance phone call).

How does e-mail work? It's actually a lot like the Postal Service. E-mail uses addressing and a "store and forward" mechanism. This means that there is a standard way of addressing, and the mail is routed from one place to another until ultimately it appears at its destination. Along the way, if necessary, a machine can store the mail until it knows how to forward it.

Of course, there is a little more than that to sending e-mail on its way, but not much. The address in your e-mail header, much like the address on a postal letter, contains all the information necessary to deliver the message to the recipient. In the world of the Internet, a person's e-mail address is made up of two parts: a user name and a computer name, indicating where the user's ID is located. In the example `kmfez@schwartz.com`, `kmfez` is the user portion of the address, and `schwartz.com` is the name of the location (actually a host machine). The last part of the location's name, `.com`, is known as the *high-level domain*—in this case `.com` tells you that it is a *com*mercial organization. If `.edu` appeared instead, you'd know it was an *edu*cational organization.

An address can actually contain many domains, which you see separated by periods, like this: `joke.on.you.com`. If more than one domain appears in an address, they move in hierarchy from right to left. As you read to the left, the domains get smaller in scope.

The Domain Name System and Packets

There is a system responsible for administering and keeping track of domains and (believe it or not) it's called the Domain Name System (DNS for short). DNS is a distributed system that administers names by allowing different groups control over subsets of names. In this system, there can be many levels or domains, but the top-level domains are generally standardized, making it easy for mail to be routed.

In addition to the more familiar "English" names, all machines on the Internet have an Internet address in the form of four numbers separated by decimals; this is because, while a user might change the "English" address, an address is needed that will never change. This numeric address is organized in a system commonly called *dotted decimal notation*. An example of a host computer's address would be 130.19.252.21. These numeric addresses work fine for machines communicating with each other, but most people find them cumbersome to use and tricky to remember. To help people out, host computers were given names, such as *ruby* or *topaz*, making it easier to remember and to facilitate connecting.

However, other factors came into play, such as making sure that each machine on the Internet had a unique name, registering the names in a centrally managed file, and distributing the file to everyone on the Internet. This system worked adequately when the Internet was still small, but as it grew in size, so did the size of the file keeping track of all the host names.

The common standard American domains are as follows:

com   Commercial business, company, or organization

edu   Educational institution (university, etc.)

gov   Nonmilitary government site

mil   Military site

net   Any host associated with network administration, such as a gateway

org   Private organization (nonacademic, nongovernmental, and noncommercial)

These domains are referred to as *descriptive* domains. In addition, each country also has its own top-level domain, commonly called a *geographical* domain. Here in the United States, we are in the us domain. Other examples of countries represented with domains include:

au   Australia

ca   Canada

fr   France

Just as you need not know the internal workings of the U.S. Postal Service to use the system and get your mail, you don't need to know all about TCP/IP to use Netscape. But it does help to have some understanding.

TCP/IP is not part of Netscape; it's part of your local network if you're on one. If you're not on a local network, though—if, for example, you're using your stand-alone machine at home or at work—you can still use Netscape. In that case, you have to have special network drivers loaded (not to worry, Chameleon Sampler, provided on the disk that comes with this book, includes them). These drivers make things go back and forth over the phone connection using the protocol Netscape understands. We'll talk more about this in Chapter 9.

If you're using a PC on a LAN that's already connected to the Internet you're probably already set up with the TCP/IP software you need to run Netscape and you can just use your company's connection. Your Network Administrator can clue you in to the details of running TCP/IP-based software like Netscape. <u>Don't install Netscape on a networked machine without notifying the network administrator</u>.

What Netscape Recognizes

Netscape has many big selling points, one of which is that it provides one-stop shopping for the Web by handling a variety of *data types*. Data types are just that—types of data. Having standard types of data makes it possible for one machine (indeed, a program) to recognize and use data that was created on another machine (and maybe even in another program).

The data types recognized by Netscape include:

- ◆ HTML
- ◆ Graphics
- ◆ Sound
- ◆ Video

The data type that the Web was designed around is HTML, the type the Hyper-Text Transfer Protocol we've talked so much about was designed to transfer.

HTTP servers, the servers that make up the World Wide Web, serve hypertext documents (coded with HTML, as we've discussed). These documents are not just what you view; these HTML documents actually guide you through the Web when you're cruising.

When you view hypertext documents using a line-mode browser (see Figure 1.1), you'll see the links displayed as item numbers, or as reverse-video, depending upon your display. When you view hypertext documents using Netscape, you'll see the links displayed as text that's either underlined or in a different color than the main text in the document.

Clicking on the underlined or colored text pops you to the next link, which may be another hypertext document or a graphic, or even a sound or video file.

Netscape's Use of Viewers

For those data types that it can't handle directly, Netscape uses external "viewers." (In this context, a *viewer* is software that might specialize in displaying a graphic or playing a sound, a movie, or both.) Viewers are independent applications developed for viewing, opening, or accessing a particular type of information.

You can configure Netscape to work with specific viewers. For example, you might configure audio files to be played by WHAM, a Windows-based audio application that's available as freeware. (See Chapter 10 for more information on getting and using external viewers.)

Netscape version 1.1 includes a very credible sound "viewer."

How Viewers Work

Briefly, here's how viewers work: Netscape looks at the first line (the *header*) in the file; the header tells Netscape what it needs to know to deal with the file appropriately. Text files are displayed on screen, in the very attractive way Netscape displays them. Compressed files, such as graphics, are uncompressed and then displayed. But when Netscape encounters a sound or video file, the program "knows" it needs help and it launches the appropriate viewer to "play" the file—if you have the viewer on your machine, you won't see much evidence of this; you'll just hear the sound or see the movie on screen.

Many viewers are available in the public domain from many Internet sources (including anonymous FTP servers, Archie servers, and the Web) and for all types of files. NCSA, for example, makes it clear that it neither maintains nor formally distributes the viewers needed to work with the various files that Web browsers can access, but when NCSA learns of a viewer that can be freely distributed, they file a copy of it on a server in Illinois. (Remember that these public domain viewers, like all public domain programs, are supported (if at all) only by their authors and not by the sites where you got them. If you have questions about how to use any given viewer, you must go to that viewer's author to get help.)

With the help of viewers, you can play sound and video clips with Netscape, but you should avoid doing so if you have a modem connection (as opposed to a LAN connection) to the Internet. Most sound and video files are multi-megabytes in size. As a rough estimate, each megabyte takes about 15 minutes to transfer with a 14.4K bps modem (that is, on a good day with prevailing winds). It might take literally hours to access a single, relatively short video clip.

Let's talk for a minute about those types of data Netscape most commonly needs a viewer to work with. (We'll go into more detail about how to use this stuff starting in Chapter 10.)

Graphics   Usually when you encounter graphics while using Netscape, they'll be one of two kinds: those that appear in the document (called "in-line" graphics) and those that require you click on something in order to view them.

Netscape can work with many common types of graphic images, for example, GIF, TIFF, and JPEG. You will only need an external graphics viewer if you come upon a graphics file that Netscape does not support. Because most graphics on the Web are in the GIF and JPEG formats, this is unlikely.

You don't really need to concern yourself with what the names of these various file formats mean unless you plan to publish your own documents. Most of the time, all you'll be doing is looking at things; sometimes the graphic you'll see in your Netscape document window is a link to another document or a larger, compressed image. Clicking on the picture will begin the process of bringing the other file over the network.

Sound Netscape version 1.0 must be configured in order to be able to play sound files; version 1.1 comes with a sound viewer. Windows audio files (WAV) and Basic audio (AU) files will be recognized as linked data. Remember that sound files can be very large and take a long time to transfer over a slow connection.

Video Netscape can be configured to work with viewers for QuickTime movies (MOV), Microsoft video (AVI), and movie files compressed using the MPEG compression standard. Again, remember that many video files you'll come across as you begin to work with Netscape are, in the words of Tiny Elvis, "huge."

Netscape as a Consistent Interface to Other Internet Resources

In addition to providing a nice graphical user interface to linked multimedia information, Netscape also provides a consistent interface to other information types available on the Internet. In fact, many of the links in the hypertext documents on the Web will take you to information on FTP servers, gopher servers, or WAIS servers. (Read on for the gory details.) You can also read newsgroups and post messages to them from Netscape.

Let's take a quick look at the kinds of resources that make up the Web and that you can access using Netscape.

FTP: For Transferring Files

We've talked about viewing files; actually obtaining them is a different matter. To transfer a file from one machine (a server, for example) to another (yours, for example) you need FTP (File Transfer Protocol). FTP is

Wanderers, Spiders, and Robots—Oh My!

In June 1993, there were about 130 Web servers on the Internet. Six months later, there were over 200. Two months after that, there were over 600. By April 1994, there were over 1,200; in December 1994 the number hit 2,000. So, how do you find what you need in this ever-expanding haystack? Wouldn't it be great to know what's out on the Web, and where?

You can find out, by consulting World Wide Web creatures known as *wanderers*, *spiders*, or *robots*. An assortment of Web robots have been developed since the beginnings of the WWW; these programs travel through the Web and find HTTP files—the files that make up the content of the Web. With names the likes of Arachnophobia, W4, Webfoot Robot, JumpStation Robot, Repository-Based Software Engineering Project Spider, WebCrawler, WebLinker, and World Wide Web Worm, you may not see their useful purposes when you first encounter them.

Some robots, such as W4, were designed strictly to keep track of growth on the Web. The statistics cited at the beginning of this piece were gathered by W4; the W4 page of the Web keeps these figures posted and updated.

The more interesting and useful Web crawlers are those that dump the information they gather into a place that's readable by the rest of us browsers. The World Wide Web Worm is one such robot. The information is collected into an indexed database that Web users can search.

The Repository Based Software Engineering Project Spider creates an Oracle database by searching through links within the Web to find HTML files. The data that's extracted is then siphoned off into a WAIS index, which can be searched.

Check out Chapter 6 for information about accessing the World Wide Web Worm and other search tools.

one of the means by which you move files around the Internet. Both a communications protocol and an application, it is the application that is of most interest to many people, as we use FTP to obtain files (once we've located them, of course) from all kinds of Internet sources. This kind of file transfer most often works in what is known as *anonymous FTP* mode.

What's Out There?

You can retrieve a table listing available compression software with the URL `ftp://ftp.cso.uiuc.edu/doc/pcnet/compression`.

FTP itself only lets you see a list of the files on a computer, whereas something like Netscape lets you see more—the files, the contents of the files, even graphics, sounds, movies, etc. Still, FTP should not be overlooked for what it has accomplished and still does, namely, allowing users to bring home files, information, and data that otherwise would be left for browsing only.

After retrieving the file, you may need to perform some additional steps if the file has been compressed to save space. This involves using a utility to uncompress, or unzip, the file to make it usable. There are many compression formats in use, so you may find yourself cursing sometimes rather than jumping for joy when you uncover just the file you are looking for but are unable to unzip it.

Netscape presents FTP directories as a graphical menu using icons similar to those used by the Windows File Manager. Directories are represented by a folder icon; text files are displayed as the familiar sheet-of-paper-with-its-top-corner-folded-down. These items all appear as links—they are underlined so that you can click on them to move to the place in question.

Another advantage of Netscape, over say a regular FTP session, is that Netscape reads the file type, so it can display a text file on screen when you click on the link. A regular FTP session involves copying the file to your workstation and then opening it later using a text editor.

Likewise, Netscape will deal with sound, image, and video files that appear as links (in the FTP list) as it does in other contexts, displaying the text, picture, or movie, or playing the sound when you click on the link.

Anonymous FTP Explained Here

Anonymous FTP permits users to access remote systems without actually having user accounts on the systems. In effect, it allows for "guests" to visit a remote site, and permits just enough computer privileges to access the resources provided. The process involves the user starting an FTP connection and logging in to the remote computer as the user "anonymous," with an arbitrary password which, for the purposes of Internet etiquette, should be your e-mail address. The beauty of using Netscape for anonymous FTP is that with Netscape you don't have to go through all the login steps, you don't have to use a text-based FTP program on your machine, and Netscape displays all the stuff on the FTP server in an easy-to-use graphical interface. You can tell when a Web document you are viewing in Netscape comes from an anonymous FTP site, because the URL starts with `ftp:`.

Netscape may have to be properly configured with the appropriate external viewer applications in order to play sounds or movies and display pictures. Also, once Netscape plays the sound or movie, it's gone. You'll learn how to save the images, sounds, and videos in Chapter 3.

Gopher: For Searching and Finding

When you use a URL in Netscape that begins with gopher, your copy of Netscape is talking to a gopher server. Originally developed at the University of Minnesota as a front-end to telnet and FTP, gopher has since caught on as one of the more important information retrieval tools on the Internet.

When you access gopher information with Netscape you are presented with a series of menu choices, much like the directory structure one sees in the Microsoft Windows File Manager. By double-clicking on icons, you can traverse the directory structure a level at a time until you come to an item. The great thing about gopher is that you don't have to know what the item is, or even where it is (unlike FTP). If the item is a file to download,

gopher invokes an FTP session. If the item is a link to another computer, gopher invokes a telnet session so you can use that computer. If it is something to be displayed—a graphic, a text document, etc.—it will do so on your screen, provided you have the proper client software installed on your PC. All this happens without the necessity of you worrying about Internet addressing schemes, domains, host names, and such.

The other aspect that makes gopher so powerful is that gopher servers reference or *point* to each other. It really doesn't matter where the data is located, or where you start accessing gopher servers, because gopher is able to take you there seamlessly. This is an obvious step up from using FTP, because with FTP you have to know the name of the FTP machine to get anything from it.

The University of Minnesota gopher server acts as the master gopher; by registering with the university, administrators can make their gopher server available through the master, thus allowing world-wide access to their servers. Note that there is not a gopher-formatted resource per se, rather, gopher acts as a helper to collect the Internet resources into a convenient inventory that lets you find items in much the same way you use the subject card catalogs at a library. In fact, with the way the gopher servers reference one another, all this information almost appears to be on one gigantic computer.

When you use Netscape, gopher server information is presented as a graphical menu listing of folders and file icons—just like FTP server files. (See Figure 2.8.) Because gopher data is indexed, however, you can perform a gopher search. Netscape has a Find menu option; when you select it, a dialog box will pop up to enable you to describe what you're seeking. (This same dialog box appears regardless of what type of indexed data you're searching—it could just as well be hypertext or a WAIS database.)

WAIS: For Searching Text Databases

The Internet Wide Area Information Service, WAIS, lets you search indexed information to find articles containing groups of words you choose. WAIS is a lot like gopher, in that it shields you from having to know on which computer the information resides. Unlike gopher, WAIS does the searching for you. A WAIS search is not totally accomplished without some human intervention—someone has to make the text information

Gopher Menu

- About Earthquakes
- About NCEER
- About the NCEER Gopher Server
- Comprehensive listing of professional meetings
- Connect to NCEER ftp
- Connect to other Gophers
- Federal, State and Local Programs
- NCEER Information Service Resources
- Other Earthquake related ftp's
- QUAKELINE Database
- Veronica Searches (search Items in gopherspace)
- Who to contact for help
- NCEER Earthquake Engineering Highway Project

FIGURE 2.8:   When you use Netscape to access a gopher server, you will see folder and file icons much like those that appear in Windows File Manager.

available on a WAIS server by indexing it; but once that happens, anyone can gain access to it. From a WAIS client, you decide which library of information to search and which words to search on. WAIS then returns articles and documents containing those keywords.

There are a few drawbacks to WAIS. For example, because there are no special words, every word counts. That is, if you search the word *car*, everything containing any occurrence of that word is retrieved. And you can't narrow your search—there currently is no logical "and" operation, allowing you to look for, say, *Porsches and Ferraris*. Another problem is that you can't tell WAIS to discard articles that may have gone astray; you basically get a lot more at times than you bargained for, which means some sifting on your part is required. In spite of these small annoyances, WAIS is still one of the most useful search tools on the Internet today.

Netscape lets you access WAIS servers through a WWW-WAIS gateway (access to all these other services is through gateways, too), which converts the data to the appropriate format for the Web. Of course, the beauty of Netscape is, as usual, that you don't need to know about gateways or even WAIS itself to perform a search on WAIS indexes. Hypertext links may point to WAIS information. (See Figure 2.9.)

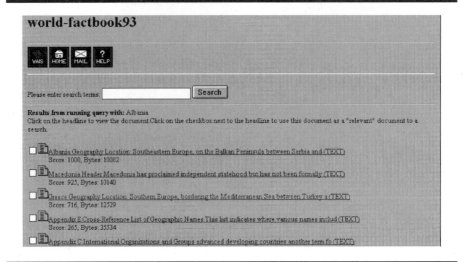

FIGURE 2.9: Using the CIA World-Factbook93 database, you can quickly find information about any country in the world.

Like other indexes (such as gopher), WAIS indexes display as searchable indexes.

Usenet: All the News You'd Ever Want

The first stop for new Internet browsers after e-mail typically used to be network news, although with the advent of graphical tools such as Netscape, this may no longer be the case.

Network news is the great question and answer, ask-and-you-shall-receive-a-reply oracle of this century. It is like e-mail in that you are reading and possibly replying to messages, but unlike it in that you are able to partake of a broader scope of public conversations and discussions, with as little or as much participation as you want. You don't even have to take part—you can just stand back and watch if you'd prefer. There are literally thousands of discussion groups on nearly every subject imaginable; you can join in or just cruise through them as you like.

Network news occurs in a format a lot like that of a private BBS system, such as CompuServe. Because it is organized into newsgroups, it is very easy to work your way through the major headings and then through the newsgroups themselves. You need a *newsreader*, a piece of software that organizes and sorts the newsgroups—there are a number available for all the major platforms. You can even download them free from the Internet.

The major (but not the only) source of network news is Usenet, which is a free service. Usenet was actually born before the Internet, and much confusion exists as to how the two interact. Usenet is not a network like the Internet, there are no Usenet computers per se, and Usenet doesn't even need the Internet. Rather, what drives Usenet is akin to an agreement set up between those who want to distribute and those who want to read newsgroups. Network administrators arrange with other administrators to transfer newsgroups back and forth, which usually occurs via the Internet, but only because that's convenient. The site that provides your site with news is called a *news feed*. Some newsgroups end up being transferred by some computers, others by other computers, and so on.

Netscape provides a very capable newsreader. You can subscribe (and unsubscribe) to your favorite newsgroups, post your own articles, and read articles (not in the order of the posting but rather by subject). We'll go over all this in detail in Chapter 3. Figure 2.10 shows links to newsgroups as they appear in a Web document.

The Human Side of Hypermedia

The Web is hypermedia-based, which is why the Web is called the Web: the notion of interconnections and multiple branching points, no beginning and no end, is implicit in the Web. The structure of the information is neither hierarchical nor linear. The Web and its hypertext underpinnings offer a rich environment for exploring tangential or directly related information because the hypertext paradigm works the way people do when they're on the road to discovery.

For example, if you were a kid in the '60s or '70s working on a book report about Native American cultures, your process might have looked like this: you began by reading the encyclopedia section on *Indians* (this, remember, is before Native Americans were referred to as such) when you came to a passage describing the dislocation of the Hopi people to a reservation near what is called today Apache Junction, Arizona.

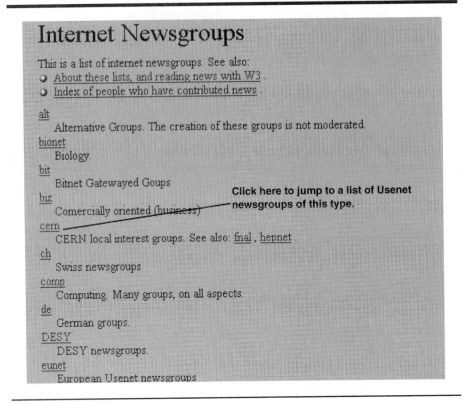

FIGURE 2.10: You will often find links to Usenet newsgroups in Web documents.

Having never been near Arizona, you decided to find out about its climate, terrain, flora and fauna. Putting the *I* volume aside on the floor, you grabbed the *A* volume and dipped into *Arizona*. Then you wondered, "What's it like today?" You called the Apache Junction Chamber of Commerce and asked for recent industrial and employment statistics. Later that day, curious about the status of any national reparations made to the Hopi in Arizona, you made a trip to your local library and had a chat with the reference librarian, who in turn brought you copies of various federal government policy statements.

Thus, the kind of discovery process supported by hypertext—and the Web—is really modeled after the way people tend to work when they're learning new things. Following our example using other tools on the

Internet, such as gopher, would be like doing the research for your childhood book report by starting each search for a distinct bit of information from the table of contents of a single book. It's easy to see why the hypertext paradigm and the Web have really taken off. In a hypertext document, if you want more information about something you can just click on its link and there you are: the linked item could be a document on a server 7,500 miles away. If you were writing that book report today, you might travel all over the world, via the Web, without ever leaving your computer.

Moving Along...

With all this backstory in place, you're ready now to hit the highway. Starting with the next chapter, we're going to dig into how you do what you do with Netscape and the Web. Let's hit the road.

Part Two:

Navigating and Publishing with Netscape

Running Netscape

Let's get working with Netscape. In this chapter, you'll learn to start the program, and then how to open and save documents, switch between documents and other hypermedia (sound and video, for example) via *hot links*, and finally how to save files to your local hard drive.

 This chapter assumes you've already installed Netscape on your PC. For information on getting Netscape, installing it, and making your Internet connection, see Chapters 8 and 9.

Launching Netscape

Launching Netscape is easy. If you follow the instructions for getting the software and setting it up in Chapters 8 and 9, you'll have two new groups in the Windows Program Manager, one for Chameleon Sampler and the other for Netscape—with these two pieces of software in place, you're ready to go.

1. In the Windows Program Manager's Chameleon Sampler group window, double-click on the Custom icon. The Custom window will appear.

Custom

SLIP and PPP: The Netscape Connection

To start Chameleon Sampler, you must first start the SLIP/PPP software that accesses the Internet, then start Netscape. This may seem complicated at first, but it's no big deal.

Here's how SLIP or PPP software works: You start your connection software—Chameleon Sampler, in this case—which then contacts your Internet service provider (which is on a machine somewhere else). SLIP/PPP "introduces" Netscape to your Internet service provider—it provides a vital link in your Internet connection. Chameleon Sampler and your service provider will then do a little dance together, passing back and forth the TCP/IP packets that make it possible for you to run Netscape (which is on your machine). Voilà—the Internet accepts your machine as a little network hooked into the bigger, more exciting network called the Internet, and you're on your way!

2. From the menu bar in the Custom window, select Connect and then click on OK. Chameleon will automatically dial up your Internet service provider through your modem and connect your machine to the Internet. Now you can run Netscape.

3. In the Windows Program Manager's Netscape group window, double-click on the Netscape icon.

Netscape

That's all there is to it.

If all goes well (and it surely will) the Netscape window will open and the N icon in the window's upper-right corner will become animated.

This tells you that Netscape is transferring data, which will appear in a second in the form of a home page. Whenever Netscape is "working" (downloading a document, doing a search, and so on) the big N is animated. It stops when the action has been completed.

When you start Netscape, you'll see the Welcome to Netscape home page, with its slick, colorful graphics. You can change this start-up home page to something else if you like; we'll tell you how to do that later, in Chapter 4.

The *home page* is where you begin, where Netscape first lands you on your Internet voyage. Think of it as one of many ports of entry into the Web—the Web, you'll recall, doesn't just go from here to there… it's literally a *web*. It doesn't really matter where you start, because everything's interconnected.

You can return to the start-up home page (the one you see when you start a Netscape session) at any time simply by clicking on the home icon on the Netscape toolbar.

If you followed the steps earlier in this chapter and have Netscape running now, try clicking on the home icon. This brief exercise will test your Internet connection. The N should become animated and you should see the start-up home page displayed again on your screen.

What's Out There?

By default, the start-up home page is the Welcome to Netscape home page. If you change the start-up home page and want to find Netscape's Welcome home page again, its URL is
`http://home.netscape.com/home/welcome.html/`.

Home, Home on the Home Page

The start-up home page—any home page, for that matter— may be located anywhere on the Web. Home pages provide a lot of information and change frequently, so you may not want to zip by the start-up home page—instead, take the time to review it when it pops up.

You are not limited to seeing the Welcome home page at startup—you can make it so that Netscape won't load a home page on startup (see Chapter 4), or you can store and start up with one of any number of home pages that you find on the Internet. You can even create your own home page. (Refer to Chapter 7 for instructions on how to do so.)

What You See: The Netscape Interface

Let's look at the parts of the Netscape window. The interface shows a window called the *document view window*. Figure 3.1 shows you what's what.

The toolbar, status bar, location bar, and directory buttons can be displayed or hidden on your screen. They are activated or deactivated via the Options menu.

Title Bar In the title bar you can see the name of the page you are currently viewing.

Menu Bar The menu bar is similar to those in other Windows applications: it provides you with pull-down menus. When you move the mouse to the menu and click on a selection, choices appear.

Toolbar The toolbar performs some commonly accessed features. It's like other Windows toolbars, in that all you have to do is click on the icon for the specified action to occur. Let's quickly go over the Netscape tool bar icons.

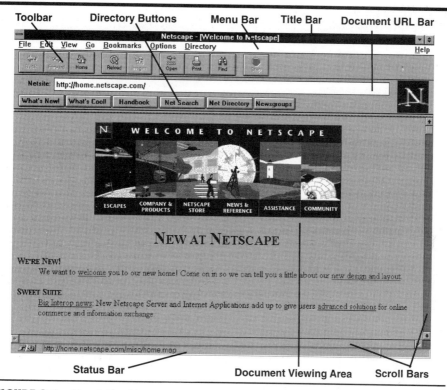

FIGURE 3.1: Here's the Netscape window with all its parts labeled so you can see what's what.

The Tool	Its Name	What You Do with It
Back	Back	Jump back to the previous page or document in your history list (i.e. the page you were viewing just prior to the current page).
Forward	Forward	Jump forward to the next page or document in your history list. (If you're on the last item in the history list this icon is *dimmed*—it looks grayed out).

The Tool	Its Name	What You Do with It
	Home	Return to the start-up home page.
	Reload	Refresh the currently loaded document. (You may need to do this if, for instance, you have a temporary communications problem with the Web server you're connected to and the page you want to see is incompletely displayed.)
	Images	Load images into the page you are currently viewing. This icon is dimmed when Netscape is set to load images automatically (that's the default setting).
	Open	Open a document via its URL.
	Print	Print the current document.
	Find	Find specified text in the current document.
	Stop	Cancel the process of loading an incoming document.

Location Bar Here you'll see the URL (the Uniform Resource Locator) of the current document. We'll get to a discussion of URLs a little later in this chapter.

Directory Buttons Below the Location Bar a row of buttons appears; clicking on any of these buttons affords you fast access to some very useful Web pages about Netscape.

Document Viewing Area This is the main portion of the screen—it's where you'll see what you came to the Web to see.

Status Bar The status bar is at the bottom of the screen. As you move the cursor about the document viewing area and come across links, the cursor changes into the shape of a hand with one finger pointing and the status bar displays the URL for the link. When a document is being transferred to your machine, you'll see numbers in the status bar indicating the progress of the transfer.

◆ The key at the left end of the status bar indicates whether a document is secure.

◆ The "fractured" key indicates an insecure document—one that is unencrypted, or in other words does not prevent a clever third party with serious hacking skills from viewing it when it's transmitted.

 Security is a topic of great concern to commercial users, who want to protect their customers who are making credit card purchases from theft. Netscape has encryption and security features that make it highly popular with commercial users. Check out A Few Quick Words on Security for more on Netscape's security features.

Scroll Bars These are just like regular Windows scroll bars: they appear on the side of the viewing area, and possibly at the bottom, when the document is too big to fit in the window. Click on the scroll bars to bring into view whatever's off the screen.

Opening Your First Document

You actually opened your first document when you started Netscape and the home page appeared. But let's dig around a little further and see what else we can open.

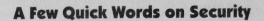

A Few Quick Words on Security

If you are new to the Web and haven't used the Internet for much more than e-mail and the occasional file transfer, you probably haven't had to concern yourself with *security* yet.

However, keeping the data that passes across the Internet safe and secure is an issue that bigwigs in both business and government are discussing now, and one that will soon become relevant to even the casual user.

You've probably noticed a lot of talk in newspapers and magazines and on TV about commercial ventures on the Web—merchants setting up shop and taking your credit card orders through their home pages. If this data (your credit card number) is not *safe*, it can be read by some electronic eavesdropper lurking in an electronic shadow somewhere...well, you can surely see the concern!

Fortunately, the designers of Netscape had this issue in mind when they designed the software. Netscape is the first Web browser to allow secured transactions to take place (between clients running Netscape and servers running Netscape's Netside Commerce server). In English this means that when you, running Netscape at home, connect to a home page on a special server that was purchased from Netscape Communications, the data sent back and forth can be secure from prying "eyes."

By now you've probably noticed the gold skeleton key icon in the lower-left corner of the Netscape window. Usually, the key appears "fractured" and displayed on a gray background. This indicates the document you are currently viewing is *insecure*, meaning that a third party sufficiently motivated and equipped can look in on the data being sent back and forth and do with it what he or she will.

If, however, you are connected to a *secure* page—one where such eavesdropping is not possible because the data is "encrypted" before it is transferred and "unencrypted" upon arrival—the key will appear unfractured and on a blue background. (In addition, a dialog box will appear both when you connect to and disconnect from that page, telling you of the secure status of the transmission.

(continued on next page)

(continued from previous page)

You can find out more about security by selecting Help ➤ On Security from the Netscape menu bar and reading the information that appears. To get a directory of sites using Netsite Commerce servers, select Directory ➤ Netscape Marketplace from the menu bar.

When money begins changing hands on the Web, you'll be prepared—Netscape's security features will stop those lurking Net bandits in their tracks.

Following Hot Links

As we've said before, hypertext is nonlinear. (That means you don't have to follow a straight path from point A to point Z, but rather you can skip around from one place to another to another, back to the first, round to a fourth, etc....) Hypertext has links—*hot links*, they're often called—to other sources of information. You follow these links through a document, or from document to document, or perhaps from server to server, in any way you like as you navigate the Web. (You can think of hypertext as both the text and the links—it's the navigational means by which you traverse the Web.)

How can you tell what is hypertext in a document? Typically, the text on your screen appears highlighted in blue and is underlined, or an image appears with an added border of color. These qualities all indicate hypertext.

Moving around the World Wide Web via Netscape is a snap, thanks to hyperlinks. It's as easy as a mouse click on the hyperlink—each hyperlink points to another document, image, sound, etc., and when you click, you jump right to whatever's represented by the item you clicked on.

If we slowed the whole business down and showed you its underpinnings, you'd see that when you click on a hyperlink, Netscape does one of these things:

◆ Gets the document which the link specifies and displays it.

◆ Goes to another location in the current document.

◆ Gets a file such as a sound or image file and through the use of an external viewer (another piece of software on your PC), plays the sound or displays the image.

◆ Gives you access to another Internet service, such as gopher, FTP, telnet, etc.

If you still have the Welcome to Netscape home page open, follow a few links between documents by clicking on the home page's hyperlinks. You'll soon see why they call it the Web. Try jumping back and forth a couple of times, too, by clicking on those tools in the tool bar. When you've had enough, just click on the Home icon to get back to your start-up home page.

 When you move back to a document you've already seen, the color of the link changes from blue to purple. This is Netscape's way of letting you know you've been to that place before.

URLS Explained Here

Remember that talk about e-mail addresses back in Chapter 2? There's a standard addressing scheme with which Netscape and the Web work, too. It's called the Uniform Resource Locator (URL). The URL pinpoints the locations of documents and other information on the Web so Netscape and other browsers can find the stuff. The structure of a URL may seem complicated at first, but it's really pretty straightforward.

The components of the URL are:

◆ The type of resource

◆ The name of the machine containing the file (the document or information) to be transferred

◆ The full path that locates the file among the directories and subdirectories on the machine

(continued on next page)

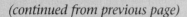

(continued from previous page)

For example, in the URL

```
http://home.netscape.com/home/welcome.html
```

the resource type and transfer protocol are `http` (which, as you know, is HyperText Transfer Protocol), the name of the computer is `home.netscape.com`, and the path and filename of the item on the computer is `/home/welcome.html`.

To you, all this navigation and addressing will be transparent most of the time; Netscape uses the URL embedded in the HTML document to locate the document via hyperlinks behind the scenes.

One thing you should keep in mind, though, is that, unlike e-mail addresses, URLs are case-sensitive—capitalization matters! This is because lots of Web servers are Unix machines; in Unix, filenames uppercase letters are not considered the same as lowercase letters.

Opening a Document Using Its URL

Sometimes you're going to want to go straight to the document—you know where it is, you just want to see it without starting on a home page and skipping through a lot of hot links. Maybe your pal just sent you the URL for the Exploratorium, a really wonderful interactive science museum in San Francisco.

To open a document using its URL:

1. Select File ➤ Open Location from the menu bar. The Open Location dialog box will appear (Figure 3.2).

2. Type the URL of interest in the Open Location text box. (In our example, **http://www.exploratorium.edu**.)

3. Click on Open, and Netscape will find the document for this URL and display it on your screen. (See Figure 3.3.)

You can jump quickly to a document by typing its URL directly into Netscape's Location bar—that is if you have the Location bar displayed.

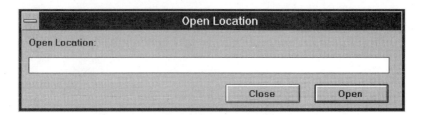

FIGURE 3.2: The Open Location dialog box

FIGURE 3.3: Here's the Exploratorium's home page. We found it using the URL a friend gave us.

The Web is <u>very</u> BIG. And it changes all the time. From time to time you might have difficulty locating or accessing a document. The original may have been removed by its owner, the machine that holds the document may be unavailable or over-worked when you try to access it, or the network path between your machine and the server might be down. If Netscape has been trying for a while to access a document without success, it will display a dialog box saying it just plain cannot locate the document (usually it will say "Unable to locate host"). You can go back to the document that was on screen before you tried making the jump by clicking on OK.

Changing the Size and Color of Displayed Text

If you work along with this chapter, you'll notice on your screen that text appears in different sizes. Usually, the text that makes up the substance of the page—the "body text"—is about the size you'd expect, while the title of the page is larger. (For a more complete discussion of the composition and elements of Web pages, see Chapter 7.)

Changing Fonts and Type Sizes

You might find that while Netscape displays body text clearly and sensibly enough, the titles on a page are too large, so that a single, short title crowds out the body text and you have to scroll around a lot to read anything. You can change the font and size of displayed text in Netscape.

Here's how you do it:

1. Select Options ➤ Preferences from Netscape's menu bar. The Preferences window will appear.
2. From the drop-down list at the top of the window, select Styles (if you have version 1.0) or Fonts and Colors (if you have 1.1). The Preferences window will be updated to reflect your choice.

3. Now, in the Window Style area (in 1.0) or the Fonts/Encodings area (in 1.1), you can make settings for either the proportional or fixed font.

The *proportional* font is the one used for most of the text—body, head, and list text. The *fixed* font is the one used for preformatted text (a rarely used HTML element). Because the fixed font is so seldom used, we're going to stick to the proportional font in our discussion.

4. Click on the Change Proportional Font button (in 1.0) or the *upper* Choose Font button (in 1.1). The Choose Base Font window will appear.

5. From the Font List in this window, select a font. (The fonts that appear as choices on this list are those that are installed on your system. If you've installed lots of fonts, they'll appear here. Otherwise, you'll see the fairly standard set of fonts that come with Windows.)

6. Now select a font size, if you like, from the Size list. As a practical matter, the size you choose should probably be between 10 and 12 points.

Leave both "encodings" set to Latin1. Latin1 is the proper setting for English and most European languages. Note, too, that while there are other choices apparent in this window, they aren't really available to you unless you have a version of Windows that's been regionalized to a specific language or country. Leave this stuff alone unless you know what to do with it.

The changes you make will take effect as soon as you close the Preferences dialog box (which you can do, of course, by clicking on OK).

You might wonder as you go along, "How does changing one font size change the style of more than one kind of text on a single page?" Good question. Basically, Netscape displays different sizes of text (the title, headings, body text, etc.) in comparison to one "measure"—the basic font size. Netscape will display the title so-and-so many times larger than this base measure, and so forth. It is the base measure that you are changing in the procedure we just described.

Changing Colors

In Netscape 1.1, you have the option of changing the *color* of text. Imagine that! To do so, follow these steps:

1. Select Options ➤ Preferences from Netscape's menu bar. The Preferences window will appear.

2. From the drop-down list at the top of the window, select Fonts and Colors. The Preferences window will be updated to reflect your choice.

You get to choose whether you want the selections you are about to make to override any existing settings in the documents you'll be viewing. For example, you might want all the text other than links in all the documents you view to be purple, even if the document's designer made the text black. Or you might want the document's designer's wishes to outweigh your own.

3. To make your upcoming color choices override any other settings, click on the Always Use Mine button.

or

To allow the settings that exist in a given document to override the color choices you are about to make, click on the Let Document Override button.

4. Now click on the Choose Color button for the element whose color you want to specify. Your choices are:

◆ Links

◆ Followed Links

◆ Text

◆ Background

The Color dialog box will appear.

5. In the Color dialog box, you can select any of a number of predefined colors by clicking on one in the Basic Colors area.

or

You can define a custom color by clicking on the Define Custom Colors button. In that case, the window will expand to include a wide

range of colors. Click in the box wherever a color you like appears. Click on the Add to Custom Colors button. The color you have specified will appear in the Custom Colors part of the Color dialog box. Click on it to make it your selected color.

6. Click on OK to close the Color dialog box. The Preferences window will reappear; close it by clicking on OK yet again.

The changes you've made will take place immediately. If you don't like the results, you can always go back and repeat the whole color-changing process, selecting something new and different.

 You can always go back to the original, default color scheme. Just deselect any custom colors you've indicated and make sure you've clicked on the Default button next to Background.

Saving Stuff to Your Local Machine

Let's say you've been skipping around the Internet and looking at a lot of stuff and you found something really nifty you want to hold on to.

 Saving takes up valuable disk space. This means you don't want to save <u>everything</u>. You do want to save things you want to keep for reference or access quickly in the future.

There are two ways to save a document to your local hard drive. We'll get to those in a second; first, a word or two on naming files in general and hypertext files in particular.

Naming the Files

Most documents you'll want to save don't conform to the standard DOS file-naming conventions. In DOS, a filename can be up to eight characters long, followed by a period and then by an extension of up to three characters.

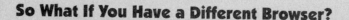

So What If You Have a Different Browser?

One line of thinking goes that Web documents should be viewable by any person with any Web browser, so pages should be thoughtfully designed to take into account the failings of browsers other than Netscape. Another line goes that one should exploit all the wonderful features Netscape has to offer, including fancy things like special colors and the use of columns, even though people using Web browsers other than Netscape might not be able to view that stuff as it was intended to appear. You can sometimes see the evidence of this "debate" on the Web in the form of messages that say something like "Use Netscape for best viewing," or "Netscape not Required." Let's take a look at what all this talk is about.

Netscape, since its nascent moment, has always pushed the envelope of what a Web browser can do. Netscape 1.0 shipped supporting HTML version 1.0 and some of the proposed HTML+ extensions, while at the time all other Web browsers were still offering only HTML version 0.9. Netscape 1.1 was released supporting the newly proposed HTML 3.0 standard, with a promise to support the final HTML 3.0 standard as soon as it's finalized. What does this mean to you? Well, by using all the advanced HTML features that Netscape supports, Web page authors can create state-of-the-art, visually sophisticated documents. For example, the gray background of a document can instead be a pattern. Small animation windows that are automatically updated can be placed in the document, and even fancy formatted tables and multicolumn lists can be created.

The only drawback in using these amazing features is that Web browsers other than Netscape cannot (yet) display them on screen correctly. A document designed to take full advantage of Netscape's advanced design features can look disappointingly different when it's viewed with some other Web browser.

(This is commonly called the 8.3 standard.) The extension often tells you what kind of file it is. An example might be READTHIS.TXT, a text file.

Filenames you find on the Web may be many characters in length and end in longer extensions. This is because they are often created and stored on Unix machines, and their names follow the Unix file-naming system. But you're using Netscape—a *Windows* product, and that means Windows

is really doing the saving. If you don't change the filename when you save the file to disk, Windows will do it for you. To meet the 8.3 convention, Windows will truncate the filename, often resulting in something that is not easy to recognize. So we recommend that you always assign your own filename to any file that you save to your local PC by typing the name into the appropriate text box (described in the sections that follow).

Saving Stuff You Can See

To save the page you are viewing at the moment to your hard disk:

1. Select File ➤ Save As from the menu bar. The Save As dialog box will appear (Figure 3.4). This is much like a Save As dialog box you'd see in any other Windows application.

2. In the File Name text box, type a filename. You'll use the usual DOS file-naming conventions (up to eight characters, then a period followed by a three-letter extension). Use the extension .HTM because this is a hypertext file and that's the extension for hypertext files.

3. Specify the drive and directory if you like, using the Drives pull-down list and the Directories box.

4. Click on OK.

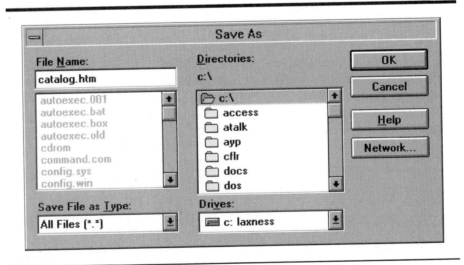

FIGURE 3.4: The Save As dialog box

Perhaps this is obvious, but you won't see the document you've saved on screen when you save it. You'll know it's been saved when you check the Directory list and see the filename there.

Saving Stuff That's Not in View

Let's say the page you are viewing at the moment includes a link to something (maybe sound or an image) you want to save to disk to check out later. You can save the stuff at the other end of the link without first having to travel that link. Just follow these steps:

1. Press the Shift key and hold it down while you click on the link that goes to the stuff you want to save. The familiar Windows-style Save As dialog box will appear.

2. In the File Name text box, type a filename. You'll use the usual DOS file-naming conventions (up to eight characters, then a period followed by a three-letter extension). If the stuff at the other end of the link is a hypertext document, use the extension .HTM. (Other types of files will take care of their own extensions.)

3. Specify the drive and directory if you like, using the Drives pull-down list and the Directories box.

4. Click on OK.

To verify that the save was successful, you can check the Directory list and see if the filename is there.

You can e-mail the contents of a Web page to someone else or even yourself. Sometimes this is a convenient way to "save" a page. Start with the Web page of interest in view on your screen, and select File ➤ Mail Document from Netscape's menu bar. In the Send Mail dialog box that appears, click on the Quote Document button to bring the text of the Web page into an e-mail message. Now, in the Mail To text box, type the e-mail address of the person to whom you wish to send the page, then click on the Send button to send the message containing the Web page on its way.

Viewing Documents You've Saved

You can view a document you've saved to your local hard drive by selecting File ➤ Open File from Netscape's menu bar. The File Open dialog box will appear; again this is a standard Windows dialog box. Select and open the .HTM file of interest by double-clicking on it. By the way, saving a file and then viewing it this way is a lot faster than accessing and viewing it when it's somewhere else in the world; the drawback is that if the owner of the document has made changes to it, you won't know about them. A really cool aspect of this, though, is that when you view a document that's been saved to your local machine, *the links have been saved with it* and you can just click on those links and start up your Web travels again.

 Using the rightmost button on your mouse, click once on any item (text, a link, anything) in the Web page you're viewing. A menu will appear offering you options pertaining to that item.

Jumping Back and Forth While Viewing a Document

The Back and Forward icons on the toolbar provide you with a convenient way to jump back and forth along the hot links you've followed.

Netscape keeps track of the documents you've visited as a history list so you can do this. If you have Netscape running, try clicking on the Back icon to jump backward along the links you've just followed, then click on Forward to jump forward.

There is an end to this—if you jump back to the first document you've viewed in this session, or forward to the last one, you've reached the end of history. The Back or Forward icon, depending on which end of history you've reached, will be grayed out. (You can, as always, create more history—click on another hypertext link to explore further.)

At the bottom of many documents you'll find a hot word that says something like <u>Go Back</u>, which, if you click on it, will quickly jump you back to the last document you viewed. It's usually quicker, however, to click on the Back icon on the toolbar to go back.

You Can Get There from Here in a Snap: Bookmarks

A big part of managing your Netscape tour of the Web is going to be keeping track of what you found and liked. One way you can revisit what's worthy is to save files to disk, a process we described earlier in this chapter. But you don't always want the stuff on your disk—it takes up valuable disk space. When you stumble across something on the Web that you want easy access to in the future, you should mark it with a *bookmark*. In the menu bar you'll find a pull-down menu devoted entirely to bookmarks. Let's take a look at it.

Bookmarking Documents

When you're viewing a page or document you like so much you want to bookmark it for viewing again later, select Bookmarks ➤ Add Bookmark from the menu bar. The name for whatever page you're so taken with will appear immediately on your Bookmark list, which is at the bottom of the Bookmarks menu, below the View Bookmarks option.

Keep in mind that it's not the page itself you save when you create a bookmark, however; it's the page's URL. This means that when you revisit the page you found so interesting, it may have changed. This can be both an advantage, in that you may find even more interesting stuff there next time, and a disadvantage, in that whatever you liked so much the first time might be gone on your next visit.

Quickly Jumping to Documents on the Bookmark List

Anytime you are using Netscape, regardless of where you are or what you're viewing, you can jump to any page you've bookmarked. Just pull down the Bookmarks menu and select the name of the page you want to jump to. There's nothing more to it than that.

Bookmark Management

After a while, when you've bookmarked a lot of pages, you'll find the list growing to unwieldy proportions. The bookmarks themselves might seem to be in no particular order. (Actually, bookmarks are listed in the order you created them, but that's not very helpful when you're digging through a long list.)

Fortunately, Netscape allows you to impose some order on all this seeming chaos. You can toss out the old and unused stuff if you want, but you can also shift things around so they make more sense. You can put related pages next to one another on the bookmark list; you can even group related pages together under headings, which then appear as submenus of the Bookmarks menu.

Rearranging Bookmarks

You can easily rearrange items in your bookmark list. Let's say we've created three bookmarks: one is the Exploratorium home page, which we saw earlier this chapter, the second is the Rolling Stones home page from Chapter 2, and the third is the home page from the National Center for Earthquake Engineering Research (NCEER) at SUNY Buffalo.

The first and the third pages might fit nicely together into a *science* category. Here's how to put them next to one another on the Bookmark list:

1. From Netscape's menu bar, select Bookmarks ➤ View Bookmarks. The Bookmark List window will appear, as shown in Figure 3.5 (where the three bookmarks are displayed).

You can use the Bookmark List window as a handy way to jump to a document you've marked. Simply highlight the bookmark for the page you want to jump to and click on the Go To button.

2. Highlight the bookmark you want to move by clicking on it and then click the Up or Down button to move it up or down one level. (In our example, move the NCEER bookmark up one level in the list by clicking once on the Up button.)

That's all there is to it.

Creating Headers

When you've created a long, long list of bookmarks, rearranging them may seem tedious. In the end, it's also a pretty poor solution to your

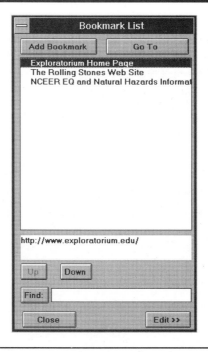

FIGURE 3.5: The Bookmark List window

organizational woes—you'll still find yourself searching line by line through the list. A better way to deal with the problem is to group bookmarks together under *headers*, which will appear on the bookmark list (i.e. the Bookmarks menu) as submenus. (Bookmarks grouped together under a header will appear as options on these submenus.)

It's a lot easier to create appropriate headers and organize your bookmarks under them if you first put your bookmarks in order using the techniques described in the preceding section of this chapter.

Here's how to create headers:

1. If it's not already open on your screen, open the Bookmark List window by selecting Bookmarks ➤ View Bookmarks from the menu bar.

2. Click on the Edit>> button. The Bookmark List window will expand, as shown in Figure 3.6.

Netscape conveniently provides useful information about any highlighted bookmark in the expanded window. You'll find the name of the marked page, its URL, and the dates when you created the bookmark and when you last visited the page. There's even a text box into which you can type your own description of the bookmarked page.

3. Click on the New Header button. This adds an unnamed header (called, unsurprisingly, *New Header*) to the Bookmark list. Note that headers appear with a dash marking them (at the left edge of the list).

4. Click on the Up or Down buttons to move the header to a position above the bookmarks you want to appear grouped together under the header. Following our example from the previous section, we moved the new header to a location above Exploratorium and NCEER.

5. In the Name: text box, give the new header a descriptive name, one that will help you find this stuff when it appears on the bookmark list. (We'll call our new header here *Science*.)

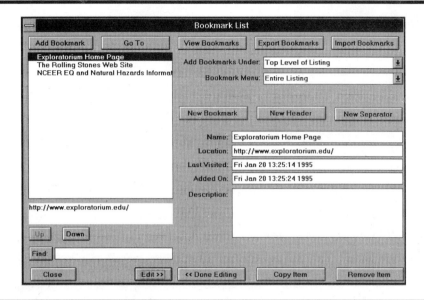

FIGURE 3.6: The expanded Bookmark List window even includes a text box where you can type a description of the page.

6. Now that you've created and named a new header, you'll have to group bookmarks under it. Use the Up and Down keys to move a bookmark under its header. Then, click once on the Up key to "indent" the bookmark, placing it neatly where it belongs.

 If you don't indent the bookmark, it will not appear under the header.

7. Repeat step 6 for each bookmark you wish to place under a header. When you've finished this, close the Bookmark List window by clicking on the Close button.

Now if you pull down the Bookmarks menu, the header you created will appear as a submenu (marked on its right side by an arrow) but the bookmarks you grouped under it won't be listed there. Not to worry—just select the new header and the grouped bookmarks under it will appear.

Displaying the Bookmark List

Netscape gives you a good deal of control over the way the Bookmark list is displayed on the Bookmarks menu. Once you've created a header, you can tell Netscape to put any new bookmarks under it. By default, you see, Netscape will put a new header at the top level of the Bookmark list, which means directly on the Bookmark list and not under any header you've created. To change this and to put any new bookmarks automatically and directly under a header, first open the Bookmark List window. Then pull down the Add Bookmarks Under list and select the header you want to use. It's that simple.

Netscape also allows you to "shrink" the Bookmark list so when you pull down the Bookmarks window, Netscape will display only the bookmarks contained under one header. This may be useful if you've got a *lot* of headers and you're only going to be using one group in a given Web session. To do this, pull down the Bookmark Menu pull-down list on the Bookmark List window and select the name of the headers whose bookmarks you wish to display. To change the list back and display all bookmarks (and headers) again, select Entire Listing from this list.

Removing Items from Your Bookmark List

Out with the old and in with the new! You can remove any bookmark or header you wish from your Bookmark list, making room for fresher material.

To delete items from your Bookmark list:

1. From the menu bar, select Bookmarks ➤ View Bookmarks to open the Bookmark List window.

2. Click on the Edit>> button to expand the window (Figure 3.6).

3. In the list box on the left side of the window, highlight the bookmark or header you wish to remove.

4. Click on the Remove Item button. If it's a bookmark you're removing, the deletion will occur with no further ado. If it's a header you're removing, a dialog box will appear asking you to confirm your action. Click on Yes to confirm and continue.

 If you delete a header from your Bookmark list, any bookmarks under that header will vanish along with it.

5. When you've finished removing, click on the Close button.

The item you deleted will no longer appear in the Bookmark list (i.e. on the Bookmarks pull-down menu).

The History Window as Bookmark List

You might think of the History window as a pseudo-Bookmark list. The History window is a log of every move you make in your Netscape session; each time you launch Netscape, the History window starts empty, then it fills up with a list of your moves as you go along. To see the History window, select Go ➤ View History from the menu bar. You can highlight anything listed there and then click on Go To to jump to that item. This makes it possible to use the History window as a kind of short-term Bookmark list.

You can also use the History window to retrace your steps. This is more convenient than continuously pressing the Back icon, but it's not *terrifically* convenient. You have to scroll through the list of places you've been, find the one you want, and click the Go To button on the bottom of the window—not as quick as using the Bookmark list, but handy in some circumstances.

The more recent part of the History window's listing is also "mirrored" on the Go pull-down menu. The name of each page you have visited appears at the bottom of the Go menu (a checkmark appears next to the name of the current page). To use the Go menu to revisit a page, select Go from the menu bar and then the name of the page you want to see.

Reading and Writing Usenet News with Netscape

Unlike many other Web browsers, Netscape provides you with fully workable access to Usenet. Usenet, which some people think *is* the Internet, is a collection of discussion groups, called *newsgroups*, each organized around a specific topic or area of interest. Using Netscape you can read and post *articles* (messages) to those newsgroups that interest you.

One Way to Get into a Newsgroup

The URLs for newsgroups start with *news:* rather than *http:*. Knowing this handy fact, you can access a Usenet newsgroup by selecting File ➤ Open Location and, in the window that appears, typing the newsgroup's URL (which is just the name of the newsgroup preceded by news:) into the text box and clicking OK. This is a quick way to get into a newsgroup, but it does not preserve your access to the newsgroup—next time you want to go there, you'll have to repeat this procedure.

 Once you've accessed a particular newsgroup using this technique, you can read articles and, using the skills described in the sections that follow (check out <u>Posting a Reply</u> and <u>Posting a New Article</u>), you can write to the newsgroup.

Another Way to Get into a Newsgroup

Netscape lets you *subscribe* to groups you read or participate in regularly. When you subscribe to a newsgroup, a link will be created to take you directly from a Subscribed Newsgroups page to the newsgroup of interest forever after.

You can subscribe to a newsgroup by following these easy steps:

1. From the menu bar, select Directory ➤ Go to Newsgroups. Netscape's Subscribed Newsgroups page will appear, as shown in Figure 3.7.

2. In the text box labeled *Subscribe to this newsgroup*, type the name of the newsgroup to which you want to subscribe. There's no need to use the URL here, just the newsgroup's name will do.

What's Out There?

There are over 10,000 newsgroups out there! Luckily, a list of those newsgroups accessible via your Internet service provider can be seen if you'll just click on the Subscribed Newsgroups page's *View all newsgroups* button. You'll also find a complete list of all the newsgroups that exist in the Usenet newsgroup `news.lists`.

The newsgroup to which you've subscribed will appear as a link on the Subscribed Newsgroups page, with a number in parentheses to its left. The number tells you how many articles in that newsgroup you have yet to read. In Figure 3.7, you can see that we've subscribed to a newsgroup called `comp.os,ms-windows.misc`, which is a hotbed of talk about Microsoft Windows.

Subscribed Newsgroups

Here are the newsgroups to which you are currently subscribed. The number to the left of the newsgroup name is how many unread articles currently exist in that group.

To unsubscribe from any of these newsgroups, select the matching toggle buttons and click the "Unsubscribe from selected newsgroups" button. To subscribe to a new newsgroup, type in the name of the newsgroup in the "Subscribe to this newsgroup" field and press Return or Enter.

Press the "Reload" button to get an up to date article listing.

```
  62  [ ] news.announce.newusers
5683  [ ] news.newusers.questions
5316  [ ] news.answers
2714  [ ] comp.os.ms-windows.misc
```

| Unsubscribe from selected newsgroups |

Subscribe to this newsgroup: [_____]

FIGURE 3.7: The newsgroups you subscribe to will appear as links on Netscape's Subscribed Newsgroups page.

Unsubscribing from Newsgroups

You won't always want to remain a subscriber to a particular newsgroup. Your interests will change; the newsgroup will grow dull. In fact, Netscape automatically subscribes to three newsgroups for you—they provide helpful information for new Usenet users but aren't really necessary once you've become accomplished, so you'll probably want to let them go after a while. Unsubscribing is really easy. Click on the box to the left of the newsgroup link—an × will appear in the box—and then click on the button labeled *Unsubscribe from selected newsgroups*. When you do this, the newsgroup link will disappear. You can always resubscribe if you want to pick up that newsgroup again.

Reading Articles in Subscribed Newsgroups

To read articles once you've subscribed to a newsgroup, click on that newsgroup's link. All of the "unread" articles in the newsgroup will appear as links in a list (Figure 3.8) you can see. To read an article just click on its link. When you do this, Netscape will transfer the contents of the article to your computer and display it on the screen.

Reading Along a Thread

Notice also in Figure 3.8 that some articles appear indented below others. Some less capable newsgroup readers display articles only in the order they were posted, but Netscape arranges articles by *subject* in the order they were posted. A message that is not indented is the beginning of a discussion on some particular topic. A message that appears indented below another is a later message about the same subject; often it is a reply.

By ordering the messages in this way, Netscape allows you to read all of the articles about a subject, one right after the other. Messages grouped together by subject in this way are called *threads* and reading messages this

Newsgroup: comp.os.ms-windows.misc

- **WINNT Mail Connection to MS-Mail Server 3.2** - Mike Owens (10)
- **Re: Apps. opening in different spot every time** - Lucien Cinc (15)
- **Re: WHEN IS WIN95 DUE OUT!** - Bob Cerelli (3)
- **Re: Can't enable 32bit FA - LoadFail NETAPI.DLL** - Bob Cerelli (4)
  - Jim Kramer (7)
- **Temp directory** - Stephanie Ann Tuck (11)
  - Hstud (18)
  - Tom Robinson (17)
    - Toralf Bakketun (25)
- **How OS/2 Warp Wins Win95 Loses ! ! ! ! !**
  - curt williams (28)
    - Victor Healey Ki4je (8)
      - Daniel Krislov (15)

FIGURE 3.8:   A few of the unread articles listed for a newsgroup called comp.os.ms-windows.misc (a general discussion group about Microsoft Windows)

way is called *reading along a thread*. A thread is essentially a string of re-lated articles—they're related in that they are usually responses that follow the original article.

To read along a thread, first open any article you want by clicking on its link. (Since Netscape lists the articles in each thread in the order they were posted, it's actually probably a good idea to start with an article that be-gins a thread—in other words, one that is not indented.)

When you're done reading the first article, you can read the next article in the thread—this can be the next contribution to the discussion or a reply to the message you just finished—by clicking on the Next Article button. If you're in the middle of a thread, you can read the article posted prior to the one you're looking at by clicking on the Previous Article button. This button, and all the others you need to read newsgroup articles, appear both at the top *and the bottom* of every displayed article.

Let's quickly go over all of the buttons Netscape's newsreader provides for reading articles.

The Tool	Its Name	What It Does
	Previous Article	Moves to the previous article in the thread you are currently reading.
	Next Article	Moves to the next article in the thread you are currently reading.
	Previous Thread	Moves to the first article in the previous thread.
	Next Thread	Moves to the first article in the next thread.
	Catchup Thread	Retrieves those articles, belonging to the thread you are currently reading, that were posted since you began reading (whether that was a minute ago or hours or even days ago).
	Go To Newsgroup	Returns to the list of unread articles in the newsgroup you are currently reading. This is the same list you saw earlier, in Figure 3.8.

The Tool	Its Name	What It Does
Go To Newsgroups	Go To Newsgroups	Returns to the Subscribed Newsgroups window, which is where you began your venture into newsgroup reading.
Post Followup	Post Followup	Allows you to post a reply to the article you are currently reading.
Reply to Sender	Reply to Sender	Allows you to send an e-mail message to the author of the article you are currently reading.

Posting a Reply

If you want to post a reply to an article you've read, follow these easy steps:

1. With an article open (presumably the one to which you want to reply), click on the Post Followup button either at the top or bottom of the article you are reading. The Send Mail/Post Document window will appear, as shown in Figure 3.9.

In the Send Mail/Post Document window's Subject: box, the subject of your post (taken from the original article) will appear. In the Post: box, the newsgroups in which the original article appeared will be listed.

2. If you'd like to include the original message in your reply, click on the Include Document Text button at the bottom of the window. The original message (the one to which you are posting a reply) will appear in the window. To make it easy for you to see what's what, each line in the original message will be prefixed with the > symbol. You can delete any part (or all) of the original message if you like.

USENET News Posting

Posting to newsgroups:
**comp.os.os2.misc, comp.os.ms-windows.misc, comp.os.ms-windows.advocacy,
bit.listserv.os2-1, bit.listserv.win3-1, talk.rumors, alt.fan.q, alt.2600**

Subject: `Re: How OS/2 Warp Wins Win95 Loses ! ! ! ! !`
Newsgroups: `comp.os.os2.misc,comp.os.ms-windows.misc,comp.os.ms-w`
Message:
```
Cary Quinn <cquinn@rmii.com> wrote:
>
> krislov@ix.netcom.com (Daniel Krislov) wrote:
> > >Q did this  Os/2 Warp is his idea of a joke on humanity.
> > >The federation will beat him by switching their computers to win
> > >Q -stop toying with the nids of men!
> > >
> > >
> > > Haven't you noticed how closely Microsoft resembles the BORG?
```

FIGURE 3.9: The Send Mail/Post Document window is your door to writing newsgroup replies

3. Type your reply to the original message in the Message text box and click on the Send Message button at the bottom of the box.

Your reply will be posted automatically to the groups in which the original article appeared.

You needn't feel compelled to quote the entire original article in your reply. It's considered good form to delete as much of the original message as necessary 'til you get down to just the part that is immediately relevant to your response. Further, you can add or delete newsgroups listed in the Post: text box as you wish. This is a simple matter of typing in the names of any newsgroups you want to add, or of highlighting any you want to delete and then wielding your Delete key.

Posting a New Article

You can post new articles to start new threads as well. Just click on the Post Article icon at the top (or the bottom) of the Newsgroup window that lists unread articles. The procedure after this point is exactly the same as that for posting a reply, except that the subject of the article is not filled in and there is no text in the Message text box, so refer to the preceding section (*Posting a Reply*) for more information.

 Newsgroups and articles will appear in the History window, just as Web pages do. There, a newsgroup will show up as a URL starting with <u>news</u>:, and an article will appear starting with <u>news</u>: but ending with the article's unique ID (identifier)—an odd-looking combination of letters and numbers that will include an @ sign. Remember, you can double-click on anything in the History window to jump to that item.

Do You Need Help?

For technical support for Chameleon Sampler, call NetManage at (408) 973-7171. For answers to your questions about Netscape, call (800) NETSITE or e-mail `info@mcom.com`.

Quitting Netscape

You can quit Netscape any ol' time—even when the N icon is animated.

To leave Netscape, simply do the following:

1. If the N icon is animated, click on the Stop button on the toolbar. This will cancel whatever Netscape is trying to do at the moment. (If the N icon is not animated, skip this step.)

2. To actually quit the program, double-click on the control button in the upper-left corner of the screen, *or* choose File ➤ Exit from the menu bar. This will quit you out of Netscape, leaving you back at the Windows Program Manager with the Custom window showing again. Remember, you are still connected to your Internet service provider and you must break this connection.

3. Click on Disconnect (in the menu bar). A dialog box will appear asking for confirmation. Click on the Yes button to confirm that you want to disconnect.

The Ol' Bookmark List Becomes a Web Page Trick

Here's a nifty trick: You can make your Bookmark list into a Web page that links you to all your favorite places. This is possible because Netscape stores your bookmarks in an HTML file that can be viewed and navigated like any other Web page. With Netscape running, follow these steps:

1. From the menu bar, select Bookmarks ➤ View Bookmarks. The Bookmarks List window will appear.

2. Click on the Edit>> button. The window will expand. Click on the Export Bookmarks button. The Save As dialog box will appear.

3. In the Save As dialog box, type a filename—something like FAVES.HTM, or whatever you like that will remind you that this is your own personal Bookmark List page. (Use the usual DOS filenaming conventions, and end it with .HTM.) Click on the OK button. The Bookmark List window will reappear. Click on the Close button, and you'll be left with the Netscape window.

Now you can open up FAVES.HTM (or whatever you called it) just as you would any other HTML file you've saved to your local machine. The first cool thing is that you'll find you have created a Web page version of your Bookmark list, which you can use as your own home page or pass on to friends and colleagues for their use. The second cool thing you'll find is that all the headings and organization you've done in your Bookmark list will be included in the page. The third cool thing is that any descriptions you've provided for individual items (in the Bookmark window's Description box) will appear as text describing the links. ...Yes, we said links. Because, of course, all the items you've bookmarked appear in this page as clickable links to those resources you found so appealing or useful that you just had to bookmark them.

Now, with your basic skills in place for navigating the Web via Netscape, let's turn our attention in Chapter 4 to some great starting points for your exploration, and then, in Chapter 5, to lots of way cool places you can visit.

Good and Useful Starting Points

You can jump into the Web from any of what seem like zillions of places. This is part of the Web's attraction, but it can be overwhelming when you start your exploration. When you're following links from one document to another, it's also easy to forget how you got to that gold mine of resources you thought you'd remember. You may find it difficult to retrace your steps later on.

Fortunately, there are some great comprehensive starting points on the Web that can really help get you going, and Netscape provides several tools that can help you retrace your electronic trail. By the end of this chapter you should have a pretty good line on how and where to jump in.

The Big Picture

In Chapter 3 we told you how to start Netscape and navigate around. The first time you start Netscape, the Welcome to Netscape page will be the default—the page you see automatically. (Later you can change things to display a different home page on startup, if you like.) The Welcome to Netscape page is a great place to start—we'll look a little more closely at what it has to offer in a second. There are many other good starting places, however, so in this chapter we'll take the time to look at:

◆ The Welcome to Netscape Page

◆ Yahoo: A subject-oriented list

◆ NCSA's Starting Points for Internet Exploration

◆ The NCSA What's New Page

◆ The Mosaic for Microsoft Windows home page

◆ The Internet Business Directory

◆ Other departure points

Before we look at these in detail, let's go over some general information about home pages.

What Is a Home Page, Really?

You can look at this in a couple of ways. To you, the user, the home page is a starting point for exploring the World Wide Web. A home page might be seen as kind of a "main menu." This analogy breaks down a bit because the Web is neither hierarchical nor linear and Netscape is by no means menu-driven; but a home page does outline your options for you—at least the options for moving along the links from the home page to other points of interest on the Web, as imagined by the publisher of this particular home page. To whomever publishes it, the home page is part advertisement, part directory, and part "reference librarian." Publishers of a home page have to think through its construction completely to make it clear what the page is about and what can be found there.

In reality, a home page is a hypertext document with links to other points on the Web. The start-up home page, the one that is automatically loaded each time you launch Netscape, should be one that helps you get going. It may be the default Welcome to Netscape page, a home page that provides a general starting point, or one that is specialized to your interests. You can even set it up so Netscape won't access and display a home page, though why you'd want to start out without the benefit of a good start-up home page is beyond us.

Changing Your Start-Up Home Page

For new users and experienced users whose purposes are fairly general, the Welcome to Netscape page or another of those we describe in this chapter might be best. For those with specialized interests, a specific home page geared to those interests might be better. Let's say, for example, that you're doing a long-term research project on the subject of language and thought. You know what you want—none of this general stuff. For the duration of your project, you might set your start-up home page to the one published by Stanford University's Linguistics Department. That way, each time you launch Netscape, you'll immediately see the Stanford Linguistics Department's home page and you can begin your research from that point. When you've finished that project and begin another—this time writing environmental assessment reports for a large government contractor—you instead use the U.S. Geological Survey's home page as your start-up page.

To speed up Web access you might want to choose as your start-up home page one residing on a nearby server—the closer the better. This is getting easier to do, with the Web's rate of growth—perhaps you work for a company that has its own home page. Remember: you can actually get anywhere on the Web from almost anywhere else on the Web, so it makes sense to make your start-up home page as convenient for you as possible. You can even construct your own custom home page using HTML, as you'll see in Chapter 7.

To change your start-up home page you'll use Netscape's Preferences window—this handy window is your entrance way to changing many facets of Netscape's behavior on your machine.

Here are the steps for changing your home page:

1. Start Netscape by clicking on its icon, without bothering to start Chameleon Sampler or set up your Internet connection. (What we're doing here is strictly a local operation.)

2. Select Options ➤ Preferences from the menu bar. The Preferences window will appear.

3. Pull down the list at the top of the window and from it, select Styles.

4. Roughly in the middle of the window, beneath the option labeled *Home Page Location*, you'll find the URL for the home page currently slated for display at startup. It appears in the text box (Figure 4.1). Highlight that URL and type in its place the URL for the home page you want.

5. Click on the OK button. The Preferences window will close and the Netscape window will appear.

When next you start Netscape, you'll see the home page you just designated as your start-up page rather than the original default start-up home page.

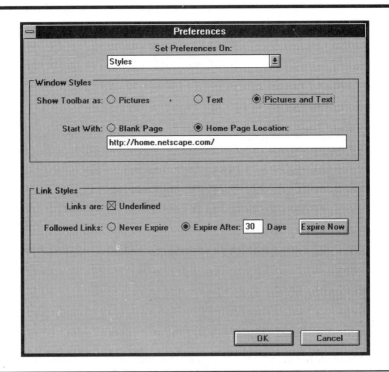

FIGURE 4.1: Type in the URL for the home page you want to appear at startup.

Let's say you have some reason for not wanting to see any home page at all when you launch Netscape. The steps you'll follow to do this are very similar to those for changing the start-up home page:

1. With Netscape running (you don't need to start Chameleon Sampler or be connected to the Internet while you do this), select Options ➤ Preferences from the menu bar. The Preferences window will appear.

2. Select Styles from the list at the top of the window.

3. In the box area labeled *Window Styles*, find *Blank Page* and click on its radio button.

4. Now click on the OK button. The Preferences window will close and the Netscape window will appear.

What could be easier? When you launch Netscape again, you should see absolutely no home page at start-up. Instead you'll see an empty document window.

 Just because you've changed your start-up home page or arranged for none to appear at startup doesn't mean you can't access the Netscape Welcome page whenever you want. It's available by selecting Directory ➤ Welcome! from Netscape's menu bar or by clicking on the Welcome directory button just above Netscape's document window. In addition, you can always bookmark the Welcome to Netscape page, as described in Chapter 3.

Now let's take a look at some good all-purpose home pages, starting with the default start-up home page you've heard so much about.

The Welcome to Netscape Page

The topmost part of the Welcome to Netscape page—with its slick graphics and friendly message—should be familiar to you from Chapter 3 (Figure 3.1).

What's Out There?

You can always go home again. The URL for the Welcome to Netscape page is `http://home.netscape.com`.

If you scroll down the page, you'll see links to information on Netscape products and the company itself, along with more links to instructions on basic Web navigation skills (we've already got that covered in this book). Of most interest to us here, however, are the links that lead to exploring other stuff on the Internet. Check them out.

Netscape Communications, the folks who bring you Netscape, are changing their Internet name from `mcom.com` to `netscape.com` as we write this book. While both names may work for you, it is also possible you'll encounter some trouble with the old name. Just replace the `mcom.com` part of any Netscape-related URLs with `netscape.com` and that should solve the problem.

The Netscape What's New Page

Netscape provides a What's New page, which includes (what else?) links to new items on the Web. You can access Netscape's What's New page by clicking on the What's New! directory button or by selecting Directory ➤ What's New! from Netscape's menu bar. The What's New page will appear, showing links for what's new. The length of this listing at any given time depends on how many Web sites have been announced in the current month.

What's Out There?

Netscape's What's New page is easily found at the URL `http://home.netscape.com/home/whats-new.html/`.

Registering Netscape

The first time you start Netscape, take the time to read the licensing agreement that appears on screen and register the program. It's the honest, right thing to do, and it couldn't be easier. You can check out the licensing agreement and get registered via links that appear on the Welcome to Netscape page.

The agreement says that Netscape is free for the use of students, faculty members, staff of educational organizations, employees of nonprofit corporations, and *for individuals evaluating the program*. If you fall into the latter group, you must pay a license fee of $39 once your evaluation period is up.

Filling out the registration form is terrifically simple; really it's just like filling out a paper registration card, except that you're doing it on screen.

Follow links on the Welcome to Netscape page or open the URL `http://order.netscape.com/order.html` to get to the Netscape Order Form page. Here you can fill out the simple forms to order and pay for a copy of the latest version of Netscape Navigator (a.k.a "Netscape") or any number of other software products Netscape offers.

What's Way Cool!

Netscape's What's New page doesn't just tell you what's new, but also what's truly *outstanding*. Check out the What's Cool! page by clicking on the What's Cool! directory button or by selecting Directory ➤ What's Cool from Netscape's menu bar. You'll find a page filled with links to outstanding Web pages grouped month by month (for the last few months).

Yahoo: A Subject-Oriented List

Yahoo, begun at Stanford University, is a complete and extensive list of sites on the Web, organized by subject (Figure 4.2). Yahoo puts forth a hierarchical list of a whopping 35,000+ sites on the Web. (The number's growing at a phenomenal rate, so don't quote us.) To get to this amazing resource,

1. Select Directory ➤ Internet Directory from the Netscape menu bar or just click on the Net Directory button. In either case, Netscape's Internet Directory page will appear.

2. Click on the Yahoo link and you'll soon see a wonder of a page with hundreds of links, each representing a different category of information available on the Web.

Another way to get to Yahoo, of course, is simply to

1. Select File ➤ Open URL from the Netscape menu bar and type the Yahoo URL into the Open URL dialog box, then click on OK.

What's Out There?

You can mosey on over to Yahoo with the URL http://www.yahoo.com.

Some of the categories we found when we looked were:

◆ Art
◆ Business
◆ Computers
◆ Economy
◆ Education
◆ Government
◆ Law
◆ News
◆ Science
◆ Sports

ESCAPES

SUBJECT DIRECTORIES

These directories present probably the widest range of information on the Internet. Most are organized by subject matter, but the groupings vary from site to site - you might want to explore all of them to see which one presents information and updates topics of most interest to you. The geographic sites offer yet another way of searching for information, as well as a chance to see the Internet's growth around the world.

YAHOO

David Filo and Jerry Yang at Stanford have been offering their directory of Internet sites for over a year now. It currently features over 32,000 entries. Yahoo also offers listings of the most popular pages, the ability to search the directory of services, and (if you're up for adventure) a way to visit any Net page at random.

Yahoo

[What's New? | What's Cool? | What's Popular? | A Random Link]

[*Yahoo* | Up | Search | Suggest | Add | Help]

- Art *(730)* [new]
- Business *(9540)* [new]
- Computers *(3433)* [new]
- Economy *(993)* [new]
- Education *(1962)* [new]
- Entertainment *(9965)* [new]
- Environment and Nature *(283)* [new]
- Events *(64)* [new]
- Government *(1280)* [new]
- Health *(648)* [new]
- Humanities *(269)* [new]
- Law *(243)* [new]
- News *(333)* [new]
- Politics *(212)* [new]
- Reference *(531)* [new]
- Regional Information *(5192)* [new]
- Science *(3554)* [new]
- Social Science *(130)* [new]
- Society and Culture *(1066)* [new]

There are currently **35288** *entries in Yahoo.*

FIGURE 4.2: Click on the Yahoo link (above) to get to Yahoo's subject-oriented list (below), and then click around until you find what you seek.

There are plenty more. Clicking on any link on the Yahoo page will take you to yet another page of links focused on the selected category. Just keep clicking through the links 'til you find what you seek.

If you know of a page that is not in the Yahoo lists, click on the <u>Add</u> link at the top of any Yahoo page. A form will appear into which you can type the URL of the page you want included in Yahoo. You can also enter a description of the page and the Yahoo category under which you believe the link should go. The people that run Yahoo will review your submission and, if they like the page, it will become part of Yahoo's list.

Searching through Yahoo

Searching is the subject of another chapter (that'll be Chapter 6) but let's just pause here for a moment because Yahoo is not just clickable, it's *searchable*! To search Yahoo,

1. Click on the Search link at the top of any Yahoo page. The Yahoo Search page will appear (Figure 4.3).

2. In the text box, type one or more words (separated by spaces) describing what you seek. Make selections to indicate

◆ Whether you want to find pages that include *all* of the words you entered or *any* of them

◆ Whether you want to search only URLS, only titles of pages, only descriptions of pages, or any combination of these items

◆ Whether you want the search to be case-sensitive

◆ Whether you want the search to look for whole words or pieces of the words

◆ The maximum number of documents you want to see as the result of your search

3. Click on Search. A page will appear showing a listing of pages (all appearing as links) that match the criteria you set out for the search.

Yahoo Search

[*Yahoo* | Up | Search | Suggest | Add | Help]

Find all matches containing the *keys* (separated by space)

[   ] [Search] [Clear]

Find matches in ☒ Title ☒ URL ☒ Comments
☐ Case sensitive matching
Find matches that contain
　　　○ At least one of the *keys* (boolean **or**)
　　　⊙ All *keys* (boolean **and**)
　　　○ All *keys* as a single string
Consider *keys* to be
　　　⊙ Substrings
　　　○ Complete words
Limit the number of matches to [100   ▼]

FIGURE 4.3:　Yahoo is searchable!

To check out the pages that appeared in the listing as the result of your search, just click on their links. If you click around a while and get away from the page listing the result of your search, you can always go back to that page by selecting Go from the menu bar and then selecting Yahoo Search from the list that appears.

NCSA's Starting Points for Internet Exploration

NCSA's Starting Points for Internet Exploration is a document that includes links to information about the Web and Mosaic. Near the top of

◆ Subject Information

◆ Data Sources by Service

◆ Directory of Web Servers

This is a handy all-purpose set of links to services new Web users will find helpful. Each of these categories contains likely candidates for your start-up home page; let's take a closer look at them one by one.

What's Out There?

Jump off from NCSA's Starting Points for Internet Exploration at the URL `http://www.ncsa.uiuc.edu/SDG/Software/Mosaic/StartingPoints/NetworkStartingPoints.html`.

Information by Subject

The Starting Points page has many links to subject-oriented pages of information, enough so that we don't have space to go into detail about all of them, but here's the gist of it.

To get a subject list of available information, select the Information By Subject link. The World Wide Web Virtual Library will appear (Figure 4.4). You can click on any category in the Virtual Library to see a list of resources for that category. If you have an idea of what topic you want to explore, here's where to start.

What's Out There?

The URL for the World Wide Web Virtual Library: Subject Catalog page is `http://info.cern.ch/hypertext/DataSources/bySubject/Overview.html`.

The WWW Virtual Library

This is a distributed subject catalogue. See <u>Summary</u>, <u>Library of Congress Classification</u> (Experimental), <u>Top Ten most popular Fields</u> (Experimental), <u>Statistics</u> (Experimental), and <u>Index</u>. See also arrangement by <u>service type</u> ., and <u>other subject catalogues of network information</u> .

Mail to <u>maintainers</u> of the specified subject or www-request@info.cern.ch to add pointers to this list, or if you would like <u>to contribute to administration of a subject area</u>.

See also <u>how to put your data on the web</u>. All items starting with ! are *NEW!* (or newly maintained). New this month: ※ <u>African Studies</u> ※ <u>Cross-Connection Control/Backflow Prevention</u> ※ <u>Collecting</u> ※ <u>Irrigation</u> ※ <u>Sociology</u> ※ <u>Standards and Standardization Bodies</u> ※ <u>Tibetan Studies</u> ※ <u>United Nations and other international organisations</u> ※ <u>U.S. Federal</u>

FIGURE 4.4: Click on the Subject Catalog link in the NCSA Starting Points for Internet Exploration page to open up the World Wide Web Virtual Library: Subject Catalog page shown here.

For example, if you're interested in geology, click on Earth Science; after the N becomes animated, the Earth Sciences listing will be displayed. You can make further choices from there—for example, you can explore sublistings of earth sciences organizations around the world; delve into pertinent current events; or unearth useful resources, software, and references. Figure 4.5 will give you an inkling of the possibilities.

What's Out There?

You can dig up the Earth Sciences list with the URL `http://www.geo` `.ucalgary.ca/VL-EarthSciences.html`. The United States Geological Survey's home page can be unearthed at `http://www.usgs.gov/`.

Data Sources by Service

Another useful way to view all the information on the Web is by service—that is, FTP, gopher, and WAIS, in addition to http. If you know *where* you

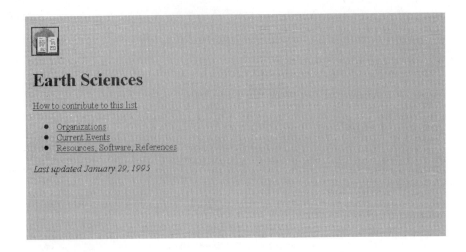

FIGURE 4.5: Clicking on the **Organizations** link in the earth Sciences page (above) will take you to the list in the Earth Sciences Organizations page (below).

might find whatever you're looking for—say, if you know it's on an FTP server at UC Santa Barbara—it makes more sense to look for the information organized by the *type of server* rather than by the topic.

From the Starting Points page, you can check out the services listing by clicking on the Type of Service link. A document will appear with hypertext links to additional listings for each service type:

◆ World Wide Web servers

◆ WAIS servers

◆ Network News

◆ Gopher

◆ Telnet access

Click on the service type that interests you and a detailed listing of servers of that type will appear. Click on the specific server you're looking for; a connection will be established to that server and you can then find what you're seeking. (You started out knowing what and where it was, remember?)

What's Out There?

You can check out data sources by the type of service they represent via the URL http://info.cern.ch/hypertext/DataSources/ByAccess.html.

Directory of Web Servers

The Web, as we've said, is a global network. To explore the Web's branches in other countries, you can use the Internet Directory page's directory of servers. To access it, click on the World Wide Web Servers link. The World Wide Web Servers: Summary document will appear. Here you'll find a list of known Web servers around the world, categorized by geographical areas:

◆ Africa

◆ Asia

◆ Australia and Oceania

◆ Central America

◆ Europe

- ◆ Middle East
- ◆ North America
- ◆ South America

Each of these areas is further categorized by country. What's this good for? Well, let's say you're interested in finding out the name of the head of the Computer Science Department at the University of Sydney. This is just the sort of information you're more likely to find on a server in Australia than anywhere else; why not start your search in the right country?

What's Out There?

Web Servers around the world are listed and even mapped out at the URL `http://info.cern.ch/hypertext/DataSources/WWW/Servers.html`.

For a more graphical approach than the list offers, click on <u>clickable world map</u> and you'll get a view like that shown in Figure 4.6.

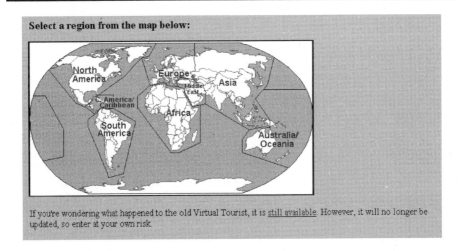

Select a region from the map below:

If you're wondering what happened to the old Virtual Tourist, it is <u>still available</u>. However, it will no longer be updated, so enter at your own risk.

FIGURE 4.6: Click on a continent to start tracking down Web servers located there.

The NCSA What's New Page

The Web is a happening place—new Web servers come online every month. To find out what's new any ol' time, check out the NCSA What's New page. When schools, companies, or individuals set up new http servers they send out announcements with basic information about their server. This information gets anchored to the What's New page and a link is born—that is to say, the informational listings on the What's New page are (what else?) hyperlinks to the respective new server.

 The NCSA What's New document can be quite long. It may take a very long time for the entire document to appear, but the information it contains is plenty useful. It's well worth the wait.

What's Out There?

You can get hip to what's happening via the NCSA What's New page at `http://www.ncsa.uiuc.edu/SDG/Software/Mosaic/Docs/whats-new.html`.

The archive of old NCSA What's New pages is another useful stopping off place; turn to Chapter 6 for more information.

The Mosaic for Microsoft Windows Home Page

The folks at NCSA were the original creators of Mosaic, and they maintain a home page (Figure 4.7) filled with information about their version of Mosaic for Microsoft Windows. Mosaic, you remember, is the granddaddy of all the Web browsers and was a precursor to Netscape.

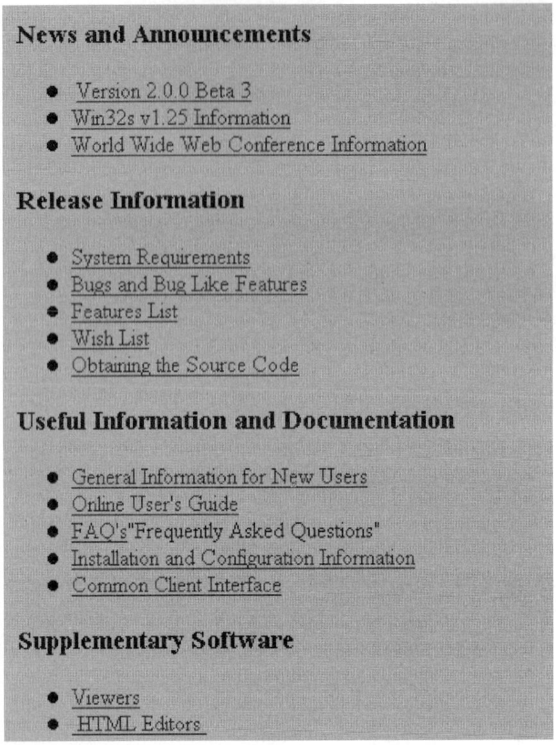

News and Announcements

- Version 2.0.0 Beta 3
- Win32s v1.25 Information
- World Wide Web Conference Information

Release Information

- System Requirements
- Bugs and Bug Like Features
- Features List
- Wish List
- Obtaining the Source Code

Useful Information and Documentation

- General Information for New Users
- Online User's Guide
- FAQ's "Frequently Asked Questions"
- Installation and Configuration Information
- Common Client Interface

Supplementary Software

- Viewers
- HTML Editors

FIGURE 4.7: The Mosaic for Microsoft Windows home page includes information about the Web, Mosaic, and viewers that will enhance your Netscape experience.

This is a very good place to visit, in that there are also links here to other software you might want to use with Netscape—those external viewers discussed in Chapters 2 and 10, for example.

However, this is *such* a fountain of basic information that pretty much everyone starts here, and that's not good. This is a heavy traffic area, so much so that Mosaic's developers at NCSA/UIUC would like you to use some other start-up home page to take the weight off this one. If you make up your mind to change your start-up home page from the Netscape home page to another, this is not your best bet.

Let's look at what makes this home page so useful in your Web travels.

Mosaic for Microsoft Windows and NCSA Mosaic: A Tale of Two Home Pages

The Mosaic for Microsoft Windows home page is different from the NCSA Mosaic home page. If you want information about Mosaic for Windows—the application, new features, bug fixes and enhancements—you'll find it in the Mosaic for Microsoft Windows home page. The NCSA Mosaic home page was the original default home page, covering not just the Windows product but Mac and UNIX, too. When traffic became overwhelming a split was deemed necessary and was carried out.

You'll know which of these home pages is which not only by the difference in content, but by the URL. The Mosaic for Windows Home Page, with links to information specific to Mosaic for Windows, has this URL:

```
http://www.ncsa.uiuc.edu/SDG/Software/WinMosaic/HomePage.html
```

The NCSA Mosaic home page—which contains stuff like general information about the Web, hyperlinks to catalogues, indexes of information that's available by subject—has the following as its URL:

```
http://www.ncsa.uiuc.edu/SDG/Software/Mosaic/NCSAMosaicHome.html
```

Downloading Viewers and Other Software

When the folks who developed NCSA Mosaic have new versions available, an announcement is posted on the Mosaic for Microsoft Windows home page. Likewise, when new viewers become available, an announcement is posted. In fact, the people at NCSA will tell you about pretty much whatever they find that they think you might want, as long as they think it's good stuff. Your option, then, is to take advantage of this opportunity by downloading whatever you think you can use. (See *Mosaic for Microsoft Windows and NCSA Mosaic: A Tale of Two Home Pages*.)

When you're looking over the Mosaic for Microsoft Windows home page and you see an announcement telling you about new software, you'll be

told in the announcement more or less how to get the software. Here are two possible scenarios:

◆ The announcement will say something like "...you can get it here:" and will be followed by a blue, underlined word. This indicates that the link is to the software file itself.

◆ The announcement will say something like "...you can get it from X-Y-Z place" and X-Y-Z will be blue and underlined. This indicates that the link is to wherever the software file is located.

In either case, all you have to do is click on the link. If the link is to the software file itself, the Save As dialog box will appear, allowing you to save the file to your local machine. If the link is not directly to the software but rather to its location, some sort of page will appear, probably telling you about the software; in turn, that page will have a link for you to click on, and when you do, the Save As dialog box will appear.

Saving software files with the Save As dialog box is a very straightforward Windows operation; you probably won't have to (or even want to) rename the files but you may want to specify the drive and directory you want them to land in.

 Downloading software is a lot like saving files to your local machine, which we described in detail in Chapter 3.

Compressed Files

Often you'll find that the software files you download from the Web are *zipped*—they've been compressed with a utility like PKZip or LHarc—which you'll know because the filename ends in either .ZIP (for PKZip) or .LZH (for LHarc). Files are zipped (*compressed, shrunk,* or *compacted*) to make them smaller, so that they can be transmitted more quickly. Compressed files often can be $^1/_2$ the size of the original file; some files can be compressed to as little as $^1/_{20}$ their original size. If a file has been compressed, you'll need a companion program to uncompress the file. PKZip/PKUnzip are available commercially; LHarc is downloadable freeware. Other compression/decompression programs are also available—some emulate or are compatible with their commercially available cousins (Zip/Unzip, for example, will compress and uncompress PKZip files).

What's Out There?

You'll find a table full of information about available compression software at the URL `ftp://ftp.cso.uiuc.edu/doc/pcnet/compression`.

The Internet Business Directory

As the Internet has expanded from its roots as a network of academic and military computers, commercial use has become more and more a reality. The Internet Business Directory page is a useful resource for investigating commercial use; it has links providing access to and information about businesses that maintain an Internet presence.

While it is still not terribly common to find products sold directly on the Internet (at least not yet), you can get information about businesses and the products they offer from the Internet Business Directory page, shown in Figure 4.8.

Welcome to the
Internet Business Directory

- Catalogs
- How to join the IBD
- Search IBD, UseNet News, Resumes
- Directory of Resumés
- Resumé Service FAQ
- Rumor E-Mail Database

FIGURE 4.8: The Internet Business Directory provides links to business-related resources.

What's Out There?

The Internet Business Directory is located at the URL http://ibd.ar.com/.

Other Points of Departure

There are literally dozens (if not hundreds) of places from which you can launch your Web explorations, and the list is growing every day. Individuals like Scott Yanoff and John December maintain lists that are very worthwhile.

What's Out There?

Scott Yanoff's list of Internet resources is at the URL
http://slacvx.slac.stanford.edu/misc/internet-services.html.
John December's list is at the URL
http://www.rpi.edu/Internet/Guides/decemj/text.html.

Check out the inside front cover of this book for even more starting places.

Now What?

With Netscape starting-point basics under your belt, let's take a wider look at what's available on the World Wide Web. In Chapter 5, we're going to have a look at some sites so hot they sizzle.

Spots on the Web You Won't Want to Miss

Those home pages we talked about in Chapter 4 are great places to get going in your Web exploration, but they sure aren't the be all and end all. Browsing the Web is what Netscape's all about, and browsing is all about happening across the unexpected. As we've said, the Web changes every day; you'll find things we've never dreamed of in your own Web travels. Here to get you started are some hip, happening, and downright amazing things we found on the Web when we were just looking around.

Some Real Roadmarkers

Along the Infobahn, there are many places you'll want to visit. Let's start our survey by looking at what's "best," what's new, and what-makes-it-easy-to-find-what-you-want.

The Best of the Web

Here you'll find hyperlinks to winners of the annual *Best of the World Wide Web* competition, which was spawned at the International World Wide Web Conference in Geneva in May 1994. The winners are selected during a two-month period of open nominations followed by a two-week period of open voting. More than 5,000 votes were cast to select the first year's winners. The point of the contest—and the point of displaying the winners on this server—is to highlight the Web's potential to new users and to information providers. The *Best of the World Wide Web* competition shows what can be done with the Web's underlying technology: the Hyper-Text Markup Language (HTML) and the HyperText Transport Protocol (HTTP).

What's Out There?

You can see winners of the *Best of the World Wide Web* competition through the URL `http://wings.buffalo.edu/contest/`.

The Best of the Web page is a good place to begin exploring the Web. Winners are organized into categories—General, Application, and Technical—within which these awards are given:

◆ Best Overall Site

◆ World Wide Web Hall of Fame

◆ Best Campus-Wide Information System

◆ Best Commercial Service

◆ Best Educational Service

◆ Best Entertainment Site

◆ Best Professional Service

◆ Best Navigational Aid

◆ Most Important Service Concept

◆ Best Document Design

◆ Best Use of Interaction

◆ Best Use of Multiple Media

◆ Most Technical Merit

Some of the winners are included in this book—for example, the Xerox PARC Map Viewer we talk about later in this chapter was the *Most Technical Merit* winner in 1994. In Figure 5.1 you can see another winner, the World Wide Web Sports Information Service. Be sure to check out the Best of the Web; you can use the current winners as handy starting points for your Web travels.

What's New with NCSA Mosaic

We talked about the NCSA Mosaic What's New document briefly in Chapter 4, but it's worth another mention here. This dynamic document covers recent changes and additions to the Web. When new information providers go online, they can submit an announcement to the Keepers of this Page. With the appropriate reference in place in the form of a hyperlink, the new material is accessible from this list simply by clicking on the hyperlinked name in the listing.

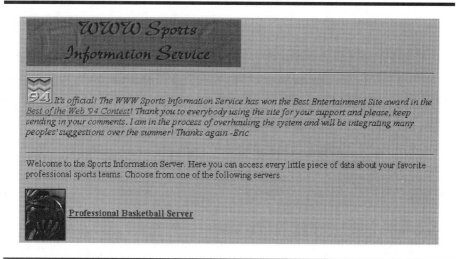

FIGURE 5.1: World Wide Web Sports Information Service provides information about professional basketball and football.

The What's New page is a great place to see the range of material becoming available on the Web. The URL is `http://www.ncsa.uiuc.edu/SDG/Software/Mosaic/Docs/Whats-new.html`. New information providers can submit announcements to the keepers of What's New via the URL `http://www.ncsa.uiuc.edu/SDG/Software/Mosaic/Docs/submit-to-whats-new.html`.

What's New pages going as far back as June 1993 are available as of this writing.

The World Wide Web Worm

As you'll recall from Chapter 2, there are Web wanderers, robots, and other automated processes scurrying through the Web to document the numerous Web sites available. The most useful of these is probably the World Wide Web Worm (Figure 5.2). Because the Worm (WWWW) creates an indexed database, and because Netscape provides a way for you to query data through its *forms* mechanism, you can send a request to the Worm and it will search the Web all over the world to find out whatever you've requested.

What's Out There?

Find out about the Worm and set it into motion through the URL `http://www.cs.colorado.edu/home/mcbryan/WWWW.html`.

There is one caveat here: the Worm is another overworked resource, and because of this it's sometimes unable to return the listing you want. See Chapter 6 for more on the World Wide Web Worm, including tips for getting the most from it.

WWWW - the WORLD WIDE WEB WORM

Best of the Web '94 - **Best Navigational Aid.** Oliver McBryan

Last Run: Sept 5. **Users: 500,000 per month.**
Introduction, Definitions, Search Examples, Failures, Register a Resource, WWWW Paper.

Select:
| 1. Search only in Titles of citing documents |
| 2. Search only in Names of citing documents |
| 3. Search all Citation Hypertext |
| 4. Search all Names of Cited URL's |

Keywords: [   ]   Start Search

FIGURE 5.2: The World Wide Web Worm will help you search the Web efficiently.

Blinded by Science

The Web, and in fact the Internet, started as a research tool, though of course it's grown into much more than that. You can see the effects of these beginnings, though, in the wide range of information on the World Wide Web about everything from nuclear physics to genetic engineering to cancer research to… well, you get the idea. Here's a sampling of some Web servers that are chock full o' fascinating and useful data.

The Exploratorium

Here's a real beauty. The Exploratorium is a hands-on, interactive science museum in San Francisco. To call it a museum, though, is a *bit* misleading—it's a really FUN place for the whole family. The only problem is that if you live outside the San Francisco Bay Area, it may be difficult to get there. No longer. The Exploratorium, which has been on the Internet for a while now (it *is* a science and technology showplace, after all) now has its very own Web server! Much of the fun (and educational) experience you'd go to the Exploratorium for now is not only online, but also graphical and interactive, in the true Exploratorium spirit (Figure 5.3).

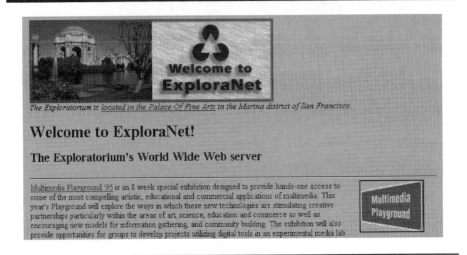

FIGURE 5.3: The Exploratorium offers online interactive fun for everyone.

Once you've accessed the Exploratorium's home page, you can click on the Digital Library and then select from a page of offerings ranging from photos of current exhibits to actual interactive versions of electronic exhibits and even (if you have the right sound drivers) a sample of the Doppler effect (you know—how a train sounds as it passes you).

MIT SIPB Home Page

Forage for days at the MIT SIPB home page (Figure 5.4), with links to just-about-everywhere-else on the Web, all *very* well organized and easy to access. After all—where better to look into science and technology than that granddaddy of science and technology academia, the Massachusetts Institute of *Technology*?

What's Out There?

The MIT SIPB home page, a real doozy, is available at the URL
`http://www.mit.edu:8001`.

MIT SIPB World Wide Web Server

Welcome to the Student Information Processing Board World Wide Web server.

New to the World Wide Web? Maybe you don't know Mosaic from HTTPD? Check out The World Wide Web for the Clueless, a quick, **non-jargon** intro to WWW and our server. (These are hypertext links; just click on them to follow them.)

SIPB will be offering a number of computer-related courses over IAP '95. Check out our IAP Course Guide for more information.

We welcome any and all feedback you'd like to make, via our (optionally anonymous) comment gateway.

MIT has an official MIT web server with all sorts of information about MIT.

FIGURE 5.4: A home page for that granddaddy of science and technology, MIT

Here you'll also find the latest version of PGP (Pretty Good Privacy), a free public-key encryption mechanism for noncommercial use. You'll also find a hyperlink to a great listing of online resources for women—women in computer science and engineering, women in academia and industry, gender and sexuality, women's studies programs and women's centers (click on Interesting Documents and then click on "A collection of writings and resources on *women* in computer science and engineering, women on the Net, women's studies, etc.").

Back at the MIT SIPB home page, click on Other Information Servers around MIT to display the More Neat Servers document. You'll find links to pages providing information about MIT departments, admissions, administration, and other such issues. Scroll further down the page to the

MIT Laboratories heading. This is lab-coat city, with links to:

◆ The MIT Laboratory for Nuclear Science

◆ The MIT Microwave Subnode of NASA's Planetary Data System, a subsidiary of the Geosciences node of NASA's Planetary Data System

◆ The MIT Earth Resources Laboratory

◆ The MIT Research Laboratory for Electronics

◆ The MIT Artificial Intelligence Laboratory

◆ The MIT Laboratory for Computer Science, which among several other ventures, has joined forces with CERN in guiding the future direction of the World Wide Web

◆ The MIT Microsystems Technology Laboratories

◆ The MIT Weather Radar Laboratory

◆ The MIT Computational Aerospace Sciences Laboratory

◆ The MIT Plasma Fusion Center

◆ The MIT/Whitehead Center for Genome Research

Theses, general information about the research centers, and links to additional subgroups are all available by following links within a specific laboratory area.

What's Out There?

The URL for direct access to the MIT Microwave Subnode of NASA's Planetary Data System is `http://delcano.mit.edu/`. Among other things, pictures of the Shoemaker-Levy comet are available here.

MIT Media Lab

The MIT Media Lab is widely known as a happening place in the field of technology, particularly regarding human interaction with technology. If you want to learn about current research in *collaborative interface agents*—semi-intelligent systems that will help you with computer-based tasks—check out the Autonomous Agents Group on the MIT Media Lab's home page. Details of several of the Lab's ongoing research projects are available from there, including complete papers.

What's Out There?

You'll get direct access to the MIT Media Lab through the URL `http://www.media.mit.edu/`.

Academia Is Only Mouse-Clicks Away

Several other worthwhile university home pages are readily available. One that's especially interesting is the home page for the ANU (Australian National University) Bioinformatics Facility, which is part of ANU's Centre for Molecular Structure and Function, Centre for Information Science Research (CISR), and Supercomputer Facility. The ANU's URL is `http://life.anu.edu.au`. Geographically closer to home, but no harder to get to via Netscape, you'll find:

◆ University of North Carolina at Chapel Hill (`http://sunsite.unc.edu`)

◆ Legal Information Institute, Cornell Law School
(`http://www.law.cornell.edu/lii.table.html/`)

◆ Ohio State University (`http://www.cis.ohio-state.edu`)

◆ Honolulu Community College (`http://www.hcc.hawaii.edu`)

◆ Northwestern University (`http://www.acns.nwu.edu`)

◆ Carnegie Mellon University (`http://www.cmu.edu`)

Each of these offers links to a variety of useful and remarkable documents—check 'em out.

Mars Atlas Home Page

Cybernauts who are really frustrated astronauts can get vicarious thrills looking at Viking Orbiter shots of Mars (Figure 5.5). The Mars Atlas home page gives you entrée to a browsable, zoomable, and scrollable Mars atlas, providing access to literally thousands of high-resolution Viking Orbiter images.

What's Out There?

Your astronaut's-eye view of Mars can be found at the URL
`http://fi-www.arc.nasa.gov/fia/projects/bayes-group/Atlas/Mars/`.

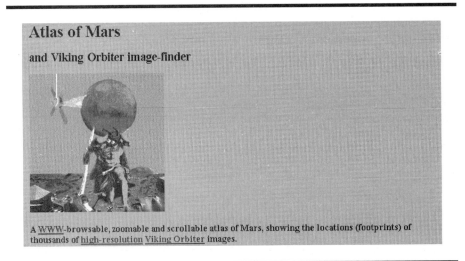

Atlas of Mars

and Viking Orbiter image-finder

A <u>WWW</u>-browsable, zoomable and scrollable atlas of Mars, showing the locations (footprints) of thousands of <u>high-resolution</u> <u>Viking Orbiter</u> images.

FIGURE 5.5: Care to take a gander at Mars?

You can start your search through the Mars atlas in one of three ways:

◆ From a small (600x300-pixel) map

◆ From a larger (1440x720-pixel), more detailed map

◆ From a list of topographical features—mountain, ridge, canyon, and so on

Just one caveat: the file's big maps are *really big*. For this gizmo to really work, you're going to have to wait a while for the maps to be transferred. (Go get coffee.)

Sometimes with all the scrolling around you're doing, the display gets a bit mucked up. That is, the screen may not repaint the document window very cleanly, some words that you saw just a second ago may seem to disappear, and so on. To straighten out your screen display, select View ➤ Reload from Netscape's menu bar. This should do the trick.

NASA Information Services via World Wide Web

Do you want advance information about upcoming Space Shuttle missions? You can find this or access one of many images made public from the Hubble Space Telescope. Just go to the NASA Information Services home page and click on <u>Hot Topics</u> for these and many more links.

What's Out There?

Space, the final frontier, is yours to explore through the NASA Information Services home page. Its URL is `http://www.nasa.gov/`.

This is a terrific home page for would-be explorers. Those interested in NASA's strategy for its future (and in the future of space exploration as it proceeds into the next century) can click on <u>NASA Strategic Plan</u>. <u>Human Exploration and Development of Space</u> details the history of space exploration in terms of NASA's mission and goals. Online educational resources are also available, all through the NASA Information Services home page. Also very cool, very fresh, is the "live" map of NASA centers around the country (Figure 5.6) in the NASA Information Services home page.

What's Out There?

In the "live" map of NASA centers around the country in the NASA Information Services home page, you can click on <u>Ames Research Center</u> in California (`http://www.arc.nasa.gov/`) or <u>Jet Propulsion Laboratory</u> in California (`http://www.jpl.nasa.gov/`), or <u>Johnson Space Center</u> in Houston (`http://www.jsc.nasa.gov`) or <u>Kennedy Space Center</u> in Florida (`http://www.ksc.nasa.gov`), to name a few. You'll jump right to the respective home page for the Web server at that location, where you can tootle around some more.

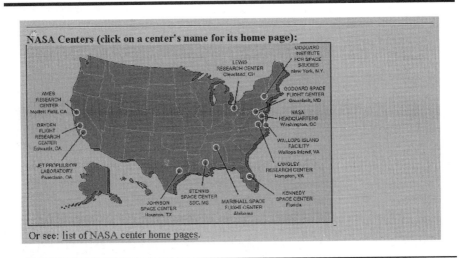

FIGURE 5.6: To find out what's up at any NASA center in the country, just click on the name of that center in this map.

HyperDoc: The National Library of Medicine

Here's the World-Wide-Web way to look into the National Library of Medicine, part of the U.S. National Institutes of Health in Bethesda, Maryland.

The library houses over 4.5 million books, journals, reports, manuscripts, and audio-visual materials, making it the largest medical library in the world.

What's Out There?

Everything you ever wanted to know about Western health and medicine (and perhaps even alternatives to it) can be learned from the U.S. National Library of Medicine. Its home page can be found at the URL http://www.nlm.nih.gov/.

Of special interest to the general Net "cruiser" might be the History of Medicine exhibit (Figure 5.7) and the searchable database of nearly 60,000 images from the National Library of Medicine's History of Medicine division. To get to these from the home page, select <u>OnLine Information Services</u> (NLM, NIH, the World). Scroll halfway down the document and when you see <u>Hypertext/multimedia exhibits</u>, click on it.

Stanford University

If you want to find out what's happening at Stanford, or if you had hoped to send your kid to Stanford but know you'll never have the dough, take a look at the Stanford University home page.

What's Out There?

You can look into Stanford and what's happening there via the URL http://www.stanford.edu/.

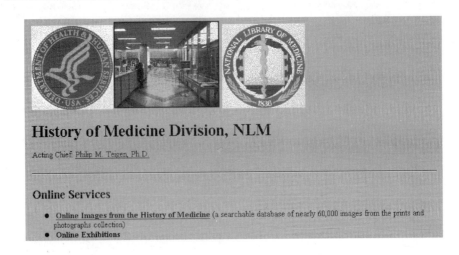

History of Medicine Division, NLM

Acting Chief: Philip M. Teigen, Ph.D.

Online Services

- **Online Images from the History of Medicine** (a searchable database of nearly 60,000 images from the prints and photographs collection)
- **Online Exhibitions**

FIGURE 5.7: Be sure to stop by the History of Medicine exhibit.

This is a very broad home page with links to many a place. Big categories include:

- General information about Stanford University, including an overview of faculty
- Schools and Departments, which is a hypertext listing of the schools that make up the University, with more links to even more information
- Centers, which is a listing of centers associated with Stanford (like the Bechtel International Center, for example)
- Academic Organizations, which links you to pages for academic organizations on campus
- Extracurricular Organizations, which links you to pages for extracurricular organizations on campus
- Just Off Campus, which links you to pages for stuff off-campus that might be of interest to the campus community (the Future Fantasy bookstore, City of Palo Alto, and so on)

What's Out There?

From the Stanford home page, you can get to lots of other interesting locales, including the Hoover Institution on War, Revolution, and Peace (`http://hoover.stanford.edu/www/welcome.html`), the Stanford Linear Accelerator Center (`http://slacvm.slac.stanford.edu/FIND/slac.html`), and the U.S.-Japan Technology Management Center (`http://fuji.stanford.edu`).

U.S. Geological Survey

The U.S. Geological Survey (USGS) boasts as one of its purposes the publishing of information about the United States' mineral land and water resources, which it has done through traditional means for many a decade. Now the USGS has a Web server.

You'll find links listed on the USGS home page for geologic information, minerals information, map sales, and book sales. If you live in earthquake

What's Out There?

The USGS home page, providing links to resources and data related to geology, is at the URL http://www.usgs.gov.

country, you'll want to size up the seismic activity stuff—there are some nifty maps showing up-to-date earthquake information (Figure 5.8).

The USGS home page also has lots of useful information of special interest to those who work in fields related to geology. Most helpful is the directory of USGS personnel, which is an indexed, searchable database.

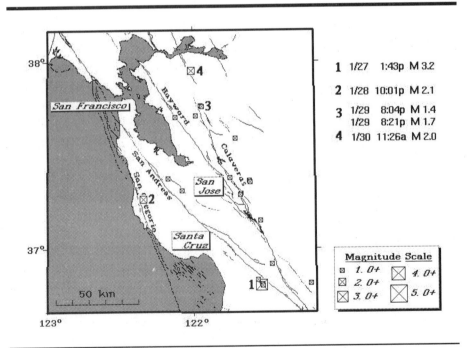

FIGURE 5.8: If you live in earthquake country (or if you're just curious) you'll want to check out the USGS's cool maps.

World Health Organization

Headquartered in Switzerland, the World Health Organization is an international organization dedicated to "the attainment by all peoples of the highest possible level of health." Its home page contains hyperlinks to the World Health Organization's press releases and newsletters, including the Environmental Health Newsletter, the Global Programme on AIDS Newsletter, the Influenza Newsletter, and research newsletters on malaria and leprosy, as well as the Library Digest for Africa.

What's Out There?

The World Health Organization provides loads of information on the Web by publishing its newsletters at the URL `http://www.who.ch`.

Xerox PARC PubWeb

The Xerox Palo Alto Research Center (PARC) is well known as the brain trust that created such technical advances as the mouse (the one you're using as you putter on your PC), the graphical user interface, and much, much more. While you're here, be sure to check out the map viewer (Figure 5.9), which was developed by Steve Putz of PARC.

What's Out There?

Pull off the Infobahn and PARC for awhile at the URL `http://pubweb.parc.xerox.com/`; if you do, you can check out the way cool map viewer (`http://pubweb.parc.com/map`).

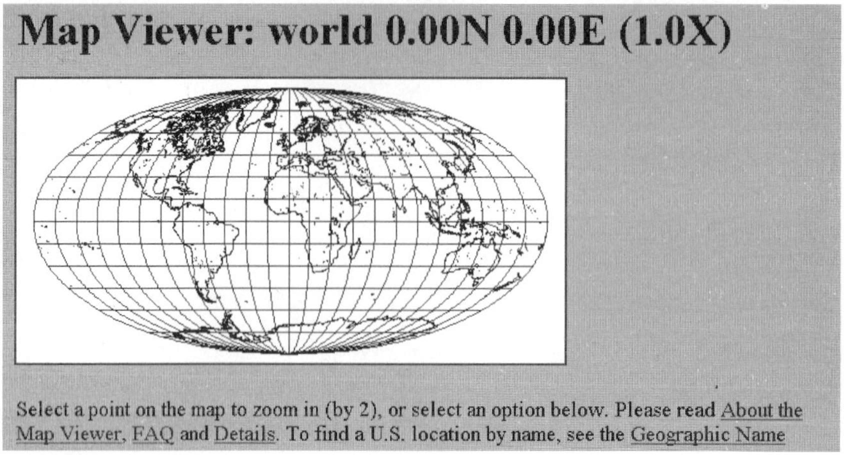

Map Viewer: world 0.00N 0.00E (1.0X)

Select a point on the map to zoom in (by 2), or select an option below. Please read About the Map Viewer, FAQ and Details. To find a U.S. location by name, see the Geographic Name

FIGURE 5.9: This map viewer is worth a pit stop.

Computer Geek Stuff

So you want to upgrade your modem? Reconfigure and upgrade your entire computer system? Find *free software*? All you need to know is where to go for all the technical and product-specific information you'll ever need. Here are some places to go—you can do your homework on the Web before you write that check to the computer store.

Cryptography, PGP, and Your Privacy

Privacy on the Net has become a major concern in the past couple of years, particularly since the U.S. Government designed the "Clipper chip," a microchip for use in digital communications devices. (Remember, Internet connections take place over *phone* lines, and as time goes on, phones are more and more often *digital* phones.) The Clipper chip is able to encrypt phone calls, making them more private than they have been, which is good news. The bad news is that the Clipper chip includes a back door that would enable "them"—U.S. intelligence and law enforcement agencies—to eavesdrop with greater ease.

Other encryption methods, such as Pretty Good Privacy (PGP), are being touted as alternatives to the government's proposed Clipper standard. (PGP is a software package that allows you to communicate securely even when you're using an insecure communications channel like e-mail or the telephone.)

The Cryptography, PGP, and Your Privacy home page (Figure 5.10) will provide you with all the background you'll need to understand these issues. It will also give you a place to get involved in grass-roots electronic activism if you care about privacy.

What's Out There?

To find out about privacy issues as they might affect you, pop in on the home page at `http://draco.centerline.com:8080/~franl/crypto.html`.

 Cryptography, PGP, and Your Privacy

This page is part of the WWW Virtual Library. Send email to Fran Litterio <franl@centerline.com> if you have any suggestions about how to improve this page.

 Up to *WWW Virtual Library Subject Catalogue*

> *Civilization is the progress toward a society of privacy. The savage's whole existence is public, ruled by the laws of his tribe. Civilization is the process of setting man free from men.* -- Ayn Rand, *The Fountainhead* (1943)

Cryptography is the study of *encryption*. Paul Fahn defines encryption as "the transformation of data into a form unreadable by anyone without a secret decryption key".

PGP is Pretty Good Privacy, a program created by Phil Zimmermann. It's a widely-used tool for performing public key encryption and managing the associated keys. PGP is available for a wide variety of computer systems (see Where to Get PGP).

FIGURE 5.10: About your privacy

CUI W3 Catalog

The Centre Universitaire d'Informatique (CUI for short) is a computer science research center in Geneva, Switzerland. The Centre's W3 Catalog is a searchable listing of Web resources created from several manually maintained World Wide Web lists available all over the WWW. You can enter a search string (like a list of key words) into a text box to indicate what you want to find information about, and the catalog will search its database, turning up whatever seems related to the key words you entered.

What's Out There?

You can access the CUI W3 Catalog (and through it, lots and *lots* of stuff on the Web) via the URL http://cuiwww.unige.ch/w3catalog.

We did a lot of the research for this chapter using the CUI W3 Catalog. Be prepared for some real serendipity to take place here. It was while we were searching for anything on women and minorities that we discovered the Little Russia and Death of Rock 'n' Roll home pages we discuss later in this chapter.

Linux: A Unix-Like Operating System for Your PC

If you're interested in fiddling around with Unix on your PC (Intel 386, 486, or Pentium), you can use Netscape to gopher to a site where you can get your very own Linux software package, *for free*. Linux is a complete Unix clone that includes Emacs, X11R6, gcc, TeX/LaTeX, groff, TCP/IP, SLIP, NFS, UUCP—the works.

What's Out There?

You'll find Linux for download at gopher://sunsite.unc.edu/11/.pub/Linux. The Linux Documentation Project home page is at the URL http://sunsite.unc.edu/mdw/linux.html.

The Linux Documentation Project home page dishes up background information and "How To" documents about Linux and its features. Don't leave DOS without it.

For more on Linux, which is a terrific operating system that's no picnic to install but a real delight to use, check out our book The Complete Linux Kit (Sybex, 1995). In it we talk about the ins and outs of installing and using Linux, and we even provide you with a copy of the software.

PC Week Labs

Now, even if your name isn't on the in-house routing slip, you can glean the benefits of product testing by PC Week Labs' experts. PC Week is a controlled-circulation weekly newspaper targeted at the folks who evaluate and recommend computer hardware and software for large, networked sites; PC Week Labs is a department of PC Week that conducts the testing on which reviews and technology backgrounders are based.

What's Out There?

You can get hip to PC Week Labs online through the URL
`http://www.ziff.com/~pcweek/`. Check out PC Magazine, too; it's at
`http://www.ziff.com/~pcmag`.

People Everywhere

Nothing says the Web has to be gender-specific, Euro-centric, or confined to the interests of the academic elite. Looking for the international Web, the alternative Web, the politicized Web? It's there, and it's growing.

The International Web

Cruise the world by Web; it's not *really* the same as going to another country, but it's faster and cheaper. The Web is global, so you can find plenty about cultures other than your own. Curious about Russia? Check out the Little Russia home page, where you can see images and documents that not only describe the culture, but give you a hyperlinked, regularly updated peek into that culture's humor through real, live translated Russian *jokes* (Figure 5.11). (You're even provided with links to explanations of the jokes, many of which will leave you scratching your head in confusion if you don't know the cultural context.)

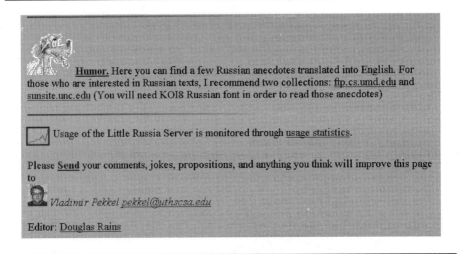

Humor. Here you can find a few Russian anecdotes translated into English. For those who are interested in Russian texts, I recommend two collections: ftp.cs.umd.edu and sunsite.unc.edu (You will need KOI8 Russian font in order to read those anecdotes)

Usage of the Little Russia Server is monitored through usage statistics.

Please **Send** your comments, jokes, propositions, and anything you think will improve this page to

Vladimir Pekkel pekkel@uthscsa.edu

Editor: Douglas Rains

FIGURE 5.11: A sampling of Russian humor is available in Little Russia. You'll "get" the jokes when you click on the links to explanations that place them in their correct cultural context.

Australian universities are big contributors to the Web, with home pages on aboriginal studies (The Coombslists: Aboriginal and Indigenous Peoples Studies) and Asian Studies, as well as other information of interest to those who want find out about pan-Pacific cultures.

Amnesty International is an international human rights organization. It publishes a home page with information about how to contact the group and what membership involves.

What's Out There?

The Little Russia home page will clue you in to that culture; its URL is
`http://mars.uthscsa.edu/Russia/`. Find out about Aboriginal or Asian
Studies by starting at the URL
`http://coombs.anu.edu.au/CoombsHome.html`.
And to get the latest on human rights developments, turn to Amnesty
International at the URL
`http://cyberzine.org/html/Amnesty/aihomepage.html`.

Women, Gays, and Minorities on the Web

One home page that seems at first glance to be about (just) women and
computers (Women and Computing, Women and Computer Science) actually also includes information on African Americans and computing, too.
It's a great starting point for the exploration of such issues as the ability of
women and minorities to break into and succeed in the world of computers and computer science. Other Infobahn stops that might be of interest
include:

◆ The African American Culture and History home page, with sections
on colonization, abolition, migration, and the WPA (and with plans
to present a major exhibition on the impact of African American culture on the American identity).

◆ The Society and Culture: Sex home page, which provides paths to a
host of lesbian, gay, and bisexual resources, ranging from pages on
Domestic Partnership and Same Sex Marriage to the "CyberQueer
Lounge."

◆ Amnesty International's page on Lesbian and Gay Concerns.

The Conservative Web

On the other side of the political coin, you can check out a home page devoted to convincing liberals of the correctness of the ultra-conservative viewpoint. The Right Side of the Web home page, featuring a photo of Ronald Reagan, is a directory of places on the Web that promote a politically conservative point of view. Topics covered include the National Review Archives and Whitewater information. There's also a link to the Newt Gingrich WWW Fan Club home page.

The Hip, the Cool, and the Groovy

The Web isn't just a network, it's a state of mind, a subculture, and an emerging scene. It's the electronic fast lane, where you can find out not just what's happening now, but also what's on the minds of the creative and the just plain crazy. For the truly hip and the groovy wannabes, here are some Web locales that just can't be overlooked.

Art on the Net

To get to a true art space, where artists gather, create and "hang" their work online, go to Art on the Net (a.k.a. Art.Net). Here, a variety of galleries and art styles can be seen. One piece from the online gallery is shown in Figure 5.12.

What's Out There?

To get to Art on the Net, use the URL `http://www.art.net`. To go straight to the group show gallery, use `http://www.art.net/the_gallery.html`.

Each month, Art.Net features a visual artist, a band or musician, and a poet in its <u>Featured Artists</u> gallery. In addition, there are group shows in the Art.Net Gallery. Find out about art happenings, classes, and events around the world. (Any art-related activities can be sent to `webmaster@art.net` for posting on this server.)

CyberSight

Don't let the URL for CyberSight fool you (we thought we were going to see spaceshots of planets). CyberSight (Figure 5.13) gives you a spaceshot of the cyber*chic* planet. Here the Web is in-your-face with genuinely eccentric style. We first found this baby while tootling around the Library of Congress home page (we talk about the Library of Congress elsewhere in this chapter).

What's Out There?

CyberSight, which is not really easy to describe other than as a doorway to what's ultra-cool and amusing on the Web, can be found using the URL `http://cybersight.com/cgi-bin/cs/s?main.gmml`.

FIGURE 5.12: Art on the Web appears at ART.NET.

Our first visit to CyberSight included playing several rounds of interactive games (*Hangman* on the Web is charming; you can get a glimpse of it in Figure 5.14), and participating in a public opinion poll on a murder scandal that was currently grabbing a lot of media attention. This is also where we found a link to Roadkill R Us, which we describe in an upcoming section of this chapter.

Enterzone

There are lots of "literary" magazines on the Net and the Web; most of them lean more toward science fiction than real literary fare. Enterzone is a hyperzine that breaks the mold, providing a thoughtful selection of not just fiction, poetry, and essays, but also photography, paintings, and even interactive art forms (Figure 5.15). It also solicits and publishes responses to the work, adding the dimension of a salon to the basic magazine structure.

What's Out There?

Enterzone presents writing and artwork of true merit. Use the URL `http://enterzone.berkeley.edu/enterzone.html` to find Enterzone.

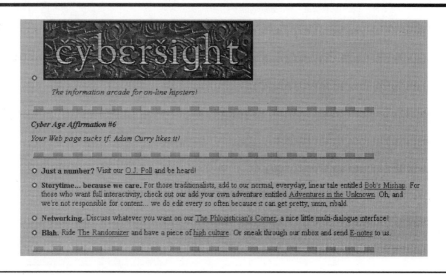

FIGURE 5.13: CyberSight's home page

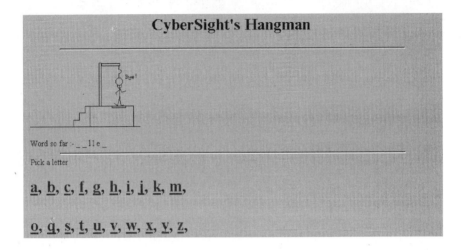

FIGURE 5.14: Hangman is one of many interactive games on the Web.

FIGURE 5.15: Enterzone, a literary showcase

Wired Magazine and HotWired

Dubbed "Wired Magazine's Rest Stop on the Infobahn," the HotWired Web server offers complete back issues of the very trendy publication, *Wired*. *Wired* was an immediate smash when it was launched in 1993. Devoted to the cybernaut subculture, this rag is high-tech with an attitude. Its progeny, HotWired, was launched in late 1994. You can see the Hot-Wired home page in Figure 5.16.

Perhaps unsurprisingly, HotWired is even cooler than its parent. Let's face it, HotWired *is* what *Wired* is *about*. HotWired's content in just one issue ranged from a calendar of events in Tokyo to an article about life in the South Pole.

FIGURE 5.16: HotWired is a project of Wired magazine. You can get HotWired for free via Netscape on the World Wide Web.

What's Out There?

Get HotWired via the Web server for this journal of the cybernaut sub-culture; the URL is `http://www.hotwired.com`.

To access HotWired, you'll have to go through the simple hoops of setting up a (cost-free) account. Just follow the simple on-screen directions the first time you jump in to the HotWired world; you'll have your free account in a moment or two and you won't have to go to any trouble at all next time.

Welcome to the Metaverse

This Web server (Figure 5.17) is the creation of an ex-MTV video jockey turned Internet entrepreneur; it's definitely got that Generation X edge, providing you with links to the kinds of music and weirdness this guy only talked about as a vee-jay before he got into the Web-home-page game.

The Metaverse home page is chock full o' big graphics, which move slo-o-owly across a modem connection. Accessing this home page in its entirety is going to take a while. To make the Metaverse home page show up faster, select Options ➤ Auto Load Images from the menu bar. This toggles off image loading, which means you won't see any pictures, but the page will be there a lot sooner. To load pictures into a text-only display, click on the Images icon on Netscape's toolbar.

When we took a look at Metaverse, we found a hyperlinked list of space kitsch ("collectibles and merchandise"):

◆ Starseekers Limited Edition Lithograph

◆ Skylab Space Station Fragment in Lucite Pyramid

◆ Apollo 11 25th Anniversary Video Set

◆ Apollo 11 Press Kit

What's Out There?

The Metaverse universe is right next door through the URL
`http://metaverse.com`.

FIGURE 5.17: Click in the sky portion of the image to go shopping in the metaverse.

Here's the deal: any of this stuff can be ordered via the Web! Maybe you want to order the "Space Shuttle Flight Suit, a replica of the same flight suit issued to the NASA Space Shuttle Astronauts, including patch, American flag, and NASA logo—all for $59.95 for Internet users plus $8.00 s/h and sales tax if required. The retail price is $80.00 at space centers through-out the U.S." It's yours, through the simple act of clicking the link and then providing the requested information: name, mailing address, credit card number, that sort of thing.

If you're not in a shopping frame of mind but would rather reminisce—for free—you can hyperlink your way back to the '60s via Woodstock '94. (We mentioned the Woodstock '94 home page back in Chapter 2.) Just click on an icon of two doves on a guitar handle, and (assuming you've got the sound drivers to deal with this) you'll hear some of Jimi Hendrix's most famous riffs. You can also explore some of the facts and figures of the "real" Woodstock and see statistics describing its economic fallout.

 Keep in mind that things change on the Web at the whim of the folks who publish there. This and other home pages (and the pages they're linked to) will change to reflect the times. This is part of the Web's attraction. Don't worry, be happy: you might stumble across one truly amazing thing while you're looking for another.

That's (Sheer) Entertainment

To augment your subscriptions to entertainment rags, turn to the Web. There you'll find a variety of entertaining stuff about Tinseltown, celebrities, and products of the entertainment dream machine. As BD said, "Fasten your seatbelts, it's going to be a bumpy night," as you glide from one star-studded page to another.

Elvis Aron Presley Home Page

Die-hard Elvis fans who can't make the real trip to Memphis can take a tour of Graceland from their desktops, thanks to Andrea Berman and David Levine, creators of this Elvis home page, "created to honor Elvis and his cultural and musical legacy...." (This isn't the *only* Elvis page, incidentally. Elvis home pages crop up almost as often as Elvis sightings.)

What's Out There?

Elvis is remembered, commemorated, even revered, at the URL http://sunsite.unc.edu/elvis/elvishom.html.

From this page, you can immerse yourself in Elvis—see a picture of his driver's license, hear sounds, share sightings, get a biography—almost more than you can imagine (unless, of course, you were already immersed in Elvis before you got to this page). There's even a guestbook to sign (Figure 5.18).

WARNING As always, your machine must have the appropriate sound capabilities (lots o' memory along with a sound card, drivers, and maybe even speakers) to play sound files. <u>Don't try to play sound files if you don't have the stuff to do it</u>. Sound files are enormous and trying to play them without the right capabilities will crash your system.

FIGURE 5.18: Sign here to register as a visitor to the online Graceland tour.

Movie Browser Database

For the starstruck or the plain old curious, a searchable, indexed database of movie-related stuff might be just the ticket. Query it by the name of an actor or actress, the title of the film, the genre, or a quote from the movie. From here you can also go to a hypertext listing of the Academy Award winners in many key categories, dating all the way back to 1920.

What's Out There?

You'll find a searchable database of movie information at the URL `http://www.cm.cf.ac.uk/Movies/` or at the URL `http://www.msstate.edu/Movies/`. A categorized list of Academy Award winners is available at `http://www.cm.cf.ac.uk:80/Movies/Oscars.html`.

World Wide Weirdness

We hardly know what to say about this. Anybody can publish a home page, and sometimes you'll run into the strangest, most wigged out stuff in the world.

Off the Beaten Web

Roadkill R Us bills itself as an Internet-based Disinformation Center and a misapplication of the World Wide Web. It seems to provide a place for folks to post pages as diverse as one on the Jihad destroying Barney and another describing a "Smut Shack."

The Death of Rock 'n' Roll presents excerpts from a book on the untimely deaths and morbid preoccupations of pop and rock personalities from Elvis to Sid Vicious and beyond. (We haven't seen Kurt Cobain there yet, but it seems inevitable.)

More Practical Purposes

Not all of life is fun and games. To keep yourself informed, check out the online version of your favorite newsrag (if they publish one), or browse the Library of Congress database to single out any of millions of publications, or—if you're interested in either the broad or fine points of the Constitution—check out the doings of the U.S. Supreme Court.

The Gate

Tired of cleaning ink off your fingers after wading through the morning paper? Check out the electronic versions of the San Francisco Chronicle or Examiner. (Maybe your own town paper is on the Web, too.)

Even if you don't live in S.F., you might be interested in the interactive weather map for temperatures around the U.S. and Canada published in these papers—great for planning your wardrobe before a business trip or vacation.

Thomas—Congress' New Legislative Database

Perhaps you've heard that the U.S. Congress is moving into the modern world—well, here's evidence: Thomas, the new Congressional database service, makes available information about the House and Senate, the e-mail addresses of all members of Congress, and (especially juicy) the full text of legislation beginning with the 103rd Congress.

What's Out There?

The Thomas home page includes access to the complete text of United States legislation beginning with the 103rd Congress. Catch Thomas at the URL `http://thomas.loc.gov`.

Start at the Thomas home page, and then select <u>103rd Congress</u>. Here you'll find a searchable database of all legislation passed by that Congress. To find a specific item you can search the database by typing in a *search string* (a few words to indicate what you want to search for), as shown in Figure 5.19. Just type into the Enter Query text box a few words that you believe will appear in the laws you want to read, and then click the RUN QUERY button. In a few seconds a screen filled with data will appear—the result of your search (Figure 5.20).

Supreme Court Decisions

A project of Cornell's Legal Information Institute (LII), the Supreme Court Decisions document provides a searchable database of recent Supreme Court decisions (from 1990 on) indexed by topic. You can also conduct a search based on key words. Figure 5.21 shows the bare beginning of a lengthy list that resulted from a search for matches to *irs*.

103rd Congress

FULL TEXT OF LEGISLATION

<u>ABOUT SEARCHING LEGISLATION IN THOMAS</u>

SEARCHING BY KEY WORDS IN BILLS

To search by key words, type as many significant words as you wish in the space below. Press the **RUN QUERY** button to start the search.

Enter query: `automatic weapons`

| RUN QUERY | Clear Query |

FIGURE 5.19: We typed a phrase referring to a hot political issue in the Enter Query text box...

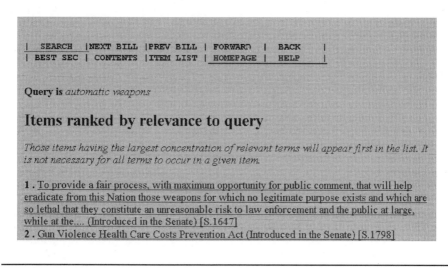

| SEARCH | NEXT BILL | PREV BILL | FORWARD | BACK |
| BEST SEC | CONTENTS | ITEM LIST | HOMEPAGE | HELP |

Query is *automatic weapons*

Items ranked by relevance to query

Those items having the largest concentration of relevant terms will appear first in the list. It is not necessary for all terms to occur in a given item.

1 . To provide a fair process, with maximum opportunity for public comment, that will help eradicate from this Nation those weapons for which no legitimate purpose exists and which are so lethal that they constitute an unreasonable risk to law enforcement and the public at large, while at the.... (Introduced in the Senate) [S.1647]
2 . Gun Violence Health Care Costs Prevention Act (Introduced in the Senate) [S.1798]

FIGURE 5.20:   ...And up popped a listing of related legislation!

What's Out There?

A searchable database of Supreme Court decisions is available at the URL
`http://www.law.cornell.edu/supct/supct.table.html/`.

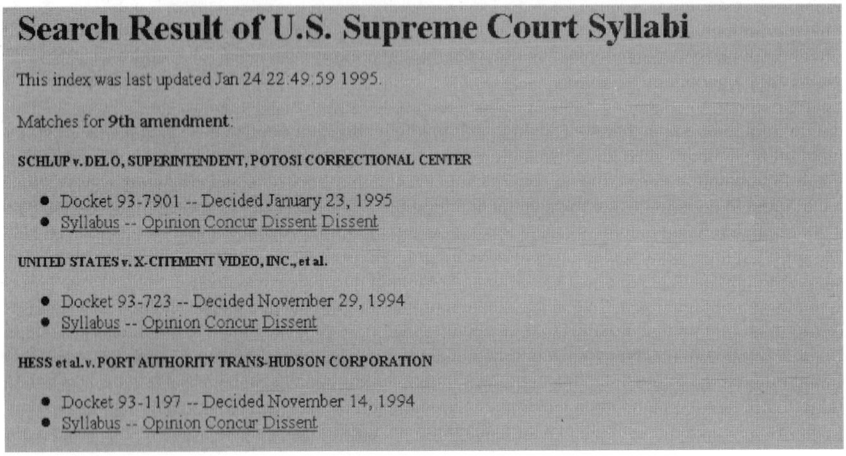

Search Result of U.S. Supreme Court Syllabi

This index was last updated Jan 24 22:49:59 1995.

Matches for **9th amendment**:

SCHLUP v. DELO, SUPERINTENDENT, POTOSI CORRECTIONAL CENTER

- Docket 93-7901 -- Decided January 23, 1995
- Syllabus -- Opinion Concur Dissent Dissent

UNITED STATES v. X-CITEMENT VIDEO, INC., et al.

- Docket 93-723 -- Decided November 29, 1994
- Syllabus -- Opinion Concur Dissent

HESS et al. v. PORT AUTHORITY TRANS-HUDSON CORPORATION

- Docket 93-1197 -- Decided November 14, 1994
- Syllabus -- Opinion Concur Dissent

FIGURE 5.21: If you want to look into what the U.S. Supreme Court thinks and decides, this is the place for you.

NASDAQ Financial Executive Journal

This quarterly (the NASDAQ Financial Executive Journal) is a joint project of Cornell's Legal Information Institute and the NASDAQ Stock Market, which should clue you in to what it covers. The journal provides legal and financial information to CFO-types and the investor-relations officers of NASDAQ-listed companies. This stuff might also interest other folks grappling with or interested in such issues as disclosure of preliminary merger negotiations and strategic analyses of proposed rulings by the Financial Accounting Standards Board (FASB). Does that sound like your cup of tea?

What's Out There?

To further investigate the NASDAQ Financial Executive Journal, check out the URL http://www.law.cornell.edu/nasdaq/.

One Thing Leads to Another

The beauty of the World Wide Web is... well, its webbiness. You can start at any point on the Web and get anywhere else, anywhere in the world, because it's all interconnected. We can't tell you about everything you'll find on the Web, and we wouldn't want to. Things change. The Web changes all the time—new stuff appears there daily, and part of the wonder of Web exploration is accidentally coming across the unexpected, the unusual, or even the outrageous as you tinker about.

After looking through these last two chapters, you should have some ideas about where to get started and about the range of stuff that's available. Cruising the Web is your game now—have a grand old time.

Now you probably want to know how to find just what you're looking for without cruising. In the next chapter, we'll look into some great tools for searching and finding whatever you're looking for on the Web.

Tools and Techniques for Searching and Finding

Okay, so everyone knows the World Wide Web is growing at a mind-boggling rate. Then how does the intrepid Net cruiser find what he or she is looking for among all of what's out there? How does anyone know even where to *begin* a search? As you use the Internet—especially the Web—you may find yourself sucked into a black hole of pointing-and-clicking, following hyperlinks with complete abandon and fascination, yet coming up with little information that's relevant to the project at hand. (That's why they call it *cyberspace*....)

Let's step back for a second and take a look at gathering information in ways that aren't so willy-nilly. The Web is a bona fide research tool, after all—let's find out how it can be used to find information on focused topics. Say, for example, you work in the planning department of a large corporation and you need to write a business report about the current cause célèbre of corporate America—"reengineering."

Say you want to pepper your report with statistical data—productivity levels in American business over the past ten years, unemployment levels, inflation rates, and so on. You also want to describe the viewpoints of financial, economic, and business experts, and to address forecasts for the future of business.

The Web is gigantic, webby, and *growing*. (We've said this before.) You just can't expect everything on the Web to be contained in any one place or searchable through any one tool. To do your Web research, whether it is on our example topic or any other topic, you'll use a number of tools:

♦ The archive of past NCSA What's New pages

♦ The World Wide Web Worm

♦ Veronica, the complete gopher index

In the rest of this chapter, we'll describe each of these tools, what it's good for, and when its use is appropriate.

Searching the NCSA What's New Archive via the CUI W3 Catalog

We've talked earlier in this book about the NCSA What's New document—it lists new services on the Web and it's updated monthly, so it's always a great starting place for your Web travels. Now what do you suppose happens when the NCSA What's New document is updated? All those handy announcements don't just go away, they're moved (by the Internet's invisible helpers) from the current What's New document into a database. Here's the big news: you can use Netscape to search this archival database.

The archive of What's New pages is kept in a comprehensive database by the people at the Centre Universitaire d'Informatique (CUI), at the University of Geneva in Switzerland. Here you'll find not only the announcements from the NCSA What's New pages, but also items of interest they've gathered from other Web indexes. Searching this database will give you quick entrée to a wide variety of topics and sources of information.

To access and search the NCSA What's New document, you'll use the CUI W3 Catalog page as a tool.

What's Out There

You can access the searchable archive of What's New pages with the URL `http://cuiwww.unige.ch/w3catalog`.

About the Search

Searching the NCSA What's New page archive is a snap. All you have to do is open the CUI W3 Catalog, type in some text that describes what interests you, click a button, and sit back and watch a page of links appear on your screen. Let's take a closer look.

Opening the CUI W3 Catalog

To search the What's New page archives, you must first open the CUI W3 Catalog:

1. Select File ➤ Open Location from Netscape's menu bar. The Open Location dialog box will appear.

2. In the Open Location dialog box's text box, type **http://cuiwww.unige.ch/w3catalog**.

3. Click on the Open button. The dialog box will disappear, the N will become animated, and in a few seconds the CUI W3 Catalog page will appear (Figure 6.1).

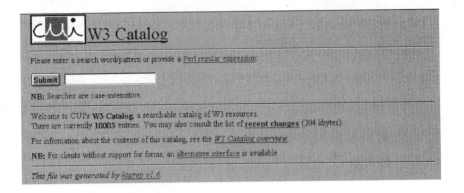

FIGURE 6.1: The CUI W3 page is your path to old (but still valuable) NCSA What's New pages.

Performing the Search

With the CUI W3 Catalog page on screen, now is the time to start searching.

1. A text box will be visible near the middle of the page. Type a word or two that describes what interests you into the text box. (For example, to find information about baseball, type **baseball** into the text box.)

2. Click on the Submit button. This will send the text you typed to the database, where a search will be performed like magic. If the topic of interest is part of any entry in the database, a page containing information (or at least a mention) of that topic will appear. (Figure 6.2 shows what we found when we searched for *baseball*.)

 The CUI W3 Catalog searches many Web resources, not just the NCSA What's New page archives. When you do a search, don't be surprised if you get a page that includes items from other sources in addition to NCSA What's New pages.

In the pages you see as a result of your search, you'll find the now familiar blue underlined text that represents links to other pages. These links behave just like the links in any document—click on a link to go directly to the item it describes.

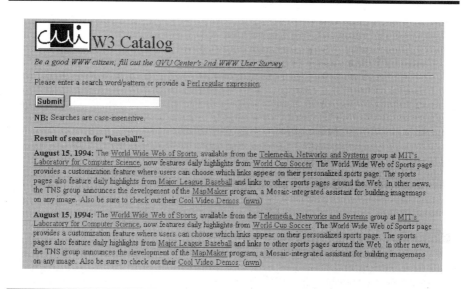

FIGURE 6.2: Searching for <u>baseball</u> came up with these entries, each of which has links to the actual pages.

Performing More Complicated Searches with CUI W3

You aren't limited to searching for simple words like *baseball* or *linux* with the W3 Catalog. You can type far more complex *strings* (lists) into the text box to make your search more specific. This is no simple matter, however; it involves entering a combination of text and special symbols, along with having some knowledge of discrete mathematics. The techniques of performing a complex search are beyond the scope of this book, but you can find a how-to discussion on this topic by clicking on the <u>Perl regular expression</u> link on the CUI W3 Catalog page.

The World Wide Web Worm

A CUI W3 Catalog search of NCSA What's New pages is a great way to search out some terrifically useful pages on the Web, but it's far from your only option. To broaden your search beyond what's known to the NCSA What's New folks, use the World Wide Web Worm (the *Worm*). The heart

of the Worm is a program that burrows through the Web, searching thousands of home pages for links to other pages, then compiling both the URL and title of each of these pages into one *gigantic* searchable database. At the time of this writing, the World Wide Web Worm database includes references to some 300,000 objects on the Web; it is accessed well over 2,000,000 times a month.

Opening the World Wide Web Worm Page

To search the World Wide Web Worm database, you must open the Word Wide Web Worm page. Here you'll find an on-screen form into which you'll type in the *search criteria* (what you want to search for). Then you'll "submit" the search to the database. When the search is complete, a page will appear with links to other pages that match your search criteria.

The first step in using the World Wide Web Worm is to open its page in Netscape.

1. Select File ➤ Open Location from the menu bar. The Open Location dialog box will appear.

2. In the Open URL dialog box's text box, type the URL for the World Wide Web Worm page:

http://www.cs.colorado.edu/home/mcbryan/WWWW.html

3. Click on the Open button. The dialog box will disappear, the N will become animated, and in a few seconds the World Wide Web Worm page will appear (Figure 6.3).

What's Out There

The World Wide Web Worm can be surfaced with the URL
http://www.cs.colorado.edu/home/mcbryan/WWWW.html.

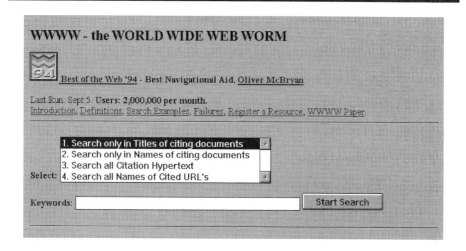

FIGURE 6.3: The World Wide Web Worm is a powerful search utility that searches the Web and catalogs the URL and title of every page that it finds, making a database of that information available to you.

Worm Words

The World Wide Web Worm uses its own lingo to describe Web pages. The Worm uses the term *name* for the URL of a Web page. A home page that the Worm has searched is a *citing document*. The text in a home page that describes the linked page is *citation hypertext*. Finally, a URL used to link a home page to another page is a *cited URL*. When in Rome....

Searching the World Wide Web Worm Database

With the World Wide Web Worm page open, you are ready to start digging up dirt ...er, *data*. Take a look at the page; it includes links to text that tells you about the Worm and even shows some example searches.

> **NOTE**
>
> A lot of pages are known to the Worm, but not every page is. Only those that are on a home page the Worm knows about or those that are referenced by a home page will be in the Worm's database. That's why you may not find something now that you think you've seen before. A hypertext reference or page that isn't a home page or doesn't appear anywhere on another home page won't be in the list.

To perform a search using the Worm:

1. In the World Wide Web Worm page, the box labeled *Select* controls the way the Worm's database will be searched for documents. The options are:

> **Search only in Titles of citing documents** searches the titles of all the home pages in the Worm's database.
>
> **Search only in Names of citing documents** searches the URLs of all the home pages in the Worm's database.
>
> **Search all Citation Hypertext** searches the text in the home pages that is linked to other pages.
>
> **Search all Names of Cited URLs** searches those URLs in the home pages that are linked to other pages.

> To select an option, click on its name. (The selected option will always be highlighted.)

You'll have the best luck if you select either *Search only in Titles of citing documents* or *Search all Citation Hypertext*. Either of these searches the English text that describes a page, not the URL for that page. (What you'll get back is a list of documents that contain the text you specified in either their titles or their descriptions.) If you know part of the URL you're looking for, select *Search only in Names of citing documents* or *Search all Names of Cited URLs*. Either of these options (see Figure 6.4) searches the URLs for specific documents. (What you'll get back this time is a list of documents that match the URL you specified in part.)

Select:
```
1. Search only in Titles of citing documents
2. Search only in Names of citing documents
3. Search all Citation Hypertext
4. Search all Names of Cited URL's
```

Keywords: finance   Start Search

FIGURE 6.4: The Worm is going to search its database for <u>finance</u>.

2. Now that you've told the Worm how it should search, you'll tell the Worm what it seeks. In the *Keywords* box, type some text to point the Worm on its way.

The developer of the Worm, Oliver McBryan, recommends keeping your searches to a single word rather than a string of text so they will go faster.

3. Click on the Start Search button to begin the search. In a few seconds a new page will appear listing everything it found in the database that matched what you told the Worm to find. (Figure 6.5 shows the result of a search for *finance*.)

Sometimes your search of the Worm will turn up a page saying that nothing was found. This happens not just when nothing matched your search criteria, but sometimes when the Worm is overcrowded. (The folks who maintain the Worm are working on this problem.) If a search that you believe should have worked comes up with nothing, try the search again later.

Performing More Complicated Searches with the Worm

You don't have to limit yourself to entering simple text as search criteria in the Keywords box. To conduct more complex searches, you can use a

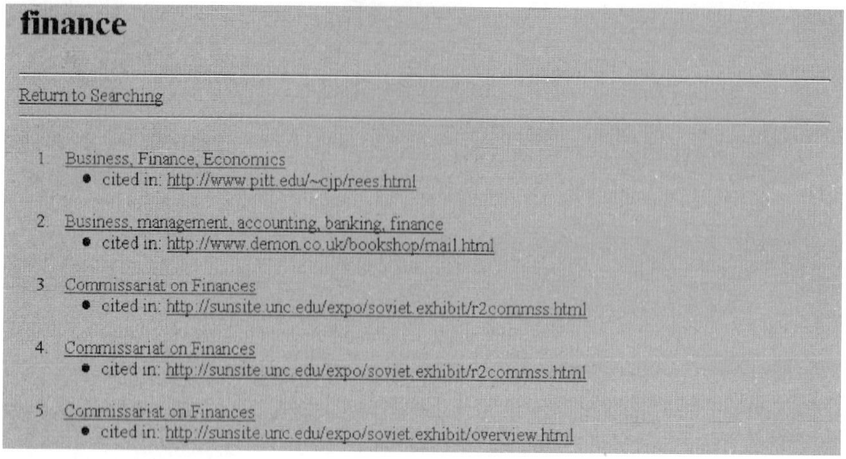

FIGURE 6.5: This list of financial things on the Web is the result of our search for finance.

number of special characters. The Worm page itself contains information on using these techniques to make your searches more powerful and specific. Here are a couple of examples:

What You Can Type	What It Means
Apple.*Mac	Anything with *Apple* followed by *Mac* (like *Apple PowerMac* or *Apple Macintosh*)
(Microsoft | Novell) DOS	Anything that includes *Microsoft DOS* or *Novell DOS*

Usually you won't have to resort to these kinds of complex search criteria; searching the Worm using simple text is often the best way to go.

Veronica

Veronica is a self-updating database of gopher documents. Gopher documents, as you'll recall from previous discussion, are usually text files (but sometimes telnet links to other computers, searchable databases, or graphics files). *Veronica* is an acronym that stands for Very Easy Rodent-Oriented

Net-wide Index to Computerized Archives. (The rodent reference is, of course, *gopher.*) Often you'll hear old-timers (essentially people who've used the Net for more than a year) say something like "You can gopher to Veronica to find that."

 Netscape can access gopher servers, making the use of Veronica a breeze, but you'll find the CUI W3 Catalog and the World Wide Web Worm to be far more useful Web-searching tools.

Like the World Wide Web Worm, Veronica locates things on the Web by searching through words in titles, rather than by a doing a full-fledged search of the document. For purposes of a Veronica search, the *title* is the name of the resource as listed on its home gopher server. Veronica "knows" about an incredible 10 million documents stored on 5,500 different gopher servers!

You can access Veronica from any of scads of gopher servers (remember, you can access any menu on a gopher server just like it was any other "page" on the Web) but we're going to concentrate here on just one page—the one kept on the University of Minnesota gopher server—as an example.

Gopher History in a Nutshell

The University of Minnesota gopher server is the mother of 'em all; that's because the University of Minnesota *invented* gopher. Gopher had its origins in an idea similar to the one that inspired HTML—gopher's inventors wanted a way to organize information. The solution they came up with was to use menus from which you could pick items that led to documents—it's the same concept as hyperlink, but without the nice graphics and "lightning fast" linking HTML offers by actually placing the links in the documents.

As Web browsers like Netscape (and the use of HTML) become more common, you might think gopher would fade away. But gopher is a mature and workable system that's being incorporated into the Web. You can use gopher with Netscape as another one of your Net cruising tools.

Opening Up a Veronica Page

To use Veronica, you must open up a page in Netscape that includes links to Veronica. Here we are using a page from the University of Minnesota's gopher server to get to Veronica. As you cruise around other gopher servers using Netscape, you'll probably find other places to gain entry into Veronica.

To open up a page in Netscape with links to Veronica:

1. Select File ➤ Open Location from the menu bar. The Open Location dialog box will appear.

2. In the Open Location dialog box's text box, type the URL

    **gopher://gopher.c.umn.edu/11/
Other%20Gopher%20and%20Information%20Servers/Veronica**

Okay so this URL is long. Remember, gopher was originally designed as a menu system. The URL shown has as its task opening layers of menu choices. To make opening Veronica faster in the future, add this URL to your Hotlist.

3. Click on the Open button. The dialog box will disappear, the N will become animated, and in a few seconds a gopher page like the one shown in Figure 6.6 will appear.

What's Out There

You can call on Veronica using the URL gopher://gopher.tc.umn.edu/
11/Other%20Gopher%20and%20Information%20Servers/Veronica.

Gopher Menu

🏛 Find GOPHER DIRECTORIES by Title word(s) (via NYSERNet)
🏛 Find GOPHER DIRECTORIES by Title word(s) (via PSINet)
🏛 Find GOPHER DIRECTORIES by Title word(s) (via SUNET)
🏛 Find GOPHER DIRECTORIES by Title word(s) (via U. of Manitoba)
🏛 Find GOPHER DIRECTORIES by Title word(s) (via UNINETT/U. of Bergen)
🏛 Find GOPHER DIRECTORIES by Title word(s) (via University of Pisa)
📄 Frequently-Asked Questions (FAQ) about veronica - January 13, 1995
📄 How to Compose veronica Queries - June 23, 1994
📁 More veronica: Software, Index-Control Protocol, HTML homepage
🏛 Search GopherSpace by Title word(s) (via NYSERNet)
🏛 Search GopherSpace by Title word(s) (via PSINet)
🏛 Search GopherSpace by Title word(s) (via SUNET)

FIGURE 6.6: Here is the University of Minnesota's gopher menu, which includes access to Veronica.

Searching Veronica

Great. We'll start searching in a minute. But first, take a look at the Veronica page and notice that from this page you can search Veronicas located at many different places (such as PSInet in the USA, University of Manitoba in Canada, and the University of Pisa in Italy). All these Veronicas should provide essentially the same information, but they're all maintained by different people at different times, so the information might not be completely in sync from one Veronica to another. Also, one server may be busier at any given time than another, so response time may vary from server to server.

A big trick to using Veronica is to select a Veronica based on its proximity to you while taking into account whether that Veronica shows fast response speeds right now. (The only way for you to know about the response speeds is to use Veronica enough to get a feel for which places are faster and when.)

A search of gopherspace (all gopher servers throughout the Internet) by keywords in titles will turn up all types of resources—text documents, image files, binary files, gopher directories, and so on— whose names contain the specified search word or words. On the other hand, a search of gopher directories by keywords contained in titles only looks at gopher <u>directories</u>, not documents. That provides fewer places from which to choose, but those places may be more focused.

To start your search of Veronica:

1. With your gopher page open, click on one of the following links to Veronica:

Click On	To Search For
<u>Search GopherSpace by Title word(s) (via PSINet)</u>	Gopher documents by using the Veronica server at Performance Systems, Inc. in New York State.
<u>Find GOPHER DIRECTORIES by title word(s) (via PSINet)</u>	Directories containing gopher documents by using the Veronica server at Performance Systems, Inc. in New York State.
<u>Search GopherSpace by Title word(s) (via SUNET)</u>	Gopher documents by using the Veronica server at Swedish University Network in Sweden.
<u>Find GOPHER DIRECTORIES by title word(s) (via SUNET)</u>	Directories of gopher documents by using the Veronica server at Swedish University Network in Sweden.

Click On	To Search For
Search GopherSpace by Title word(s) (via U. of Manitoba)	Gopher documents by using the Veronica server at the University of Manitoba in Canada.
Find GOPHER DIRECTORIES by title word(s) (via U. Of Manitoba)	Directories of gopher documents by using the Veronica server at the University of Manitoba in Canada.
Search GopherSpace by Title word(s) (via UNINETT/U. of Bergen)	Gopher documents by using the Veronica server at the University of Bergen in Norway.
Find GOPHER DIRECTORIES by title word(s) (via UNINETT/U. of Bergen)	Directories of gopher documents by using the Veronica server at the University of Bergen in Norway.
Search GopherSpace by Title word(s) (via University of Pisa)	Gopher documents by using the Veronica server at the University of Pisa in Italy.
Find GOPHER DIRECTORIES by title word(s) (via University of Pisa)	Directories of gopher documents by using the Veronica server at the University of Pisa in Italy.

A page will appear that lets you then search the selected Veronica database. Figure 6.7 shows what happened when we selected Search GopherSpace by Title word(s) (via PSINet).

2. In the Enter search keywords text box at the bottom of the page, enter the text for your search. For example, to search for information about photography, type either **photo** or **photography**.

Don't worry about using upper- and lowercase letters; Veronica searches ignore capitalization.

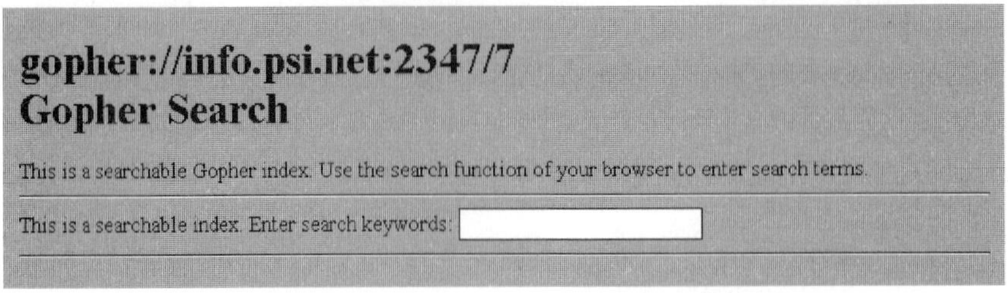

gopher://info.psi.net:2347/7
Gopher Search

This is a searchable Gopher index. Use the search function of your browser to enter search terms.

This is a searchable index. Enter search keywords:

FIGURE 6.7: Type whatever you're looking for into the Enter search keywords text box.

3. Press Enter. The N will become animated and in a few seconds a page will appear listing documents that contain text matching what you typed in as search criteria (see Figure 6.8).

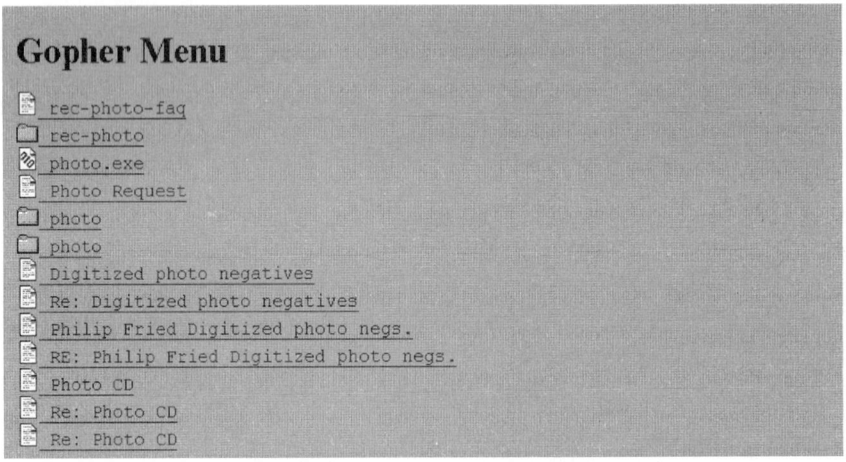

Gopher Menu

rec-photo-faq
rec-photo
photo.exe
Photo Request
photo
photo
Digitized photo negatives
Re: Digitized photo negatives
Philip Fried Digitized photo negs.
RE: Philip Fried Digitized photo negs.
Photo CD
Re: Photo CD
Re: Photo CD

FIGURE 6.8: We searched gopherspace for the word photo and came up with this list of items.

When you construct your search, keep in mind that if you use multiple words as your search criteria (like <u>women in photography</u>) only items that contain <u>all</u> of the words you indicated will be considered matches. This may keep you from finding everything out there that's related to your topic, or it may help you to find only what you need. At the same time, think about the type of information you're looking for and into what broader categories it might be filed, then tailor your search to your needs. For example, a specific topic such as <u>Honda</u> might be found by searching for the more general <u>automobile</u>.

With your page of items matching your search criteria in view, you can click on links to cruise around just as you would with any other page.

Performing More Complicated Searches with Veronica

Veronica lets you control aspects of the search by adding what it calls "flags" to your search string.

Using Flags to Search for Files

Flags are made up of dashes followed by letters and numbers. They can control things like the type of file you want to search for (for example, text files or GIF graphics files) or the number of items to find. The Veronica screen itself provides links to more information about the use of flags. Here are a couple of examples of useful flags.

Maximum Number of Documents You can use the m (for maximum) flag to control the maximum number of documents returned from a search. Without using the flag, Veronica will return up to the first 200 documents that match the search criteria. By adding the m flag, you can either increase or decrease this number. To use the m flag, add mn (where n is the number of matches to return) to the end of your search criteria.

Type of Document The Type of Document flag, *t*, controls what type of document you wish to find. To use it, add t*n* to the end of the search string; *n* is a number or letter that specifies the type of document you want to find. The following table summarizes the more common documents you can search for:

Replace <u>n</u> With	To Find
0	Text file
1	Directory
4	Mac HQX file
5	PC binary file
7	Gopher menu
8	Telnet Session
9	Binary file
s	Sound file
I	Non-GIF image file
M	MIME multipart/mixed message
g	GIF image
h	HTML file

Using -m at the end of your search criteria without a number or letter following it will find all the objects that match the other search criteria—in other words, there could be well more than 200 and this may slow you down considerably.

Using Operators to Refine or Broaden a Search

If you enter as your search criteria a simple multiple word search like *American business*, Veronica will search for instances of both words together, *American* and *business*, in either order. The search will, for example,

find objects categorized as *business, American*. Veronica interprets the entry *American business* as *American* AND *business*, where AND is a "logical operator" being used to establish a relationship between the two words for the search.

You can also use the operators NOT (to indicate to Veronica that you want *business* NOT *American*, for example) and OR (to indicate to Veronica that you want *business* OR *leisure* or some such thing). You can even make things more complex by using opening and closing parentheses. As an example of this,

```
((business OR leisure) travel) NOT American
```

will find anything pertaining to *business or leisure travel*, excluding *American business or leisure travel*.

Search strings are interpreted from right to left, and operators are interpreted as they are encountered.

It's probably best to avoid using OR alone because of the wide range and volume of stuff that search might produce. Instead, use OR in conjunction with parentheses to tightly focus your search.

Now You Know

Having read this far, you now know everything you need to know to check out what's on the Web. Maybe at this point you'd like to find out how to publish your own Web pages, including how to make your own home page. In the next chapter we'll look at HTML and how to use it.

You Too Can Be a Web Publisher

By now, having used Netscape to roam the World Wide Web, you've seen the power of hypertext firsthand. You've seen that hypertext acts as both the Web's glue and its strands—binding it together yet hiding the complexities of Internet cruising. HTML (the Hypertext Markup Language) is the *standard* (the agreed-upon system of marking up text to create pages and links) that makes the Web possible. What started out as an experiment has been embraced by the Internet as *the* means of providing information. It will probably come as no surprise that HTML, in the spirit of the Internet, is published and readily available. *Anyone* can use this standard to publish hypertext documents.

Maybe now you want to get into the act. This chapter will tell you how to get started as a Web publisher. There are five basic steps to creating your own Web page:

◆ Organizing your concepts and materials

◆ *Storyboarding* (sketching out) the page(s) you intend to create

◆ Building a prototype

◆ Testing the prototype and making adjustments

◆ Putting your page on a server

This stuff isn't impossibly difficult—it helps to have a little experience, but, *hey*, everybody's got to start somewhere. Let's look at how HTML works and how you, too, can write HTML documents.

 Don't expect to do this on your PC with a dial-up connection to the Internet. To actually publish a document for public viewing on the Web, you'll need access to an http- or ftp server. Many Internet service providers provide access to an http- or ftp server at little or no additional cost. (We'll go over this in more detail at the end of this chapter.

What's Out There?

You'll find a highly insightful style guide devoted to the use of HTML at `http://www.w3.org/hypertext/WWW/Provider/Style/Overview.html`.

About HTML: The Hypertext Markup Language

There is plenty to know about HTML and creating and publishing Web documents. Sadly, we'll have to leave the finer points to the bigger books, but let's go over the basics: how to make the heads in your documents appear in big, bold letters; how to link your documents to other documents; and how to embed pictures in your document.

The documents you see on the World Wide Web via Netscape look nice, but there's quite a bit of minor technological magic going on. In actuality, the files for these documents are stored on a machine somewhere as plain ASCII text files—unlike word processing files, these ASCII text files include no formatting, and they employ no fancy fonts or attributes like bold or italics. They are plain as plain can be. (See Figure 7.1.) All the special effects that you see in a Web document—bold, italic, links to other documents—are represented in the ASCII text files with special codes that also are made up of plain text characters.

What's Out There?

You'll find loads of resources for creating Web pages at the WWW & HTML Developer's JumpStation—the URL is
`http://oneworld.wa.com/htmldev/devpage/dev-page.html`.

This means, luckily, that you can use any word processor (Word, Word-Perfect, Ami Pro, whatever) or text editor (DOS Edit, Windows Notepad) to create your HTML documents. We use Microsoft Word for Windows to create our HTML documents; you can use any word processor or text editor you like. The only inflexible condition here is that you must save the file as plain ASCII text before Netscape—or any other Web browser—can display it. So make sure your word processor can do that (most can).

---

10 PM
by Brenda Kienan

How many women lie in darkness in Quakertown, Lansdale, Perkasie; considering their pasts, with the undusted rifle rack hanging over the bed and the green afghan heaped and dragging from the arm of a chair onto the carpet where the kids pulled it down and went on. Through the drawn shades the sound of a thousand crickets and wind sweeping between this trailer and the next. These are the elements of redemption: the wind rising,

---

```
10 PM
by Brenda Kienan

     How many women lie in darkness in Quakertown, Lansdale, Perkasie;
considering their pasts, with the undusted rifle rack hanging over the
bed and the green afghan heaped and dragging from the arm of a chair
onto the carpet where the kids pulled it down and went on. Through the
drawn shades the sound of a thousand crickets and wind sweeping between
```

FIGURE 7.1: The document shown on the top was created in a word processing program; shown on the bottom is the same document in ASCII text format. Notice that all the attributes (bold and italic) and all the formatting (indenting, for example) are lost in the transition.

Okay, so we just made the big point that you don't need a special HTML editor, yet there are HTML editors available. Though unnecessary for writing basic HTML documents, an HTML editor certainly would prove beneficial when you're dealing with hundreds of pages of text. While not strictly necessary, a good HTML editor can help you enter HTML commands and verify that you have all the details correct, making it easier to ensure that your Web documents will be displayed correctly in a Web browser.

What's Out There?

A number of freely available programs and add-ins to word processors exist to help you write HTML documents. These can be of great use when you are writing longer document or complex Web pages. CU_HTML, a template that works with Word for Windows (versions 2 and 6) was developed at the Chinese University of Hong Kong, is available at the URL `http://www.cuhk.hk/csc/cu_html/cu_html.htm`. The Internet Assistant for Word 6 is available from Microsoft at `http://www.microsoft.com/pages/deskapps/word/ia`. HoTMetaL PRO for Windows from SoftQuad (a favorite) is available at `http://www.sq.com/`, and html-helper-mode for EMACS is available at the URL `http://www.santafe.edu/~nelson/tools`.

The Elements of Web Page Design

Your Web home page will be accessed by anywhere from dozens to hundreds-of-thousands of people per day. You'll want it to convey clearly and concisely the message you intend to promote (whether that's your resume, your company's policy on hiring technical professionals, or an account of what's happening at the local soda pop machine). In this section, we'll cover some basic guidelines for successful Web page design, tossing out for your consideration all the big-hitting tips we've picked up in our Internet travels.

Just What Is a Markup Language?

Traditionally, a markup language uses defined sequences of control characters or commands embedded within a document. These commands control what the document looks like when it is output to, say, a printer. When you print the document, the control character sequences or commands format the document, displaying such elements as bold headlines, subheads, bulleted items, and the like. IBM's Document Control Language (DCL) and Microsoft's Rich Text Format (RTF) are two examples of markup languages used by many word processing programs to create the effects you see on screen and in print like bold headlines, subheads, bulleted items, and the like.

HTML differs from other markup languages, however, in its overall approach. HTML is unlike typical markup languages in that it is not so much concerned with typefaces and character attributes, but rather the internal document makeup itself. In a language like DCL, you would use commands to indicate the typeface, font size, and style of the text *in a document*. In HTML, the commands indicate the headings, normal paragraphs, lists, and even links *to other Web pages*.

HTML is derived from the Standard Generalized Markup Language (SGML), which has come into increasingly common usage in word processing and other programs for creating print documents. HTML follows the SGML paradigm in that it uses *tags* to do its formatting. Tags are pieces of coding that usually, but not always, come in pairs consisting of a start-tag and an end-tag for marking off *elements*.

When you create HTML documents, bear in mind that the HTML "standard" is in a state of development, with changes happening to accommodate changes in the World Wide Web and its attending software. If you try something that works one day and not the next, it may be that the standard has changed.

Another minor annoyance is that not all Web browsers support all HTML extensions, or they may support other aspects of the HTML language differently. Be this as it may, the basic HTML structure that is presented in this chapter should work well in most instances.

Get Organized

The best way to get started in the design of your home page is to organize your assets: the existing documents and images you want to work with, for example. Think about the message you want to convey and what types of images or text might be appropriate (is it fun and lighthearted or seriously corporate?).

What's Out There?

You'll want to find out everything you can about copyright issues; this will come up both when you want to protect your own material and when you want to use something you've "found" on the Net. (That's not always legal.) A U.S. copyright law page published by Cornell University is at the URL `http://www.law.cornell.edu/topics/copyright.html` and a FAQ (frequently asked question) list published by Ohio State is at the URL `http://www.cis.ohio-state.edu/hypertext/faq/usenet/Copyright-FAQ/top.html`.

Create a Storyboard

With the stuff you want to work with in hand, sit down with paper and pencil (or some nifty drawing software) and plot the thing out. *Storyboard* (sketch) your home page and each page it will link to; include all the elements you're considering (text, images, buttons, hotlinks), and don't be afraid to make adjustments. If your original concept doesn't flow nicely, can it and start again. *You can't do too much advance planning.*

Build a Prototype and Test It

When you've got your pages planned, go ahead and build a prototype. Then test it, test it, and *test it again*. Ask friends and colleagues to try it out and comment, and do all the fine tuning you can. You want to make your best work public, not some funky work-in-progress.

18 Top Tips for Winning Page Design

You have two seconds to grab your reader's attention. That's common knowledge in advertising and publishing circles. You can't go wrong if you follow these basic tips for designing an attention-getting, successful home page:

◆ Before you start, organize your concepts and materials; create a storyboard that sketches out your ideas and how they'll work.

◆ Make the title precise, catchy, and descriptive.

◆ Keep the page active but loose; don't let it get crowded with images, text, or "doo-dads."

◆ Put the important items at the top of the page; don't assume anyone will ever scroll down.

◆ Balance white space; balance large and small images and blocks of text.

◆ Avoid using too many fonts.

◆ Anything that looks like a button should behave like a button.

◆ Avoid links that go nowhere; don't create two links with different names that go to the same place.

◆ Make your links descriptive and accurate words or images. Avoid the generic: Don't link on the word "here."

◆ Use images that contain less than 50 colors.

◆ Include thumbnails of larger, downloadable images.

◆ Remember that people will access your page using different browsers (Netscape, various types of Mosaic, Cello, etc.) and different platforms (Windows, Unix, Mac).

◆ Keep filenames short; make them consistent.

◆ Tell people the sizes of downloadable files if you include them.

◆ Find out if you need permission to use text or images created by someone else.

(continued on next page)

(continued from previous page)

◆ Establish who's going to be Webmaster and make a link on your page leading to the Webmaster.

◆ Build a prototype and test it thoroughly. Do the fine tuning before you announce your page.

◆ Announce and publicize your page wherever possible.

You can test your prototype without making it public. At the end of this chapter you'll find a section titled <u>Using Netscape to Check Your HTML Document</u> that tells you how.

A Quick Look at Successful Web Page Designs

The best way to get ideas and to explore creating a winning Web page is to study examples. We've been showing you Web pages throughout this book; here we're going to take a look at a few especially well-designed pages, pointing out what makes them so terrific.

Some of the Web pages we show here are a bit out of an amateur Webspinner's range—we're including them anyway, to give you an idea of the possibilities.

A Sleek, Space Age Wonder

NASA has developed an understandably strong Web presence. Here's a sleek page (Figure 7.2) that uses a large, striking graphic with links to other pages (in the form of thumbnails) embedded in it. While the graphic in this page is large and takes a while to load, the result is pretty eye-catching and very easy to use. This home page provides access to a wealth of information about NASA.

What's Out There?

The NASA universe is yours to explore at the URL http://www.nasa.gov.

An Understandable Book Metaphor

While the graphics aren't slick, Novell used a very apt book metaphor (Figure 7.3) as the entry way into its Web offerings; users can click on the "title" of any "book" for information on the topic of interest.

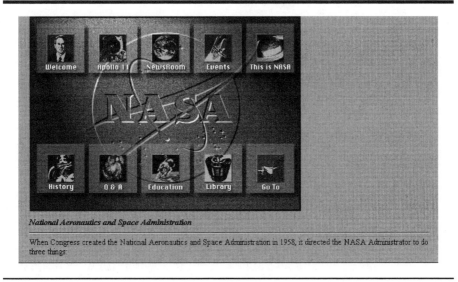

National Aeronautics and Space Administration

When Congress created the National Aeronautics and Space Administration in 1958, it directed the NASA Administrator to do three things:

FIGURE 7.2: The NASA Public Affairs home page is a real beauty.

What's Out There?

Novell makes volumes of information available at the URL
`http://www.novell.com`.

FIGURE 7.3: In the Novell home page you can select the "book" that interests you; click on the book's title and its pages will appear.

Small Graphics and Lots of Buttons

Rocket Science uses its home page to promote its product: video games. The page (shown in Figure 7.4) relies on a mixing of text with colorful custom-made graphics to grab your attention. There are plenty of buttons, providing action and also appearing in nice graphical ways. Each graphic is small, however, so it doesn't take long for this page to load.

What's Out There?

Fly on out to the Rocket Science home page; it's at the URL
`http://www.rocketsci.com`.

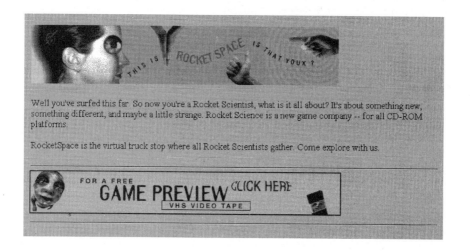

FIGURE 7.4: The Rocket Science home page is as lively and colorful as a game company's page should be.

A Stately Symmetry

The Welcome to the White House home page (Figure 7.5) uses a large image with hot spots to lead to more information on different pages. This page provides no bureaucratic runaround, it's in a simple (perhaps even *dignified*) symmetrical layout.

What's Out There?

Tour the White House interactively by checking in at the URL
`http://www.whitehouse.gov`.

FIGURE 7.5: Welcome to the White House is your entry point to a variety of topics and an electronic tour.

Colorful Graphics as Links

The Internet Underground Music Archive (Figure 7.6) uses lots of small, interesting looking graphics as links. There are West Coast, East Coast, and European versions of the archive.

What's Out There?

Whether you're a bigtime music fan or just a Web wanderer looking for some cool design, check out the Internet Underground Music Archive at the URL http://www.iuma.com.

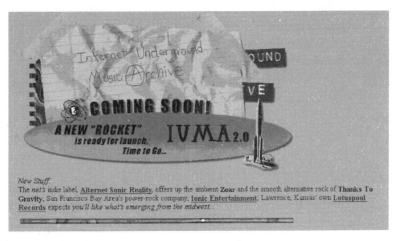

FIGURE 7.6: Take a look (when you get online) at the Internet Underground Music Archive's fun, colorful pages.

File Types and Sizes Identified for Your Convenience

Kevin Hughes is a bona fide Best of the Web hall of famer. We followed links from the Best of the Web page to find his own personal page—a useful

exercise, as it turns out, because Kevin's claim to fame is his HTML expertise and innovations. His page illustrates an important point: Kevin provides information on the size and type of each link that goes to a graphic, video, or sound (Figure 7.7).

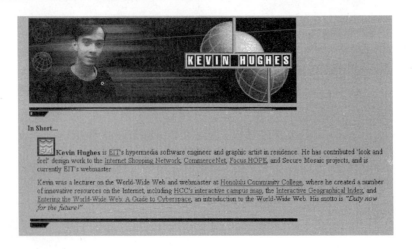

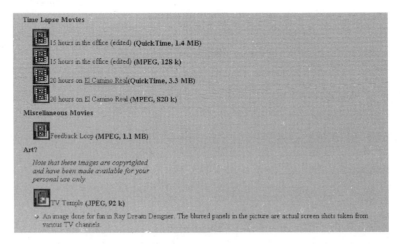

FIGURE 7.7: Kevin Hughes' home page has all the important introductory stuff at the top. If you scroll down the page, you'll find links to video and art, with file types and sizes shown.

What's Out There?

You can see the work of a genuine Web innovator (check out his fancy ruled lines) at the URL http://www.eit.com/people/kev.html.

Interactivity at Its Best

One of the most famous (and, in our opinions) *best* examples of use of the Web is the interactive frog dissection shown in part in Figure 7.8. The menu in the frog dissection home page lets you choose which phases of the dissection you'd like to see; you can follow the entire process one scene at a time in lifelike color. Of course an added bonus is that millions of people can experience this dissection without killing millions of frogs.

What's Out There?

You can experience a brilliantly innovative interactive frog dissection at http:// curry.edschool.virginia.edu/~insttech/frog/.

Using HTML to Mark Up a Document

Now let's take a look at how all this is done. Marking up a document is a pretty simple matter of identifying what you want any given element to be and then literally *marking* it as that type of element (Figure 7.9).

The mark-up, or commands, in HTML documents are surrounded by angle brackets, like this:

```
<title>
```

These commands usually come in pairs and affect everything between them. For example, surrounding a heading you'll see <h1> at the beginning, matching the </h1> at the end. ...More on this as we go along.

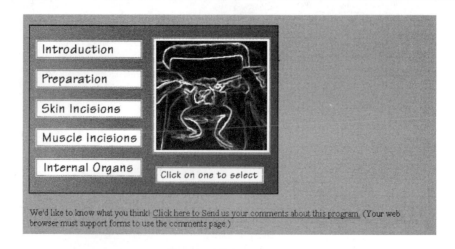

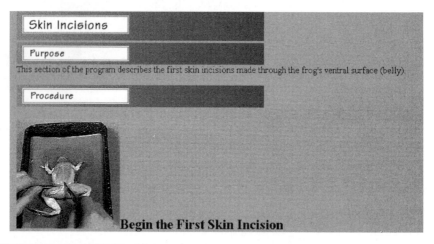

FIGURE 7.8: This interactive frog dissection is one of the best uses of the Web we've ever seen. Bravo!

 One major exception to the pairing of HTML commands can be found in the New Paragraph command, <p>, which stands alone at the beginning of a new paragraph.

```
<html>
<head>
<title>10 PM</title>
</head>
<body>
<h1>10 PM</h1>
<h2>by Brenda Kienan</h2>
<p>
        How many women lie in darkness in Quakertown, Lansdale, Perkasie;
considering their pasts, with the undusted rifle rack hanging over the bed and the
green afghan heaped and dragging from the arm of a chair onto the carpet where the
kids pulled it down and went on. Through the drawn shades the sounds of a thousand
crickets and wind sweeping between this trailer and the next. These are the elements
of redemption: the wind rising, rattling the corrugated plastic roof of the neighbor's
carport, the husband coughing over the droning tv news, the washer clicking and
getting louder as the clothes inside it spin out of balance. This is an ordering of events
that carries one day to the next.<p>
        How many women, each in her own separate darkness, surveying what might
have happened, while the rushing wind finds its way into heating ducts and whistles
through tin.<p>
        <i>Papa, it is vanishing.</i> The blue June evenings and the scent of dusty
pavement as a long-awaited rain falls. <i>I thought I'd still know, but I'm
drifting.</i> White tulips. Gold star confetti sprayed across starched tablecloths.
The priest's thick fingers holding a book.<p>
        How many women making a list, of the ways they might have gone, of the
friends they see in markets, marriages lost, pushing carts full of children, sugary
cereals, cheap meats. How many mornings of driving: her own child to another's care,
her husband (who's lost his license) to work, herds of teenagers in a yellow bus to
school. How many times the red-haired boy pushing his way to the seat behind her,
bringing her gifts of novelty pencils, a sandwich, cloisonn&eacute; earrings.<p>
        How many women wondering, each in her cool separate darkness, if the news
is yet over, if the wind will grow still.<p>
<h3>Copyright 1995 Brenda Kienan</h3>
</body>
</html>
```

10 PM

by Brenda Kienan

How many women lie in darkness in Quakertown, Lansdale, Perkasie; considering their pasts, with the undusted rifle rack hanging over the bed and the green afghan heaped and dragging from the arm of a chair onto the carpet where the kids pulled it down and went on. Through the drawn shades the sounds of a thousand crickets and wind sweeping between this trailer and the next. These are the elements of redemption: the wind rising, rattling the corrugated plastic roof of the neighbor's carport, the husband coughing over the droning tv news, the washer clicking and getting louder as the clothes inside it spin out of balance. This is an ordering of events that carries one day to the next.

How many women, each in her own separate darkness, surveying what might have happened, while the rushing wind finds its way into heating ducts and whistles through tin

Papa, it is vanishing. The blue June evenings and the scent of dusty pavement as a long-awaited rain falls. *I thought I'd still know, but I'm drifting.* White tulips. Gold star confetti sprayed across starched tablecloths. The priest's thick fingers holding a book.

How many women making a list, of the ways they might have gone, of the friends they see in markets, marriages lost, pushing carts full of children, sugary cereals, cheap meats. How many mornings of driving: her own child to another's care, her husband (who's lost his license) to work, herds of teenagers in a yellow bus to school. How many times the red-haired boy pushing his way to the seat behind her, bringing her gifts of novelty pencils, a sandwich, cloisonné earrings.

How many women wondering, each in her cool separate darkness, if the news is yet over, if the wind will grow still.

Copyright 1995 Brenda Kienan

FIGURE 7.9: In an HTML-coded document (above) you see commands (within angle brackets) surrounding the element to which they refer. In the resulting Web document (below), you do not see the commands—you see only the effect they have on the document displayed.

In Figure 7.10 you see all the elements of a basic HTML document and how it turned out when viewed on the Web with Netscape. Take note of:

◆ The entire document enclosed between <html> and </html>

◆ The title of the document enclosed between <title> and </title>

◆ The header of the document enclosed between <h1> and </h1>

◆ The body of the document enclosed between <body> and </body>

In the sections that follow, we'll look at the basic HTML commands you can use in your documents. Remember as we go along that these commands are the same whether you are marking up a document in a word processor or in an HTML editor.

```
<HTML>                                                    Beginning of document
<TITLE>The Page's Title Goes Here</TITLE>                 Title
<H1>The Page's Title Is Usually Repeated Here</H1>        Header
<BODY>
Here is the body of the page.                             Body of document
</BODY>
</HTML>                                                    End of document
```

FIGURE 7.10: Here you can see the HTML coding for the most basic elements of a Web document.

 If you're using a word processor to create an original document you intend for Web publication, you can of course simply write in the HTML coding as you go along; you don't have to write the document first and enter the codes afterwards.

Every Document Must Have the "Required" Commands

Every HTML document must include certain commands, which essentially identify the document as an HTML document and as such, show its beginning and end. Note that even these most fundamental HTML commands come in pairs—the <html> at the beginning of the documents matches the </html> at the end of the document.

Marking Up Heads

HTML supports six levels of heads. Each level of head will look different when it's displayed in a Web browser like Netscape. The highest level (let's call this the "1" head) will be larger and more obvious, the lowest level (the "6" head) will be smallest and most discreet.

 The actual way each head looks is different from one browser to the next. In other words, HTML allows you to say what text is a head, but not what the head will look like when User A accesses it with Netscape, User B with Air Mosaic, and User C with NCSA Mosaic or Cello.

The text of the head should appear between two head codes <h*n*> and </h*n*>, where *n* can be any number between 1 and 6. It is customary to start your document with a head of level 1, to indicate the important topic that comes first in your document. You can follow a level 1 head with heads of lower levels; you can also place new level 1 heads further down in your document, as you please.

Beginning New Paragraphs

You must explicitly code each and every new paragraph of text by placing the <p> code at its beginning. You needn't close a paragraph with any coding, however. As noted previously, this new paragraph business is one of the major exceptions to the "opening and closing" paired codes that are the general rule in HTML.

 Web browsers will not start a new paragraph if you do not include the <p> code, regardless of how your document looks in your word processor.

Inserting Ruled Lines

Rules, or ruled lines, are horizontal lines that you can use to separate parts of your document. To place a rule in your document, use the <HR> command. (See Figure 7.11.) Again, it's not necessary to indicate the end of the rule with a closing code. The ruled line you code in to your document will cross the Web page (whatever size the page is on screen) from the left margin to the right.

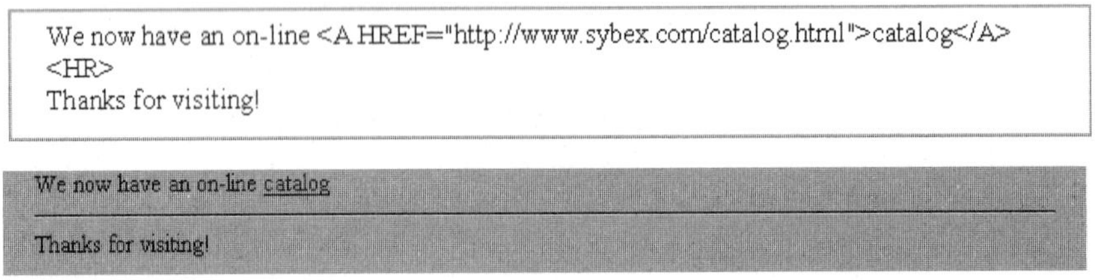

```
We now have an on-line <A HREF="http://www.sybex.com/catalog.html">catalog</A>
<HR>
Thanks for visiting!
```

We now have an on-line catalog

Thanks for visiting!

FIGURE 7.11: The coding you see in the HTML document above results in the rule you see in the Web document below.

Creating Lists

You can have two types of lists in a Web document: numbered and bulleted. In HTML lingo, numbered lists are called *ordered* lists and bulleted lists are called *unordered* lists.

Ordered Lists

Ordered (numbered) lists will be the result of text nested between the <OL> and </OL> codes. Each new item in the ordered list must start with the <LI> code. Unlike most other HTML codes, the <LI> code need not be ended with a </LI> code. For example, a numbered list of types of fruit would look like:

```
<OL>
<LI>Apple
<LI>Orange
<LI>Cherry
</OL>
```

A Web browser would display the above list like this:

1. Apple

2. Orange

3. Cherry

 When you're coding an ordered list, you need not enter the numbers. The HTML coding tells the Web browser to number the items sequentially in the order in which they appear.

Netscape also lets you control the type of numbering in an ordered list. To specify the type of numbering you want, you can embed an extra little code in the first <OL>. For example, if we modify our fruit list like this:

```
<OL TYPE=I>
<LI>Apple
<LI>Orange
<LI>Cherry
</OL>
```

Netscape will display it with Roman numerals, like this:

```
I. Apple
II. Orange
III. Cherry
```

You can use the following codes to specify the type of numbering you want:

The Code	Will Produce
A	Uppercase letters, starting with A
a	Lowercase letters, starting with a
I	Uppercase Roman numerals, starting with I
i	Lowercase Roman numerals, starting with i
1	Arabic numbers, starting with 1

Not all Web browsers "understand" the type options for numbers as Netscape does. If you create a page using these options and someone loads the page using a Web browser that doesn't allow for this, they will see the items listed using regular, Arabic numbers.

Unordered Lists

Unordered (bulleted) lists will be the result of text nested between the <UL> and </UL> codes. This, of course, is very similar to what you do to create an ordered list. Each new item in the bulleted list must begin with a <LI> code. This is *exactly* like what you do with each item in an ordered list; it is the 0 or U in the opening and closing codes that "tell" whether the list is to be numbered or bulleted—and again, you need not be bothered with placing any type of bullets. They will appear when the document is viewed on screen wherever you have placed the <LI> code in your unordered list.

 Remember that the bullets will look different and be of different sizes in the different Web browsers available.

By default, Netscape uses solid discs as bullets, and it does not indent bulleted lists. You can change the look of bullets to a square instead of a disc. This is a simple matter of embedding a TYPE=SQUARE code in your opening <UL> code, like this:

```
<UL TYPE=SQUARE>
```

Other than that one little change, you can make your bulleted list as described above. If you use the TYPE=SQUARE code in this way, all the bullets in your list will be neat, stolid squares.

Creating Links

Now we get to the heart of things. As you know well by now, the beauty of the Web is the way documents are inter-related through being linked to each other—that's what makes the Web so wonderfully webby. Let's take a look behind the scenes at the HTML underpinnings of a link.

In HTML lingo, a link is really what's called an *anchor*, the opening code for which is <A. What the anchor looks like when it appears as a link in a Web document will differ depending on which Web browser is being used, but usually it'll show up as underlined blue text. When you click on the link (the underlined blue text) the anchor is activated, and the file it is associated with (the other end of the link, if you will) is loaded and displayed on screen.

Here's an example of how this works in HTML: If you wanted the word *Catalog* to appear in a document as a link, you'd code the word like this:

```
<A HREF="http://www.sybex.com/catalog.html">Catalog</A>
```

Then, when the document is viewed with any Web browser, such as Netscape, the word *Catalog* will appear as a link. When a user clicks on it, the file CATALOG.HTML will automatically be transferred from the HTTP server `www.sybex.com`, and Sybex's Catalog will appear on screen.

What's Out There?

In your Web roamings, you've probably found links that go not to HTML documents, but perhaps instead to graphics, sounds, and videos. The URL in a link doesn't have to point to another HTML document; it can point to any type of file. For example, the anchor

```
<AHREF="http://www.iuma.com/IUMA/ftp/music/Madonna/
Secret.mpg">Madonna</A>
```

creates a link to the machine www.iuma.com, where a video clip from Madonna's Secret video is stored. When you click on the link, the video will be transferred to your computer and a player for MPEG files will start up so you can see the video—the trigger for that action is in the HTML coding shown above. You can create links to any type of file in this manner—ust include in the URL the full path to the file.

Remember, you must indicate the type of file to which you are linking; this will "tell" the Web browser employed by any given user how to deal with the file. When it comes to images, most Web browsers "out of the box" can deal only with GIF and XBM files. Netscape can also handle JPG files, but you'll need special <u>viewers</u> (as described in Chapter 10) to "view" images or sounds in other file formats.

Creating Glossaries

A *glossary* in a Web document is a special element designed to let you place definitions in your documents. Glossaries look a bit like lists when they are coded with HTML; the list of items this time must be surrounded by the codes <DL> and </DL>. Each defined *term* in the glossary starts with the code <DT>. The definitions themselves follow the term they apply to, and begin with the code <DD>. Neither <DT> or <DD> codes need closing codes.

Here is a sample of coding for a glossary:

```
<DL>
<DT>Apple
<DD>A round fruit, often red in color when ripe but some-
times green or yellow
<DT>Orange
<DD>A round, orange fruit
<DT>Cherry
<DD>A small, round, red fruit
</DL>
```

The result of this sample coding will look like this:

Apple
    A round fruit, often red in color when ripe but sometimes green
Orange
    A round, orange fruit
Cherry
    A small, round, red fruit

Inserting Addresses

Address is a special HTML element that was originally designed to hold the address of the author of the page. (The snail mail address, the e-mail address, or both.) Most Web browsers display this element in an italic font, smaller than body text. For example,

```
<ADDRESS>
Daniel A. Tauber and Brenda Kienan
<P>Sybex
<P>2021 Challenger Drive
<P>Alameda, CA 94501
</ADDRESS>
```

will appear as shown here:

> *Daniel A. Tauber and Brenda Kienan*
>
> *Sybex*
>
> *2021 Challenger Drive*
>
> *Alameda, CA 94501*

Assigning Text Attributes: Bold, Italic, and Underline

You are probably familiar with *text attributes* from word processors. Things like bold, italic, and character color, which differentiate some text from the usual, are all known as *attributes* in a word processor. You can specify attributes such as these using HTML.

Remember that none of the formatting or text attributes you might have in your word processed document will carry over to your Web document—you must specify what you want using HTML coding.

The types of attributes you can specify using HTML are broken down into two classes:

◆ Physical

◆ Logical

The *physical* attributes specify how text characters will look: italic or bold, for example. They will be italic or bold no matter which Web browser is used for viewing. The *logical* attributes specify the amount of emphasis you want to give to important text; you can choose to make text *emphasized* or *strongly emphasized*. In many cases, this will turn out to be just italic or bold, but some Web browsers will have different ways of showing logical attributes. (Maybe strongly emphasized text will be red, or in a slightly larger size, for example.) The choice of using logical or physical attributes is yours. Some people prefer to use physical attributes because they want to control the way the text finally looks. Other people prefer to use logical attributes because they convey "meaning" without specifying what the text should look like.

Physical Attributes

You can use physical attributes to make text appear bold, italic, or underlined.

 The underline attribute is not the same as the underlining that appears under links—Netscape generates the link underline automatically when you code for a link.

The codes used to apply these attributes are summarized here:

To Get This Attribute	Use the Starting Code	And the Ending Code
Bold	<B>	</B>
Italic	<I>	</I>
<u>Underline</u>	<U>	</U>

 You can use multiple attributes together by embedding them. Just make sure the opening code that's first-in corresponds to the closing code that's last-out. For example, to make the phrase Bungee Jumping both bold and italic, use the coding `<B><I>Bungee Jumping</I></B>`.

Logical Attributes

You can use logical attributes to give emphasis or strong emphasis to text you feel is important. The way the text actually appears when viewed in a browser depends on the browser's individual way of handling these attributes. The logical attributes that you can use are:

To Get This Attribute	Use the Starting Code	And the Ending Code
Emphasis	`<EM>`	`</EM>`
Strong Emphasis	`<STRONG>`	`</STRONG>`

Here you can see the result of making text emphasized and strongly emphasized and viewing the text with Netscape:

Emphasis and **Strong Emphasis**

Using Special Characters

Some special characters are available in HTML. For example, you'll often want to use the special character for the copyright symbol (©); but HTML files are really plain text files, so you don't have access to some other special characters, the symbol that's used to indicate copyright for digital audio, a letter P enclosed in a circle, to name one unfortunate example.

Some "special" characters you'd use fairly regularly in word processed text, such as the angle brackets and ampersand, have special meanings in HTML, as you know if you've read earlier sections of this chapter. To include characters such as these in your HTML document, you'll have to insert special escape codes for them in your file. Here are some examples:

For the Symbol	Which Means	Use the Code
&	Ampersand	`&amp;`
>	Less-Than	`&lt;`
<	Greater-Than	`&gt;`

What's Out There?

You can get a complete list of special characters and how to code for them at the URL `http://info.cern.ch/hypertext/WWW/MarkUp/ISOlat1.html`.

Embedding Images

Images that appear as part of a Web page are called *inline images*. While it is possible to place many, many inline images in your document, remember that including them will greatly increase the time required to load and view the document.

It's best in some circumstances to place thumbnails of images in your page—thumbnails load a lot faster than larger images—and link the thumbnail to the larger image, allowing users to download the bigger image if they want to and have time to wait for it. See <u>Mixing Elements</u>, the next section in this chapter.

Any image that you want to include as inline image in a Web document must be in one of three graphics file formats: GIF, JPG, or XBM. XBM is a Unix image format, and this, of course, is a Windows book, so let's look more closely at use of the ever popular GIF format in this section.

Some Web browsers (including Netscape) can display inline images in JPEG format. JPEG files are much smaller in size than other image files so they appear on screen much more quickly—a real advantage. The drawback for the publisher, however, is that not all Web browsers can display them. If you use JPEG and a user tries viewing your document with a browser that can't handle JPEG, all he or she will see is a little error message where the image should be.

You can use the `<IMG>` command to place an inline image into your HTML document. For example,

```
<IMG SRC="http://www.sybex.com/covers/1327.gif">
```

will cause the image stored in the file 1327.GIF in the directory COVERS on the machine `www.sybex.com` to be displayed as part of the Web document. A couple of other nifty things you can do with Netscape involve text wrapping around images on screen. To cause an image to appear to the left of text with the text wrapping around the image, use the `ALIGN=LEFT` command, like this:

```
<IMG SRC="http://www.sybex.com/covers/1327.gif" ALIGN=LEFT>
```

To cause an image to appear along to the right of text with the text wrapping around it, use the `ALIGN=RIGHT` command, like this:

```
<IMG SRC="http://www.sybex.com/covers/1327.gif" ALIGN=RIGHT>
```

What's Out There?

You can scope out a helpful FAQ file for extensive tips on scanning images to use in your Web documents. To find the Scanning FAQ, use the URL `http://www.dopig.uab.edu/dopigpages/FAQ/The-Scan-FAQ.html`. Transparent GIFs are GIFs in which one of the colors is invisible. (You might want to do this if you'd like the background color the user's Netscape is using to be one of the colors in the image.) To reveal how you can make your GIFs transparent, look into the URL `http://melmac.harris-atd.com/transparent_images.html`.

Mixing Elements

Just as you can create bold-italic text by embedding the italic code within the bold code, you can embed one type of HTML element within another element. For example, you might want to create an unordered (bulleted) list in which each element is a link to another Web page. In fact, if you

think about it, your entire HTML file is embedded between the <html> and </html> commands, so everything in your document is already embedded between two standard HTML commands.

Another practical use for embedded HTML commands is a link that leads to an image. In that case, the inline image command is embedded inside of the link command. (And this, dear reader, takes us to the next section.)

Using Pictures as Links

To make an image act as a link to another document, you can use the link command, <A, followed by indicators of what you're linking to, followed by </A>. In a nutshell, here's what you do: where you'd normally place the text the user will click on to activate the link, you instead place the command to display an inline image. For example, if you have an image called TOCATALOG.GIF, you could place

```
<A HREF="http://www.sybex.com/catalog.html"><IMG
src="http://www.sybex.com/tocatalog.gif"></IMG></A>
```

in your Web document to create a link to the page stored in the file CATALOG.HTML. This causes a Web browser to display the image TOCATALOG.GIF with a border around it. When a user clicks anywhere in the picture the link will become activated, and in this case, the Catalog page indicated will appear.

Creating Lists of Links

Let's say you want a list of links. To do this, create an ordered or unordered list, placing a link as each item in the list. For example,

```
<UL>
<LI><A HREF="http://www.sybex.com/sybex.html">Sybex's Home
Page</A>
<LI><A HREF="http://www.sybex.com/catalog.html">Sybex's
Catalog</A>
<LI><A HREF="http://www.sybex.com/people/dan.html">My Home
Page</A>
</UL>
```

produces a bulleted list with three items, each of which is a link to another page:

○ Sybex's Home Page
○ Sybex's Catalog
○ My Home Page

Creating a Simple Home Page

Great. Now, having read this chapter, you know all the HTML commands that go into creating a simple page. Let's go step-by-step through creating a home page. We'll use Word for Windows to do this, and when we're done, we'll save the file as a plain text file.

To follow along, start up Word for Windows and open a new, empty document window.

NOTE Just about everything we do here you can do in any word processor. If you use a different word processor—Ami Pro or WordPerfect, for example—you can follow along, substituting as necessary the functions and commands your word processor uses.

1. In your blank, new document window, type **\<html\>** and press ↵ to start your page. (Remember that all HTML documents should be surrounded by the \<html\> and \</html\> commands. We'll put in the \</html\> later, at the end of these steps.)

2. Now type **\<title\>Herkimer Uglyface's Home Page\</title\>** and press ↵. (You can replace Herkimer Uglyface with your own name, which is probably more attractive, anyway.) This will make the title of your home page appear in the title bar when your page is viewed by a user.

3. Now type **\<h1\>Herkimer Uglyface's Home Page\</h1\>** and press ↵. This will make it so the title of your home page appears at the top of your home page. (Although it's customary to use the same text for the title and the first head, you can actually enter whatever you want in place of "Herkimer Uglyface's Home Page" here.)

4. Now we are ready to enter some body text, so type **<body>**and press ↵. This will tell the Web browser that what follows is the body text of the document.

5. Type in a few paragraphs of body text. Remember as you do this to use the **<p>** command at the beginning of every new paragraph.

6. If you want people viewing your page to reach you by e-mail, you can add a link to your e-mail address. Type **<A HREF="mailto:** followed immediately by your e-mail address (with no space after mailto:). After your e-mail address (again no space should follow the address), type ">**You can send me e-mail.</A>**. (Don't type that last period. It's only there to make our editor happy.) Press ↵.

7. Once you have typed the body text for your page, and added your e-mail link if you chose to, type **</body>** to end the body text and **</html>** to end the document. These two HTML commands match their counterparts at the beginning of the document. You can press ↵ after each of these commands if you're a stickler for aesthetic consistency, but it's not necessary.

Now it's time to save the document. (Remember, we're using Word for Windows for this demo.)

1. From the Word for Windows menu bar, select File ➤ Save As. The Save As dialog box will appear.

2. In the Save As dialog box, click on the down arrow next to the text box labeled Save File As Type. A list of file types recognized by Word for Windows will appear. From this list, select Text Only (Figure 7.12).

3. Type in a path and filename for the file in the File Name text box. If you're saving the file to your hard disk, and placing it in your Netscape directory, the path will probably be C:\NETSCAPE. You're stuck with the DOS filenaming conventions in naming your file— eight characters only. Our hero, Herkimer Uglyface, named his file HERKPAGE.HTM—you can name yours what you like, but you'll have to end the file with the extension .HTM, because this is an HTML file you are saving.

4. Click on the OK button to save the file.

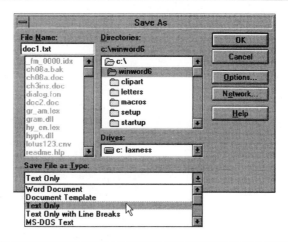

FIGURE 7.12: In the list of file types, select Text Only.

When Word for Windows is finished saving the file, the Save As dialog box will close automatically. You can now exit Word for Windows. Don't be alarmed if Word for Windows asks if you want to save changes to your file when you exit even though you just saved the file as a text file. Just answer No and continue to exit Word for Windows.

 Don't answer Yes when Word for Windows asks if you want to save changes to your file when you exit after having saved the file as a text file; if you do, Word for Windows will overwrite your text file with a Word file.

Good work. We're ready to look at the file with Netscape to see how it turned out.

Using Netscape to Check Your HTML Document

You've created an HTML document and saved it as a text file on your hard disk. Before you make public your page, you'll want to test it. You can use

Netscape to see what your finely crafted page will look like when it's viewed with a Web browser. To load a file from your hard disk into Netscape, follow these steps:

1. Start Netscape and select File ➤ Open File from the menu bar. The File Open dialog box will appear.

2. In the File Open dialog box, highlight the filename you gave your page. (The File Open dialog box works here just as it does in any Windows application.) Click on the OK button.

3. The dialog box will close, and in a few seconds your home page will appear on screen, in the form of a beautiful Web document!

You won't be able to fix typos or other errors or add things to your HTML document while you are viewing it with Netscape. If you want to make changes, close Netscape, open up your word processor, and make the changes there. Then, you can save the modified file, and re-open it in Netscape to see the changes you just made.

Making Your HTML Document Available to the World

Having created a wonderful HTML document on your own computer, you'll want to make it available to the world. As a Web publisher, you can, if you have a big pile of money, buy a machine and set it up as a web server. This is simply not practical for most people, so we're going to skip it. You can also, if you have access to a Web server at a university or elsewhere, sneak your page onto that server (but don't say we said so). A third option, more practical for a lot of people, might be to publish your page with the help of your Internet service provider. Unfortunately, this is sometimes not free—check with your service provider about costs, and if there is an unreasonable charge, *switch providers*.

Some companies, like Web Communications, will rent you space on their servers. This may be a good option if you have a service provider you want to stick with even though it offers no publishing opportunities. The URL for Web Communications is `http://www/webcom.com`.

The technical specifics of making your Web pages available to the world also vary from one Internet service provider to another, so we cannot go into *great* detail in this book. Contact your service provider to see how they recommend that you make your documents available to the Internet public.

For your HTML documents to become available to the world, they must be stored on an FTP or HTTP *server* computer that is connected to the Internet. This, for all practical purposes, is not going to be your stand-alone PC with a dial-up connection to the Internet. It'll be a specially outfitted computer that belongs to your Internet service provider. They'll tell you how to transfer your files to their machine and what URLs people should use to access your page.

When Your Page Is Ready, Publicize It

One of the worst tragedies in publishing of any sort is a wonderful piece of work that goes unnoticed because *nobody knows it's there*. Don't let this happen to your Web page. Sure, some people are bound to stumble across it; but you probably want lots and *lots* of people to see it—otherwise, why publish it on the Net?

Take a lesson from the experience of others: When Enterzone, the literary rag mentioned in Chapter 5 of this book, went "live" in late '94, it got only about 20 hits a day until it was listed in the NCSA What's New page—after the listing, Enterzone's hits-per-day increased a hundredfold. We've heard the anecdote, too, of *Virtual Vegas*, an experimental "virtual trade show booth" that went from a few dozen hits per day to tens of thousands after being listed. (*Virtual Vegas* also benefited from a short, catchy title with all the implied glitz of the casinos.)

The NCSA What's New document is visited by over 3 million users per week. We discuss it in detail in Chapter 5; its URL (for your reference one more time) is `http://www.ncsa.uiuc.edu/ SDG/Software/Mosaic/Docs/ whats-new.html.`

Another venue for announcing your page might be various carefully selected Usenet newsgroups. Choose appropriate newsgroups based on whether their topics are related to the topic of your page.

You can also announce your page via Internet mailing lists like Net-Happenings. To subscribe to Net-Happenings, send e-mail to `list-serv@is.internic.net`; in the body of your message, type: **subscribe net-happenings** and add your full name.

You can also <u>trade links</u> with others who've published pages on related topics (or even unrelated topics).

If your page is of a *commercial* nature, you can list it for free along with over 800 other companies in Open Market's Commercial Sites Index.

What's Out There?

Open Market's Commercial Sites Index can be found at the URL `http://www.directory.net/.`

What's Next?

Well. Now you know all you need to know to browse the Web, search for what you find intriguing or useful, and create your own home page. In Chapters 8 and 9, we're going to cover the nitty gritty technical details: how to install and configure Chameleon Sampler and Netscape. Then, in Chapter 10, we'll show you how to get some nifty viewers and players from the Internet itself.

Part Three:

Getting Started with Netscape

Laying the Groundwork for Installing Netscape

Roll up your sleeves, this is the part where we get down and dirty and put things together. In this chapter, we're going to get you on the Net, install and configure Chameleon Sampler (the software that comes with this book), and *go get Netscape* from the Internet itself.

What You Need

Let's face facts. Netscape just isn't one of those programs you can take out of the box and expect to install itself. Netscape has many wonderful attributes, but unfortunately that's not one of them. As we've discussed earlier in this book, to run Netscape on your Windows PC, you need:

- ◆ An account with an Internet service provider
- ◆ Netscape itself
- ◆ SLIP/PPP software to make the vital connection between your Internet service provider and Netscape

Setting up an account with an Internet service provider is up to you. Let it suffice to say here that the most important considerations in selecting an Internet service provider are

◆ Whether the service provider you're considering provides a local access phone number so you can avoid long distance charges

◆ Whether they offer SLIP/PPP accounts

You also need a Windows PC with at least 4MB of RAM (8MB or more is a lot better), 10MB of available hard disk space, and a fast modem (at least 9600 bps). Except for the modem, this is the same stuff you need to run most Windows programs, so you're probably set.

In the section that follows this one, we'll talk a bit more about choosing an appropriate Internet service provider and in Appendix B of this book we list a few major Internet service providers that offer SLIP/PPP accounts along with contact information so you can get in touch with them.

 If you need more information about Internet basics, look into <u>A Guided Tour of the Internet</u> by Christian Crumlish (Sybex, 1995). This book walks you through many aspects of the Internet and includes a comprehensive list of Internet service providers.

Getting Netscape is probably going to be a matter of going out on the Internet and downloading an evaluation copy of the software; we'll go over that in an upcoming section of this chapter. (As of this writing we have heard that Netscape may become available for sale in retail outlets, but that hasn't happened just yet, so we're going to assume that you'll be getting the software from the Net.)

Providing yourself with SLIP/PPP software may happen in one of several basic ways:

◆ It's on the disk that comes with this book

◆ You already have it if you use Netcom's NetCruiser version 1.6 or higher as your Internet service provider software

◆ You already have it if you have Windows 95

◆ You may already have it if you're on a LAN that's connected to the Internet (ask your system administrator)

In our discussion, we're going to assume you're getting set up with the software that comes with this book—Chameleon Sampler. If one of the other situations we just described fits you better, talk to the software manufacturer (Netcom or Microsoft) or to your network system administrator if you're on a LAN. They can tell you what to do.

Okey dokey. Let's get cracking. Before we do, however, a few words of caution: this chapter is going to deal with material that's a little more technically demanding than what we've done so far in this book. Setting up the SLIP/PPP software involves a lot of making little "pieces" work together. Don't let this discourage you—take your time, have patience, read carefully, and ask your Internet service provider for help if you get stuck. In the end you'll have Netscape running and it'll be well worth your effort.

Selecting an Internet Service Provider

There are things you need to think about in selecting an Internet service provider to work with Netscape; let's go over the important points.

Ask about SLIP/PPP

If you're going to run Netscape on a home computer equipped with a modem (that's what we're here for, isn't it?), you're going to need a SLIP account *or* a PPP account. *The Internet service providers that offer SLIP/PPP are different from commercial online service accounts like CompuServe, America Online, Prodigy, or Delphi.*

SLIP stands for *Serial Line Internet Protocol* and PPP stands for *Point to Point Protocol*. Some Internet service providers offer one, some offer the other, some offer both. For your purposes at home, they are equivalent; either kind of account will allow you to run Netscape just fine (that's why we talk about them as a unit, using "SLIP/PPP" for shorthand).

Do I <u>Have</u> to Use Chameleon Sampler?

In actuality, and in somewhat more technical terms, Netscape accesses the Internet via a "Winsock-compatible TCP/IP stack." (In a sense, that's just another, deeper way to say "SLIP/PPP software.") As you know by now, Chameleon Sampler, which is the software that comes with this book, provides SLIP/PPP for use on a stand-alone PC with a modem—but Netscape will run just as happily with any other software that provides a "Winsock interface." This could be gotten in the form of TCP/IP software running on a computer directly attached to the Internet, or in the form of another dial-up package, such as Trumpet or Netcom's NetCruiser 1.6, that provides a Winsock interface. You can use whatever software your Internet service provider recommends for connecting to the Internet via their service. If you choose to use something other than Chameleon Sampler, ask your Internet service provider how to get that software set up for use with Netscape.

In telecommunications jargon, SLIP/PPP allows you to send TCP/IP packets (see Chapters 1 and 2) over a serial communications device—a *modem*. Remember, while you are logged onto your SLIP/PPP account, your machine at home *is actually part of the Internet*. Maybe that's worth repeating. You're not logged onto the Internet the way you are logged on to a BBS when you call one—in that case your single machine is accessing the single machine on which the BBS resides. When you log onto the Internet, your machine becomes part of the network of millions of computers that makes up the Internet, and you can communicate with any one of them by sending and receiving e-mail, files, or whatever.

What's Out There?

To delve into the subject of SLIP/PPP, make your way to the home page maintained by Chameleon Sampler's manufacturer, NetManage Inc. Its URL is http://www.netmanag.com.

Consider the Costs

A major consideration in selecting a service provider is cost. There are essentially two costs involved: a monthly fee you pay the service provider for access (and often, whether they admit it or not, the use of their software), and the fee you pay (or do not pay if you are clever and find a service provider with local access) to the phone company for long distance charges. *Shop around for a good deal*, and when you ask about the deal, remember to ask about a local access number.

Appendix B of this book contains a list of some major Internet service providers who offer SLIP/PPP accounts, complete with contact information. If the appendix doesn't list providers who serve your area, look in local computer publications and in national computer magazines for the advertisements of more local providers—you'll find that there's no shortage of them, and one of them is bound to be perfect for you.

You can generally expect to pay somewhere in the neighborhood of $25–$50 per month for a SLIP/PPP account with an Internet service provider, plus (sometimes) a one-time setup or registration charge.

Ask about technical support, too. Is it available by telephone 7 days a week or just through e-mail? Are they fully staffed? If you have pals you can consult, ask them about the quality of support and the provider's reputation for reliability.

Make Note of Some Technical Details

Once you choose a provider, setting up your account can usually be accomplished over the telephone. It should take a few days (if that) for them to get you going.

But let's back up a minute. While you've got them on the line, find out some technical information you'll need to know to set up Chameleon

Sampler for use with Netscape. Make note of their answers as you go—we'll use this information later in this chapter. Specifically, ask them for the following information:

◆ *The IP Address of the provider's server*

◆ *The IP Address assigned to your machine at home (unless your provider "dynamically assigns" IP numbers)*

If you're already familiar with addresses in the domain.names.separated .by.periods format, you'll know that violet.berkeley.edu is a machine at the University of California, Berkeley. This is NOT what you want here, however. In our discussion in Chapters 1 and 2, we described how an address like violet.berkeley.edu is the easier-to-remember version of what's really a numerical address. You want the IP address in a *numerical* format—numbers separated by periods—such as 126.54.32.1.

Write the IP Address of the provider's server here:

_____._____._____._____

Also ask for the four-number address the provider is assigning to your computer (*every* computer on the Internet has such an address, called an *IP address*). Note that some providers will assign your machine a permanent IP address while others assign an IP address "dynamically," meaning that each time you log into your SLIP/PPP account, the provider's server automatically assigns your computer an address for use in that session only.

If your provider assigns your machine a permanent IP address, write it down here:

_____._____._____._____

If your provider assigns an IP address dynamically, write down:

1.1.1.1

We'll deal with what to do with these IP addresses when we get to the part about configuring Chameleon Sampler's Custom program.

Installing Chameleon Sampler

If it takes a couple of days for your new Internet provider is cooking up your SLIP/PPP account, you can keep busy by installing Chameleon Sampler. You'll find this software on the disk that comes with this book.

Chameleon Sampler is not <u>just</u> SLIP/PPP software—it includes a passel of useful Internet tools that have nothing to do with Netscape but everything to do with making the most of your Internet experience. Turn to Appendix A for descriptions of these tools and how to use them. Here, we're going to concentrate on one program in the Chameleon Sampler package, Custom, which is the SLIP/PPP software.

You'll recall from discussion earlier in this chapter that when your machine is connected via your SLIP/PPP account, it is actually part of the Internet. Well, if your computer is going to be part of the Internet, it has to learn to play with all of the other Internet computers, and so it must be able to send and receive data in standard TCP/IP packets. This is what the Custom program does and why it is essential for using Netscape. (See Chapters 1 and 2 for background information about *packets*.)

Here's how to install Chameleon Sampler.

1. Place the disk that comes with this book in your A: drive (or in your B: drive if that's where it fits).

2. Select File ➤ Run from the Windows Program Manager menu bar. The Run dialog box will appear.

3. In the Run dialog box's Command Line text box, type **a:\setup** (or **b:\setup** if you put the disk in your B: drive). Click on the OK button. The Chameleon Sampler setup program will start, and a warning dialog box will appear telling you that Chameleon is a TCP/IP application.

In plain English, this means that *if you are using a machine connected to a network, don't install Chameleon Sampler without first talking to your network administrator*. If you're using a networked machine, it's unlikely that you'll need Chameleon Sampler, and besides, installing it can seriously foul

things up on your network.

4. Assuming you're not connected to a network, go ahead and click on the Continue button to acknowledge the warning and proceed. The Chameleon Sampler Setup dialog box will appear.

5. Technically, you could specify a directory into which you want to install Chameleon Sampler, but the best thing to do is to click on the OK button to accept the suggested location, C:\NETMANAG. Do so now.

6. Everything at this point is automatic. The setup program copies the Chameleon Sampler files to a directory it creates on your hard disk called \NETMANAG, and setup displays its progress in the Chameleon Sampler Setup dialog box as it copies. When setup has finished copying files, it creates the Chameleon Sampler program group in your program manager and fills the group with icons. When all is said and done, a dialog box will appear saying so. Click on the OK button to acknowledge the completed installation.

Okay, so you've got Chameleon Sampler on your hard disk, and let's say for the sake of continuing that your Internet service provider has informed you that your SLIP/PPP account is ready to rock. Now you can configure Custom to work with Netscape.

If You Need Help

Technical Support for Chameleon Sampler is available from NetManage at (408)973-7171. For answers to your questions about Netscape, call (800) NET-SITE or e-mail info@mcom.com.

Configuring Chameleon Sampler's Custom Program

Once your provider has "turned on" your SLIP/PPP account, you can set up Custom. (Actually, you can set up Custom before the SLIP/PPP account is ready, but since you can't test it, and testing is necessary, there really isn't any point.) This is going to be the most technically demanding exercise in the book, but as we said before, take it slowly, read carefully, and everything will be just fine. Also, don't be discouraged if it doesn't work out on the first try. It's not unusual for it to take a few attempts to set up Custom correctly to work with a SLIP/PPP account.

The Custom Window

To begin, in the Chameleon Sampler program group, double-click on the Custom icon:

Custom

This starts the Custom program; a blank Custom window will appear. As we proceed we'll be filling in all the juicy details (Figure 8.1). From this point forward, until you get to the *Chat Login Scripts* section, you'll be working within the Custom window.

 Notice the Newt icon that appears at the bottom of the screen. Newt is an integral part of the SLIP/PPP software stack and it starts automatically when you start Custom. Later, when you close Custom, Newt will also close. You never need to do anything directly with Newt.

```
┌─────────────────────────────────────────────────────┐
│ ▢          Custom - C:\NETMANAG\TCPIP.CFG      ▾ ▴   │
├─────────────────────────────────────────────────────┤
│ File   Interface   Setup   Services   Connect   Help │
├─────────────────────────────────────────────────────┤
│ Interface:        DNAI - COM1, 9600 baud             │
│ Dial:             649-6116                            │
│ IP Address:       1.1.1.1                             │
│ Subnet Mask:      255.0.0.0                           │
│ Host Name:        twlvdzn                             │
│ Domain Name:      dnai.com                            │
├──────────────┬──────────┬──────────┬─────────────────┤
│ Name         │ Type     │ IP       │ Domain          │
│ *DNAI        │ PPP      │ 1.1.1.1  │ dnai.com        │
│                                                      │
└──────────────┴──────────┴──────────┴─────────────────┘
```

FIGURE 8.1: The Custom Window after configuration

The Interface

There are two possibilities here:

◆ Custom contains a file that tells it what to do with your Internet service provider, in which configuring the interface is fairly automatic

◆ Custom does not "know" about your particular provider, in which case you must provide this information manually

How do you know which possibility is so? Well, first you try one way and if that doesn't work you try the other way.

To find out if the information needed to configure Custom to work with your service provider is on the Custom disk already, follow these steps:

1. From Custom's menu bar, select File ➤ Open. The Open Configuration dialog box will appear.

2. Scroll down the file list on the left side of the dialog box and look for something like the name of your Internet service provider in the filenames listed there.

◆ If you see it, click once on the filename and then click on the OK button. This will automatically load the interface information you have provided manually in the section to the right.

◆ If you don't find your Internet service provider in the listing, forget it, you'll have to take the more manual approach.

3. Close the dialog box by clicking on the Cancel button.

If you were successful in attempting the more automatic approach just described, skip ahead to the section of this chapter titled *Your Machine's IP Address*.

If things didn't work out as you'd hoped, you must indicate manually whether you have a SLIP account or a PPP account. (Remember when we told you it didn't matter? Well, it only matters here for a second, and only because we must tell Custom which way to go.)

Let's give it a whirl.

1. From Custom's menu bar, select Interface ➤ Add. The Add Interface dialog box will appear (Figure 8.2).

2. In the Add Interface dialog box's Name text box, type a name that you can associate with your Internet provider and that's easy to remember. You're doing this for internal accounting purposes alone, so this can be the actual name of your provider, or if that is too long or complicated, some abbreviation.

3. From the Type pull-down list, select SLIP if you have a SLIP account or PPP if you have a PPP account.

4. Click on the OK button. The Custom window will reappear.

As an aside, Custom also works with <u>CSLIP</u> accounts. CSLIP stands for Compressed Serial Line Internet Protocol, a new, faster relative of SLIP. It is unlikely, however, that you will have a CSLIP account because most providers still offer only SLIP or PPP accounts.

Your Machine's IP Address

We discussed earlier that every computer on the Internet, including yours, must have a numeric address, known as an *IP address*. We also said that some providers will provide you with a permanent IP address and some will assign an IP address to your machine *dynamically* (meaning that a temporary address will be assigned each time you log into your account). For Netscape to run properly on your machine, it's necessary to "tell" Custom your machine's IP address (as assigned by your service provider).

FIGURE 8.2: The Add Interface dialog box

To indicate your machine's IP address, follow these steps:

1. From Custom's menu bar, select Setup ➤ IP Address. The Internet Address dialog box will appear.

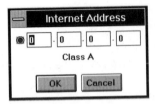

2. In the four boxes provided, enter the IP address assigned to your machine by your Internet service provider. (If your provider assigns this address dynamically, type **1.1.1.1** here; this is a placeholder address and the actual address will be assigned to your computer when you connect to your account.)

3. Click on the OK button to finish this small piece of the Custom configuration. The Custom window will reappear.

Your Provider's Domain Name Server

In a moment that might seem like déjà vu, we're now going to tell Custom the IP address for your service provider's Domain Name server, which in Internet parlance is the IP address of the domain server. The Domain Name server is a machine on the Internet that takes machine names, like www.sybex.com, and turns them into IP addresses, like 199.173.251.39, as we discussed in Chapter 1.

1. From the menu bar, select Services ➤ Domain Servers. The Domain Servers dialog box will appear, bearing a striking resemblance to the Internet Address dialog box we saw in the previous section.

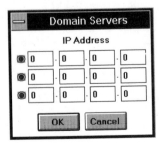

2. In the first row of four boxes, enter the four-number IP address for your provider's Domain Name server.

While most providers will have only one Domain Name server, some especially busy providers (universities and national Internet service providers spring to mind) may have multiple Domain Name servers. If your service provider has multiple Domain Name servers, enter the IP addresses of all of them in the Domain Servers dialog box.

3. Click on the OK button. The Custom window will reappear.

Your Modem

If you've worked at all with any program that uses your modem, this next bit of business should be a snap. We're going to tell Custom where on your system your modem is located and what its speed or baud rate is.

Just do this:

1. From Custom's menu bar, select Setup ➤ Port. The Port Settings dialog box will appear.
2. In the Connector area of this dialog box, click on the COM port to which your modem is attached.
3. In the Baud Rate area, click on the speed of your modem.

You'll notice that there is no setting for 14400 or 28800. That's not a problem. If you have a 14400 bps (baud) or faster modem, just select 19200.

You can probably ignore the other settings on this dialog box: Parity, Data Bits, Stop Bits, and Flow Control. Their default settings (None, 8, 1, Hardware, respectively) should be correct. See Figure 8.3.

4. To finish this part of the configuration, click on the OK button. The Custom window will reappear.

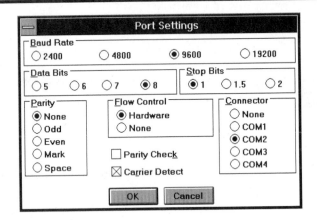

FIGURE 8.3: The Port Settings dialog box, all set up

The Telephone Number

Nothing could be more mundane or simpler than this: you must tell Custom the telephone number to dial to connect to your SLIP/PPP account.

To indicate the phone number for your Internet service provider, follow these steps:

1. From Custom's menu bar, select Setup ➤ Dial. The Dial Settings dialog box will appear (Figure 8.4).

2. In the Dial text box, type the access phone number for your service provider.

Take a quick look at the other options on the Dial Settings dialog box while you're there. The Signal When Connected option should be turned on (marked with an ×). This means that Custom will beep when it connects successfully to your account. The Redial After Timing Out option is off. If you turn it on, Custom will automatically redial the telephone number if for some reason (like a busy signal, maybe?) it did not connect on the first try.

![Dial Settings dialog box]

Dial Settings
Dial:
Timeout If Not Connected In   60   Seconds
☐ Redial After Timing Out   ☒ Signal When Connected
OK   Cancel

FIGURE 8.4: The Dial Settings dialog box

3. Click on the OK button to confirm your settings and the Custom window will reappear.

The Domain Name

The five pieces we have already put into place are critical; if they're not done correctly, your SLIP/PPP account won't work. This next piece of work, the Domain Name option, isn't so essential. Let's step back a minute for some background information. When you get connected, as we've mentioned before, your machine in cahoots with your Internet service provider "fools" the Internet into thinking your machine's a network. (This is so you can become part of the global network of networks that is the Internet, remember?) What's really happening is that you are "piggy-backing" on your service provider's network.

So... this next thing you must do is to identify exactly where on the Internet your machine is, meaning that you indicate the domain name of your Internet service provider. Here, Custom is not asking you for a numeric IP address like the one we saw above, but rather a domain name—to make things simple, remember that this is the portion of your e-mail address to the right of the "@" sign. For example, domain names for some popular SLIP/PPP providers would be `crl.com` or `clark.net`. In the e-mail address `whizkid@netcom.com`, *netcom.com* is the domain name. (See Chapters 1 and 2 for more about e-mail addressing and the domain name system.)

To enter your domain name:

1. From Custom's menu bar, select Setup ➤ Domain Name. The Domain Name dialog box will appear.

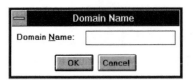

2. In the Domain Name text box, type the domain name used by your Internet service provider.

3. Click on the OK button and the Custom window will reappear.

The Host Name

Reading from right to left after the "@" sign in an e-mail address, the address lists domains from the more general to the more specific. The leftmost name in an address is often the name of a particular machine at one location (domain) that has many machines. This, the *host name* differentiates your machine from that (or those) of your service provider. Thus, `violet.berkeley.edu` is the name of one machine (*violet*) at the University of California, *Berkeley*, an *edu*cational organization. *Violet*, in that case, is the host name, identifying a single machine. If you use the host name *tex* for your machine and you have one of the service providers named in the previous section, the full name for your machine when you are connected to your SLIP/PPP account would be `tex.crl.com` or `tex.clark.net`. You can, if you wish, leave the host name blank; or you can give your machine a host name.

To specify a host name:

1. From Custom's menu bar, select Setup ➤ Host Name. The Host Name dialog box will appear.

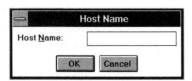

2. In the Host Name text box (the *only* text box), type a one-word name for your computer.

3. Click on the OK button to return to the Custom window.

Finding Out about Your Login Routine

To finish up our Custom configuration, we'll have to do a little research: we need to find out exactly how to log on to your SLIP/PPP account, and when we say exactly, we mean *exactly*.

 If your service provider's configuration is built into Custom (see <u>The Interface</u> earlier in this chapter), you don't have to do anything here; you're done, in fact. Skip ahead to the section titled <u>Testing the Configuration by Logging On to the Internet</u>.

When you signed up for your account, you chose a user name and a password. You know of course that you have to provide those things when you log on, but for our purposes in the next part of configuration, we need to know how your provider *asks* for them. For example, is the prompt for your user name *username:* or *login:*? Also, are there any commands that you have to give in addition to your user name and password? Some service providers require a ↵ before your user name and password. Does yours? We're going to do some research on this topic, and then we'll use the results in the two sections that follow, to tell Custom how to log into your account.

There are two ways to find out what your service provider's login routine is.

If You Have Documentation Read the documentation your Internet provider gave you. If the documentation tells you the sequence used to establish a SLIP/PPP connection, you don't have to research the matter any further. You can skip ahead to the next section, *Login Settings*.

If You Don't Have Documentation Using a general-purpose telecommunications program like Windows Terminal, dial into your SLIP/PPP account and log in manually, writing down the prompts that appear as you

do so. (You can find out how to use Windows Terminal from your Windows documentation.) Pay particular attention to capitalization and punctuation because they'll spell your success or failure. Also pay attention to when you press ↵ and how many times you do so, because this too will make a difference.

When you've logged in successfully, you'll see garbage on your screen. This is because your provider is sending TCP/IP data directly to your communications program, where there is no SLIP/PPP software operating to interpret it. When you see the garbage, hang up the phone and quit your communications program.

With your Internet service provider's exact login routine in hand, you're ready to move on.

The Login Settings

Here we'll provide Custom with the username and password you selected when you established your SLIP/PPP account, as well as any other command your provider requires for you to log in.

Follow these steps:

1. From Custom's menu bar, select Setup ➤ Login. The Login Settings dialog box will appear.

2. In the User Name text box, type the username assigned by your Internet service provider.

3. In the User Password text box, type the password assigned by your Internet service provider (Figure 8.5).

4. In the Startup Command text box, type any startup command your provider requires when you log in (it might be slip or ppp, for example). If, in your research in the previous section, you found that your Internet service provider required no special startup commands, or if it required you only to press ↵ to begin logging in, then you should leave the Startup Command text box blank.

5. Click on the OK button. The Custom window will reappear.

Login Settings

User **N**ame: twlvdzn

User **P**assword: ******

Startup **C**ommand:

OK   Cancel

FIGURE 8.5:   The Login Settings dialog box

Chat Login Scripts

OK, we're almost there; there's only one more thing to do. This last piece of configuration is not done from the Custom window, but rather from within the SLIP.INI file. We'll get to that in a second. Take a look at the Custom window while we still have it open. You'll notice that all of the information you have entered in the configuration process to this point is reflected in the Custom window. Figure 8.1 at the beginning of this chapter shows a configured Custom window that belongs to a friend of ours.

> **TIP** You don't want to have to do all this work over again, eh? Don't forget to save your configuration! To do so, select File ➤ Save from Custom's menu bar.

Now you can close the Custom window so we can do this last part of the configuration. Select File ➤ Exit and the Program Manager will appear before you.

The last thing we need to do to configure Custom is write a *login script* (a short series of commands Custom uses to log in to your SLIP/PPP account). Custom requires this procedure, by the way.

Writing a script sounds far more intimidating than it actually is. In fact, Custom has already done most of the work for you. You'll just have to make a few modifications to one line of text in the script file called SLIP.INI.

Because the SLIP.INI file is a text file, you'll use a text editor like Windows Notepad to edit it. Don't try this procedure with a word processor; Custom will not be able to read the results if you do and afterward you won't be able to log in to your SLIP/PPP account.

To make the necessary changes in the SLIP.INI file, take the following steps:

1. First, make a backup copy of your SLIP.INI file, just in case something goes wrong. Then, from the Windows Program Manager, select File ➤ Run. The Run dialog box will appear.

2. Type **notepad c:\netmanag\slip.ini** into the Run text box and click on the OK button. The Notepad window will appear, displaying the contents of the SLIP.INI file.

What you see when SLIP.INI is open in Notepad may not be terribly meaningful to you at first. You're looking at a series of three-line scripts that Custom can use to log in to many different Internet providers.

3. Scroll down to the end of the file. The last three lines in the file make up your script. They will look something like this:

```
[INTERFACENAME]
SCRIPT=login: $u$r word: $p$r -I
TYPE=SLIP
```

The first line contains the name you typed into the Add Interface dialog box in the first step of our configuration, way back in this chapter. It functions in the script as a place marker so that Custom knows where to begin.

Skipping the second line for now, the third line identifies the type of connection you specified, either SLIP or PPP. This line functions in the script to tell Custom to what kind of account you want it to connect.

The second line, the long and vaguely incomprehensible string of characters, is the only thing you have to change.

The first part of the line says

```
SCRIPT=
```

This is a marker to indicate where Custom begins looking for instructions. Do not change this part of the line.

4. Referring to the information you got from your documentation or the notes you took if you logged in manually to research your service provider's login routine, find the first thing that happened. (It was probably some kind of prompt.) Type this into the script right next to the = (with no space in between).

If, for example, the very first thing that appeared on screen was a prompt like login:, then your script should read:

```
SCRIPT=login:
```

If the prompt said user name: then your script should read:

```
SCRIPT=name:
```

You don't have to repeat the entire prompt; the last five or six letters are more than sufficient.

As a final example, if you had to press ↵ when you first logged on, your script should read:

```
SCRIPT=$r
```

$r is a command that tells Custom to send a carriage return (↵). See Table 8.1 for more about this sort of script language command.

5. Enter the second item to appear at login (it's likely that this will be your user name) after the item you entered in step 4, and on the same line.

For example, if it *was* your user name, do this:

```
SCRIPT=login: $u$r
```

These are commands that tell Custom to send your user name ($u) and then a ↵ ($r). (Remember, Custom knows your username because you entered it into the Login Settings dialog box during configuration.)

TABLE 8.1: These commands have special meaning when they're included in your chat script.

ADD THIS COMMAND	TO DO THIS
$c	Send the Startup Command you entered in the Login Settings dialog box
$n	Send a blank line
$p	Send your account password
$r	Send a carriage return (↵)
$s	Send a space
$t	Send a Tab
$u	Send your user name
$n	Cause Custom to pause for the specified number of seconds, where *n* is a number from 1–9.
-i	Accept a dynamically-assigned IP address from your provider

Now you can probably see the pattern: each thing that happens when you log on to your account is described in script language, with a space between each "event." So, let's look again at the default script you see in SLIP.INI:

```
SCRIPT=login: $u$r word: $p$r -I
```

This line describes the following logon sequence:

First, the provider prompts for your user name with the prompt login:.

Second, Custom sends your user name ($u), followed by a ↵ ($r).

Third, the provider prompts for your password with the prompt password:. (Remember, the script only needs to reflect the last few characters of the prompt.)

Fourth, Custom sends your password ($p), followed by a ↵ ($r).

Fifth and last, Custom accepts an IP Address for your machine that your provider assigns dynamically (-i).

 If your provider assigns an IP address to your machine dynamically, the last element in your script must be -i.

6. Go ahead and finish your script. If you need technical support, either contact your Internet service provider or call NetManage at: (408)973-7171.

7. When you've finished, save the newly modified SLIP.INI and quit Notepad in one fell swoop by selecting File ➤ Exit from Notepad's menu bar. A dialog box will appear telling you that the current file (SLIP.INI) has been changed and asking if you want to save the changes. Click on the Yes button to save the changes. The Windows Program Manager window will reappear.

Testing the Configuration by Logging On to the Internet

Well, we made it. That wasn't so bad, was it? Let's test our work by calling your Internet Service provider and seeing if Custom can log in to your account.

1. Start Custom by double-clicking on the Custom icon in the Program Manager's Chameleon Sampler group. The Custom window will appear.

2. From Custom's menu bar, select Connect. A dialog box will appear providing information about NetManage, Custom's manufacturer.

3. Click on the OK button and Custom will dial in to your account.

You'll hear your modem dial the phone and a dialog box will appear showing the phone number Custom is dialing. (The phone number you see is the one you entered during configuration.) If you configured Custom correctly and wrote a correct script—we trust and believe this is so, eh?—Custom will beep once, the dialog box with the phone number will disappear and then... *nothing will happen*. Custom has made the connection to your SLIP/PPP account and your computer is now a part of the Internet, awaiting further instructions.

If something goes wrong, go back through the configuration process, double-checking all your work. Your chat script is a likely place to look for errors, by the way.

 You can use Custom's Log features to track down any errors in your script file. Select Setup ➤ Log to display Custom's Log window. You can now connect to the Internet service provider as before, but everything the modem sends or receives will be displayed in the Log window. This helps you identify problems in the chat script for your Internet service provider.

Getting Netscape from the Internet

Now we can go on to our bigger purpose, getting a copy of Netscape so we can install and use it. As we mentioned earlier, you can get Netscape from the Internet itself, or more specifically, from Netscape's manufacturer's FTP site. An FTP site is basically a public archive of files accessible to anyone on the Internet who has an FTP program (like you, now that you've got Chameleon Sampler set up).

 For a complete discussion of FTP and other Internet tools included in Chameleon Sampler, see Appendix A.

Here's what you do to get Netscape:

1. Log in to your SLIP/PPP account and become a part of the Internet. If you're working along with the book, you're probably logged on right now. If not, start Custom by double-clicking on the Custom icon in the Program Manager Chameleon Sampler group. When the Custom window appears, select Connect from the menu bar—you'll be connected to the Internet in a few seconds.

2. Start Chameleon's FTP program by double-clicking on the FTP icon in the Program Manager's Chameleon Sampler group. The FTP window will appear.

If you look in the Local section (on the left side of the FTP window), you'll see a listing of all the directories and files contained on your hard disk. On the right side of the window, you'll see a blank area labeled *Remote*. When you connect to an FTP site, the directories and files on that computer will be listed in the Remote section. (In Figure 8.7, later in this chapter, you can see the window after a connection has been made.)

3. The file you are going to copy will go into the directory on your machine that's listed just below *Local Directory*; make sure the correct directory (C:\NETMANAG) appears there. If it doesn't, type **c:\ netmanag** into the text box just below the directory name, and then click on the < Change button.

4. From the FTP window's menu bar select connect. The Connect dialog box will appear.

5. In the Host text box, type **ftp.netscape.com**. This tells the FTP program the address where you'll get Netscape—it's the address of Netscape Communications' FTP site.

 Netscape's FTP server supports only so many simultaneous FTP connections. You may have to try several times or at odd hours before you connect successfully.

6. In the User text box, type **anonymous**.

7. In the Password text box, type your complete e-mail address.

Steps 6 and 7 describe the standard conventions for using *anonymous FTP* (see Appendix A). Figure 8.6 shows the Connect dialog box moments before connecting to the remote site.

8. Click on the OK button to connect to Netscape's FTP site. When you connect, a list of files contained on Netscape's FTP server will appear in the Remote section of the FTP window.

9. Navigate the directories at the FTP site by scrolling around until you find a directory called /NETSCAPE. Click on this directory's name to highlight it, then click on the Change > button to make the directory current. The contents of the /NETSCAPE directory will appear in the Remote section's Directory listing.

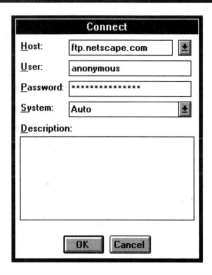

FIGURE 8.6: The FTP Connect dialog box all filled in

10. In the Directory listing, find and click on the subdirectory called WINDOWS. Then click on the Change > button. Now the files contained in /NETSCAPE/WINDOWS will appear in the Remote section's Directory listing, as shown in Figure 8.7. Netscape 1.1 for Windows 3.1 is in the file N16E11.EXE.

 Files appear in the same list for Netscape 1.1 for Windows 95 and Windows NT. While we don't talk specifically about these versions in this book, they are functionally identical to the Windows 3.1 version we do talk about. Watch for future revisions of this book that will cover Netscape 1.1 for Windows 95 and Windows NT.

11. Click on the Binary option in the Transfer section of the FTP window. This tells FTP that you are transferring a file that is not an ASCII text file.

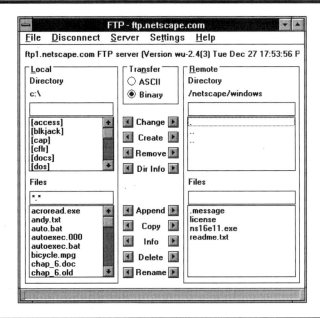

FIGURE 8.7: Connection is successful; Netscape for Windows and its related files appear in the Remote section's Files list

12. Highlight the Netscape file, N16E11.EXE, by clicking on it. Then click on the < Copy button to copy the Netscape file directly to your machine. This file is about 1MB in size; it may take 15 minutes or so to arrive. A dialog box will appear to keep you advised of its progress in transferring to your machine. When the transfer is complete, this dialog box will disappear and the FTP window will reappear.

13. When the transfer is finished and the files are on your machine, select Disconnect from FTP's menu bar to disconnect from Netscape Communications' FTP server. The Disconnect dialog box will appear.

14. In the Disconnect dialog box, click the Exit button to quit the FTP program and return to the Windows Program Manager.

Now Netscape is on your machine, so let's disconnect from the Internet and quit Custom.

15. From Custom's menu bar, select Disconnect. A dialog box will appear asking you to confirm that you want to disconnect from the Internet. Click on Yes to disconnect.

16. When you hear your modem "hang up" the phone line, quit Custom by selecting File ➤ Exit from Custom's menu bar. The Windows Program Manager will reappear.

You made it! You've got a copy of Netscape, just waiting to be installed and configured on your machine. So, when you're ready, turn the page and let's install it already.

Getting Netscape Going

In Chapter 8 we walked you through actually getting Netscape by downloading it from the Internet. In this chapter, we're going to make the software work. First, we'll install it (a simple, largely automatic process), then we'll make it run, and finally we'll show you how to make some minor changes to enhance operations.

Installing Netscape

To make things easier, we're going to break the installation procedure into two parts, neither of which is at all complicated. In the first part, we'll show you how to move the Netscape file you downloaded in Chapter 8 (N16E11.EXE) to a temporary directory in preparation for installation. (You may already know how to do this—it's a basic Windows operation.) In the second part, we'll show you just how easy it is to install Netscape.

Unpacking the Files

The file you downloaded in the last chapter, N16E11.EXE, is what is known as a *self-extracting archive* file. An archive file is one that contains one or more (often *many* more) files that are shrunk down to some fraction of their original size. This is much like the *zipping* of files we talked about when we described zipped files and compression technology in Chapter 4; we'll talk more about it in Chapter 10. Archive files and zipped files are a great convenience on the Internet; instead of downloading many large files, you can download one smaller one, which will save you scads of connect time, and therefore money.

The compressed file that contains Netscape, N16E11.EXE, contains eight files, including:

◆ The Netscape program itself

◆ Associated files that are necessary to make it run

◆ Files that contain information about the license you need to use the program

The big difference between this file and the zipped files we've already discussed is that this one is *self extracting*, which simply means that you don't need any particular unzipping software to restore the file to its original, unpacked state; the file does everything for you.

When you downloaded N16E11.EXE following the steps in Chapter 8, it wound up in your \NETMANAG directory. It's a good idea when you unpack any file, however, to do so in a "temporary" directory; this will provide you with an extra measure of insurance against mixing up the new files with files from another program or with any data you may have laying around. This is a pretty basic procedure—if you have some proficiency in Windows, you'll already know how to do most of this.

Here's how to create a directory called \TEMP and move N16E11.EXE there.

1. Open the Windows File Manager by double-clicking on its icon in the Program Manager's Main group. From the File Manager's menu bar, select File ➤ Create Directory. The Create Directory dialog box will appear.

2. In the Create Directory dialog box's Name text box, type **c:\temp**. Then click on the OK button. The new, temporary directory will appear in the directory tree displayed along the left side of File Manager's window.

3. Click on the directory (in the File Manager's directory tree) that contains N16E11.EXE to open it and then click on the N16E11.EXE to select it.

4. Drag the file over to the C:\TEMP directory and drop it there.

Okay, you've got N16E11.EXE in a directory called \TEMP. Let's unpack this baby.

1. Click on the \TEMP directory in the File Manager's directory tree. You'll see the file N16E11.EXE in the file list along the right side of the File Manager window.

2. To unpack the self-extracting archive, just double-click on N16E11.EXE

Windows will seemingly vanish for a moment, because the self-extracting archive is, strictly speaking, a DOS program and not a Windows program, so it must unpack itself in a DOS window. Not to worry. Everything will happen automatically.

 N16E11.EXE may pause while spilling its contents onto your hard disk, and say something ominous like "overwrite README.TXT y/n?" Don't panic! This means that one of the files you downloaded with N16E11.EXE is also contained in the archive. Just type N for No and unpacking will continue.

When the archive has finished unpacking itself (this should only take a few seconds), all the files that were in the archive will be in your \TEMP directory, along with the other files you downloaded when you followed the steps in Chapter 8. (See Figure 9.1.)

3. Close the File Manager by selecting File ➤ Exit from its menu bar.

You're ready to install Netscape.

Installing the Program

Installing Netscape is pretty much an automatic process that will take only a few minutes. When all is said and done you'll be cruising the Web with ease.

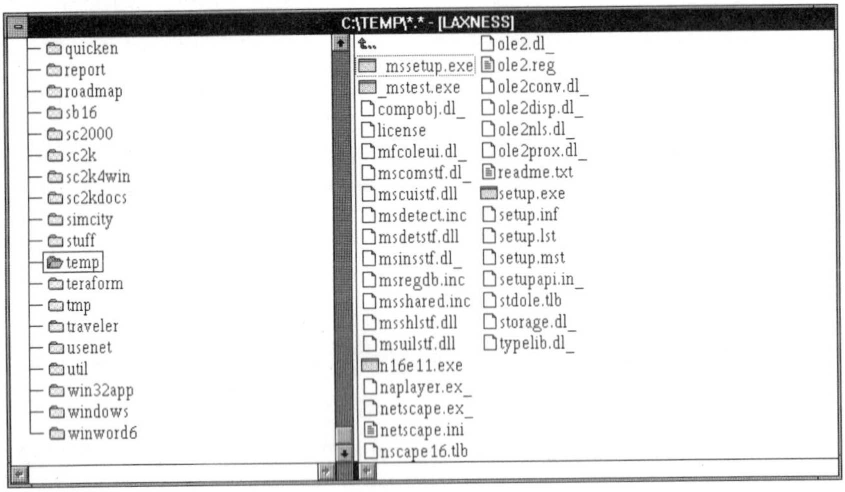

FIGURE 9.1: The Netscape program file, and the other contents of N16E11.EXE, in their temporary digs.

Here's what you do.

1. From the Windows Program Manager's menu bar, select File ➤ Run. The Run dialog box will appear.

2. In the Run dialog box's Command text box, type **c:\temp\setup**. Then click on the OK button. After waiting through a brief "Please Wait" message, you'll see the blue background common to all Windows setup programs; then a dialog box will appear welcoming you to Netscape's own Setup program.

3. Click on the Continue button to proceed. The Installation Location dialog box will appear, as shown in Figure 9.2. Netscape's Setup program will put Netscape in a directory called \NETSCAPE unless you tell it to do otherwise. It's best to let this happen, but if you really, really want to, you can type another directory name in the Location text box and Netscape will wind up there.

4. Click on the Continue button to proceed. The Program Group dialog box will appear next, as shown in Figure 9.3. Here you get to choose the program group into which you'd like to place Netscape's icon. By

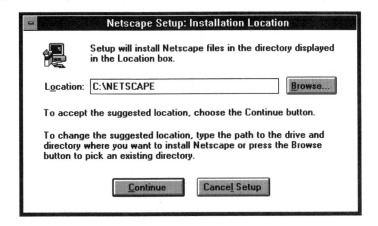

FIGURE 9.2: The Netscape Setup: Installation Location dialog box

default, Setup will create a group called Netscape (makes sense, doesn't it?), and again it's best to just let this happen. If you have some compelling reason to do so, you can create a new group with a different name and make it Netscape's home at the same time simply by typing the new name in the Program Group text box. If instead of either of these options you want Netscape to reside in a program group that already exists on your system, click once on that group's name in the Existing Groups list. Whatever your choice, when you've made your decision, click on the Continue button to go on.

From this point, Setup will proceed on its own, copying Netscape and all of its affiliated files to the directory you chose in step 3. When all this copying business is over, installation is complete. One final dialog box will appear confirming that Netscape was installed correctly and giving you the option of reading Netscape's README.TXT file. Click on the dialog box's Yes button to read the file. Clicking on the No button ends the installation program and returns you to the Windows File Manager. The README.TXT file contains important information about using Netscape, so we recommend that you read it. (The file will open in the Windows Notepad. When you're done reading it, select File ➤ Exit from Notepad's menu bar to close Notepad.)

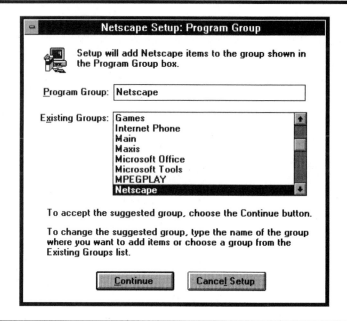

FIGURE 9.3: The Netscape Setup: Program Group dialog box

The Netscape program archive N16E11.EXE and all of its com-
ponent files are still in your \TEMP directory (or wherever you
put them). It's always a good idea to have backups—copy
N16E11.EXE to a floppy disk and store the disk somewhere
safe, just in case. Having done this, you can delete all of the
files in \TEMP and the directory itself.

Making a Netscape Connection

Now that your SLIP/PPP account, Chameleon Sampler's Custom program,
and Netscape are all online, configured, and installed, you're ready to surf!
Let's get connected and start Netscape.

 Netscape needs the file WINSOCK.DLL, which comes with Chameleon sampler, in order to access the Internet. If the file isn't there, an error message will appear saying so. We cover the installation of Chameleon Sampler, including this important file, in Chapter 8.

Starting Netscape

Remember, as we've mentioned before, starting Netscape involves first getting connected to your Internet service provider via Chameleon Sampler's Custom program, *then* starting Netscape itself. Here are the simple steps for doing this:

1. In the Chameleon Sampler program group in your Windows Program Manager, double-click on the Custom icon. The Custom window you saw in Chapter 8 will appear.

2. From Custom's menu bar, select Connect. In the NetManage information dialog box that appears, click on the OK button. Custom will dial up your Internet service provider and connect you to the Internet.

3. In the Netscape program group (or wherever you put it during installation), double-click on the Netscape icon. The first time you run the program, a dialog box will appear detailing Netscape's licensing agreement. You must abide by this agreement if you're going to use the software. Read it carefully, and then click on the I Accept button if you do in fact accept the agreement's terms.

Netscape will start and the Welcome to Netscape home page will appear. You're on the Web and free to explore. Turn to Chapter 3 for detailed descriptions of using Netscape's features and capabilities.

What's Out There?

With your Internet connection and Netscape up and running, you can find out more about Netscape by selecting Help ➤ Handbook, Help ➤ Release Notes, and Help ➤ Frequently Asked Questions from Netscape's menu bar. Each of these choices leads to a different page on the Netscape Web server; both of these pages are terrifically worthwhile.

Quitting Netscape

This is a handy piece of information that we don't want to neglect. When you're done with your travels for the day, simply do the following:

1. From Netscape's menu bar, select File ➤ Exit. This will quit Netscape, but leave you still connected to your Internet service provider, so...

2. From Custom's menu bar, select Disconnect. A dialog box will appear asking you to confirm that you want to disconnect from the Internet. Click on the Yes button to confirm.

You'll be disconnected from your Internet service provider, and free now to play with the kids, go to the gym, practice guitar, or whatever.

● Enhancing the Program's Look and Performance

Okay, we told you in the preceding sections that all you had to do was unpack the files and start up Netscape, and that's true. This is not to say you can't or don't have to configure Netscape, it's just that configuration means something a little different for Netscape than it does for Custom. You must configure Custom properly to get it to work at all. You can configure Netscape (if you like) to make it work the way you want it to work.

Configuring Netscape is quick and easy. We've already done a little configuring earlier in the book, but we didn't make a big deal of it. In Chapter 3, we told you how to change the base font to make Netscape display text in a size and color that you like, and then we told you how to get Netscape to load inline images only on demand, speeding up Netscape's performance noticeably. In Chapter 10, we'll tell you how to configure Netscape to use external viewers for viewing video and playing sound. Here we're going to make some changes to enhance the cosmetics and performance of the program.

Making the Viewing Area Bigger

Controlling the way the program looks is not just a matter of cosmetics; it can be a matter of making the viewing area larger and easier to work with. Above the document viewing window and below the menu bar you'll usually see a row of icons representing tools and features, a box showing the URL of the page you are currently viewing, and a row of directory buttons that take you to various of Netscape Communications' home pages.

These are handy things to have around. If you want to see the Welcome to Netscape home page, you can just click the Welcome button on the row of directory buttons. If you want to view the document you were looking at just a second ago, you can click on the Back button on the tool bar, and so on.

If, however, you'd rather give the Web document you're viewing more room to breathe, you can turn off the tool bar, the Location box, and the directory buttons, in any combination, including all three (Figure 9.4). Get this: you don't lose anything by turning them off; all of their functions are still available on Netscape's menu bar.

The toolbar, Location box, and directory buttons are all controlled by a "toggle switch" on Netscape's Options menu. That is, the same option on the menu turns each item both on and off; you can simply select the option once to turn an item off, then select it again to turn it back on. Fiddle around with these options as you like to see what works for you.

 When you've got Netscape's "face" configured to reflect your preferences, you can save the changes you've made by selecting Options ➤ Save Options from Netscape's menu bar. If you don't save the choices you've made, Netscape will go back to its usual configuration (with everything on the next time you start the program).

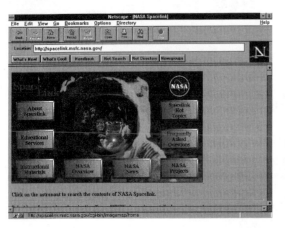 

FIGURE 9.4: The Netscape window on the left has the Toolbar, Location box, and Directory buttons turned on. The window on the right has all three turned off, making the viewing area a lot bigger.

Getting Set Up for Mail and News

Looking past the surface, you might want to tweak a few things in the way Netscape works with mail and news servers. One of the nifty things you can do with Netscape, for example, is e-mail a page that's caught your eye to some friend or colleague. To do this, and to read and write articles to USENET newsgroups, the program has to "know" where to find your Internet service provider's mail and news servers—the computers your provider uses to store and dish up mail and news.

 To find out more about sending a page via e-mail and reading and writing Usenet news, turn to Chapters 2 and 3.

What's Out There?

You can learn all the ins and outs of using e-mail from *A Beginner's Guide to Effective E-Mail*, accessible via the URL http://www.webfoot.com/advice/email.top.html.

The Mail Server

Specifying the location of your Internet service provider's mail server is an important detail of setting up Netscape, because this is how the program "knows" where to send mail. This is yet another quick and simple Netscape operation.

Just follow these steps.

1. From Netscape's menu bar, select Options ➤ Preferences. The Preferences window will appear.

2. Select Mail and News from the pull-down list at the top of the Preferences window. The contents of the window will change to reflect this choice. In the Mail (SMTP) Server text box the presumed name of your provider's mail server appears as *mail*. Chances are good that this is correct. If you later find, however, that you are unable to send a Web page by e-mail, then the most likely problem is that your Internet service provider's mail server has a different name than *mail*. Get the correct name from your provider's tech folks and type it in here.

3. In the Your Name text box, type your name—not your user name, but your real, true, human name.

4. In the Your E-mail text box, type your complete e-mail address. Figure 9.5 shows a completed Preferences Mail and News dialog box as an example.

5. If you like, you can type the name of your organization (your company or school, perhaps) into the Your Organization text box.

6. You can also arrange matters so that the contents of a short file will be appended to every e-mail message you send. This file is called a *signature* because it appears (like the signature on a letter) at the bottom of every message you send; a signature file may contain your name and e-mail address, and maybe a little bit of information about yourself. It is considered very bad form on the Internet to create signature files more than 4 lines in length. To make it so that a "signature" will appear at the bottom of your messages, create a file in your word processing program, name it with an appropriate filename, then type that filename along with its path in the Signature File text box.

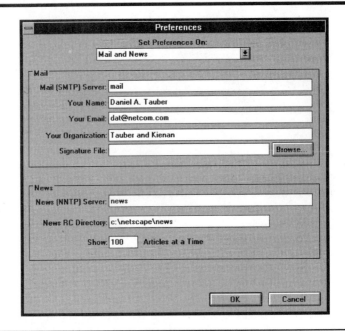

FIGURE 9.5: The Preferences Mail and News dialog box after it's been filled with e-mail information

The Your Name and Your E-mail text boxes must be filled in for you to be able to send a page by e-mail. This is because your name and e-mail address will appear in the subject header of the message you send.

Once you've got this mail business set up correctly, you won't have to change it again (unless you change Internet service providers and go to one with a mail server not called "mail"). The same is true for news, which we'll cover next. You'll be using the same Mail and News Preferences window that we just used to set up mail when you set up news in the next section, so leave the window open.

The News Server

Usenet news looks like its fully integrated into the Web when you use Netscape to access it, but it's actually delivered to your machine in an interesting way. Unlike the rest of the stuff on the Web, which is delivered to your machine from servers located all over the world, Usenet comes to you from a news server machine that is maintained by your Internet service provider. This machine has on it copies of Usenet news articles, which the service provider stores and forwards to you. Because of this structure, it is necessary to configure things to indicate on which machine your service provider is storing the stuff.

Here are the simple steps to follow to tell Netscape about which Usenet news server it can access and exactly where to find that server.

1. With the Preferences Mail and News dialog box still open (you were just using it to set up mail, right?), locate the News section at the bottom of the dialog box. In the News section's News (NNTP) Server text box the presumed news server name appears as *news*. As with mail, this is often a correct assumption and you can leave it alone. If you find, however, that you are unable to access Usenet newsgroups later (when you try), then your provider's news server probably has a different name. Get the correct name from your Internet service provider's tech-support people and type it in here.

 Just FYI: NNTP stands for Network News Transfer Protocol. This is the Internet protocol for transferring news on the Internet, just as HTTP is the protocol for transferring hypertext documents.

2. Click on the OK button and the Preferences window will close. The Netscape window will reappear.

You're Set to Go

Bingo. You're all set up. You've installed Chameleon Sampler and Netscape, you know how to start Netscape and even make it look the way you want it to, and you can access mail and news servers. In the next and final chapter, we'll get Netscape to work with video and sound viewers.

Getting and Installing Video Viewers and Sound Players

In your Web travels you've probably come across pages that include links to video and sound clips. You can click on these links to view little movies (Figure 10.1) or play sounds. We've been warning you throughout this book that the files for video and sound are really big, and that to experience the video or sound, you need external *viewers*. Viewers are special programs that enable Netscape to handle the video or sound files—really, they're just Windows programs that Netscape calls upon to "display" files it cannot display itself.

In this chapter we're going to cover downloading (getting), installing, and using the most useful viewers. With these viewers and Netscape in your tool kit, you'll be ready to handle video and sound when you encounter it on the Web.

Netscape version 1.1 includes a sound player. With version 1.1, as long as you have sound hardware (like a Sound Blaster card) and all the proper windows sound drivers installed, you can just click on a link to a sound file, and it will play. You don't have to install the sound player described in this chapter.

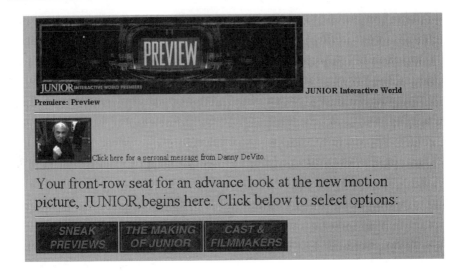

FIGURE 10.1: Stars are interviewed and trailers are shown in an online premiere of a Hollywood movie.

Just a reminder: video and sound are very exciting additions to the Web, but the files for video and sound take eons to travel over a phone line to your machine. Even with the correct viewers, be prepared to wait around a while, and make sure you have enough memory and disk storage on your machine to cope with the big files.

What's Out There?

This has nothing to do with viewers, really, but you can find a giant archive of Windows programs and other files at the Center for Innovative Computer Applications' FTP server at `ftp://ftp.cica.indiana.edu/pub/pc/win3`. There's some really useful stuff there, so check it out.

What's Available

A number of viewers are available to use with Netscape; to pump Netscape up to its best capacity, you might want a video viewer that can handle movies in QuickTime format (with the extension .MOV) and the MPEG format (.MPG, .MPEG, or .MPE), and a sound "viewer" (or *player*) that lets you play files in Sun Audio format (with the extension .AU) as well as Windows sound files (.WAV) and Macintosh sound files (.SND).

What's Out There?

NCSA maintains a listing of viewers that is somewhat biased toward NCSA Mosaic, but you can use all of the listed viewers with your copy of Netscape. The URL for NCSA's page listing viewers is

`http://www.ncsa.uiuc.edu/SDG/Software/WinMosaic/viewers.html`.

Video and Netscape

The two most popular formats for video on the Web are QuickTime, developed by Apple Computer, and MPEG, developed by the Motion Picture Expert Group. It is important to note that while QuickTime was developed by Apple, any video that has the QuickTime extension .MOV can be played by any machine that has the correct viewer (the one that works for that machine). In other words, you can play a QuickTime video clip on your PC, even if it was developed on a Mac, as long as you have a QuickTime viewer on your PC.

Functionally, MPEG is very similar to QuickTime—however, MPEG was developed by the Motion Picture Expert Group (hence, the acronym MPEG), a fine group of people who made MPEG available free of charge.

Compression Makes Video on the Internet a Reality

The big breakthrough that made it possible for users to create, transfer, and view video clips was *compression*. Simply put, there was technology available a while ago that let people create electronic videos. But there was a problem also—the files for video were so *outrageously* huge that even souped-up machines couldn't store them, no floppy disk could contain them, and transferring them over a modem would take (no joke) *days*. It's an interesting aside in our discussion of video on the Net that QuickTime and MPEG are not software products that let you shoot little movies, they are actually *compression* technologies that take the enormous files containing little movies, and shrink them adequately so they can be stored and transferred with a minimum of hassle.

This is not like *zipping* files—that's a process that crunches data into a smaller storage space—this type of compression involves sacrificing or losing some of the less important data. Not much, mind you—if you imagine an animated sequence that is very smooth, because it has many, many frames of action, and another that's just a bit choppy because some of the frames were left out, you can understand the acceptable "lossiness" of compressed video.

Now here's the difference between QuickTime and MPEG: QuickTime was developed for commercial distribution as a software product and MPEG was developed as a technology anyone can use. You'll see lots of Quick-Time video files on the Web and some MPEG files. It's best to have a viewer for each product in your Netscape tool kit.

Getting and Setting Up the QuickTime Viewer

To view QuickTime video, files with the extension .MOV, you need a QuickTime viewer that works with Netscape. Let's take a look at how to get such a viewer, how to install it, and how to set it up to work neatly with Netscape.

Downloading the QuickTime Viewer

Before you can view QuickTime video with Netscape, you must *download* (transfer to your system) the correct software. Here's how:

1. With Netscape running (you should still be connected to the Internet), select File ➤ Open Location from the menu bar. The Open Location dialog box will appear.

2. In the Open Location dialog box's text box, type **ftp://ftp.ncsa.uiuc.edu/Mosaic/Windows/viewers**. In a few seconds, the contents of a directory of viewers will appear, in the form of a Web page with a link for each viewer (Figure 10.2).

 The site `ftp.ncsa.uiuc.edu` is terrifically popular—so much so that it sometimes rejects new connections. If you try to load the viewers list and your connection is rejected, try, try again. (Try off hours, especially.)

3. Click on the qtw11.zip link. The Unknown File Type dialog box will appear. Click on the Save to Disk button, and the Save As dialog box will appear.

4. In the Save As dialog box's File Name text box, type **c:\qtw11.zip**.

5. Now click on the OK button to start downloading the QuickTime viewer software to your computer.

You can follow the progress of your transfer by watching the status bar along the bottom of the window. When the file transfer is complete, you're all set to install the QuickTime viewer.

6. Close Netscape by selecting File ➤ Exit from the menu bar. The Custom window and the Program Manager window will both appear (yes, at the same time). Now disconnect from the Internet by selecting Disconnect from Custom's menu bar and clicking on the Yes button to confirm.

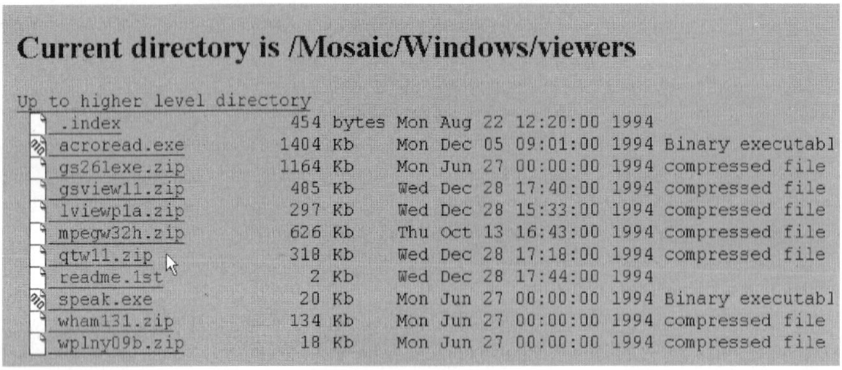

Current directory is /Mosaic/Windows/viewers

```
Up to higher level directory
     .index           454 bytes Mon Aug 22 12:20:00 1994
     acroread.exe    1404 Kb    Mon Dec 05 09:01:00 1994 Binary executabl
     gs261exe.zip    1164 Kb    Mon Jun 27 00:00:00 1994 compressed file
     gsview11.zip     485 Kb    Wed Dec 28 17:40:00 1994 compressed file
     lviewp1a.zip     297 Kb    Wed Dec 28 15:33:00 1994 compressed file
     mpegw32h.zip     626 Kb    Thu Oct 13 16:43:00 1994 compressed file
     qtw11.zip        318 Kb    Wed Dec 28 17:18:00 1994 compressed file
     readme.1st         2 Kb    Wed Dec 28 17:44:00 1994
     speak.exe         20 Kb    Mon Jun 27 00:00:00 1994 Binary executabl
     wham131.zip      134 Kb    Mon Jun 27 00:00:00 1994 compressed file
     wplny09b.zip      18 Kb    Mon Jun 27 00:00:00 1994 compressed file
```

FIGURE 10.2: A directory of viewers in the form of a Web page; click on the link for the viewer that interests you.

Unzipping Zipped Files

You can tell when you run across a file with the extension .ZIP that you've encountered a *zipped* file. Zipped files are files that have been compressed through a process that does not involve a loss of data but simply a shrinking of the space the data is stored in. Zipped files are pretty common on the Internet; this is because receiving the smaller "zipped" files costs less in transfer time and fees for online time.

One of the most popular programs available for zipping files is PKZIP. Others are WinZip and plain old Zip. To use any of these files, after you've downloaded them, you must use an unzipping program, which will expand the files to the size they had before they were zipped. To unzip files, you can use PKUNZIP, the unzip feature in WinZip, or the freely available program UNZIP. Here's the best thing: You can get Zip and UnZip from the Internet. They're available at the FTP site `ftp.oak.oakland.edu`, as well as from the Sybex CompuServe forum and scores of other sites.

(continued on next page)

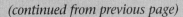

(continued from previous page)

To get a copy of Zip and UnZip from `ftp.oak.oakland.edu` using Netscape:

1. Start Custom and connect to the Internet by selecting Connect (from Custom's menu bar). Custom's Connect dialog box will appear; click on OK to continue, and the dialog box will disappear, leaving you with the Custom window and the Program Manager.

2. In the Program Manager, start Netscape by double-clicking on its icon.

3. Now, from Netscape's menu bar, select File ➤ Open Location. The Open Location dialog box will appear. (You've seen this dialog box often in earlier parts of this book.)

4. In the Open Location dialog box's test box, type **ftp://oak.oakland .edu/SimTel/msdos/UNZIP.EXE** (remebering to pay attention to capitalization!), then click the Open button. In a few seconds, the Unknown File Type dialog box will appear.

5. Click on the Save to Disk button. The familiar Windows style Save As dialog box will appear, asking you exactly where on your hard disk you want to save the file you are transferrring to your machine.

6. Select the directory C:\DOS as your choice of storage location and click on OK.

The file UNZIP.EXE will be copied to the DOS directory on your computer. The progress of copying files will be shown in the status bar along the bottom of the window. When it's finished, you'll be ready to unzip zipped files—like the ones that contain viewers you can use with Netscape.

Transferring a file is not the same as installing the software contained in the file. When you transfer the file, you are simply moving the (presumably) zipped file from its location elsewhere to your machine, where it is simply <u>stored</u> until you unzip it and actually <u>install</u> the software. Installing software these days is usually a pretty simple process—a lot of software installs itself by checking out your machine and what's already on it, then fitting itself in, and making necessary adjustments along the way.

Installing the QuickTime Viewer

Now, with the QuickTime viewer file transferred to your machine, it's time to unzip the thing and install the software on your hard disk. Here's how:

1. Beginning in the Windows Program Manager's Main group, get yourself to the DOS prompt by double-clicking on the MS-DOS icon.

MS-DOS
Prompt

You should find yourself in the WINDOWS directory, so the prompt will look something like C:\WINDOWS.

2. Now type **cd \windows\system**; this will get you into the C:\WINDOWS\SYSTEM directory, which is where the QuickTime viewer file must be stored.

3. Type **unzip \qtw11.zip** to unzip the zipped files that make up the QuickTime viewer. As the files are unzipped, their names will appear along with their sizes and a few other details that are of no concern to us here. When unzipping is complete, the DOS prompt (C:\WINDOWS\SYSTEM) will appear again on screen.

4. Type **exit** to return to Windows. The Program Manager's Main group will reappear.

You'll have to modify two of the Windows initialization files in order for the viewer to work correctly. Not to worry; this sounds more technically difficult than it is.

5. From the Windows Program Manager's menu, select File ➤ Run. The Run dialog box will appear.

6. In the Run dialog box's Command Line text box, type **notepad c:\windows\win.ini**. Click on the OK button. The Run dialog box will be replaced by a Notepad window (Figure 10.3). (Notepad is a simple text editor that comes with Windows.)

Windows configuration files like WIN.INI and SYSTEM.INI are divided into a number of *sections*. You don't need to worry about this—each section has to do with a different part of Windows, but there's no need to concern yourself with that information to do this process. Just keep in

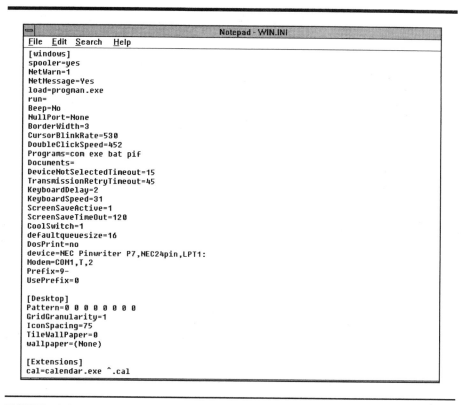

```
Notepad - WIN.INI
File   Edit   Search   Help
[windows]
spooler=yes
NetWarn=1
NetMessage=Yes
load=progman.exe
run=
Beep=No
NullPort=None
BorderWidth=3
CursorBlinkRate=530
DoubleClickSpeed=452
Programs=com exe bat pif
Documents=
DeviceNotSelectedTimeout=15
TransmissionRetryTimeout=45
KeyboardDelay=2
KeyboardSpeed=31
ScreenSaveActive=1
ScreenSaveTimeOut=120
CoolSwitch=1
defaultqueuesize=16
DosPrint=no
device=NEC Pinwriter P7,NEC24pin,LPT1:
Modem=COM1,T,2
Prefix=9-
UsePrefix=0

[Desktop]
Pattern=0 0 0 0 0 0 0 0
GridGranularity=1
IconSpacing=75
TileWallPaper=0
wallpaper=(None)

[Extensions]
cal=calendar.exe ^.cal
```

FIGURE 10.3:   Notepad is a simple text editor.

mind that each section will appear in the Notepad window with the name of the section surrounded by square brackets, like this: [Printers].

7. Look for [extensions] and under it, type **mov=mplayer.exe /play ^.mov**, then press ↵ so that what you've typed is on its own line.

8. Look for [mci.extensions] and under it, type **mov=QTWVideo**, then press ↵ again so that you've entered this on its own line.

9. Select File ➤ Save to save the changes you just made.

10. Select File ➤ Open and the Open dialog box will appear.

11. Type **\windows\system.ini** into the File Name box and click on the OK button. Notepad will load the file SYSTEM.INI into the Notepad window (Figure 10.4).

12. Look for [mci] and under it, type **QTWVideo=mciqtw.drv**, then press ⏎ to put this on its own line.

13. Select File ➤ Save from the menu bar. The changes you just made in the file will be saved.

14. From Notepad's menu bar, select File ➤ Exit to return to Windows.

15. Now exit Windows by selecting File ➤ Exit Windows from the Program Manager's menu bar. The DOS prompt will appear (something like C:\).

16. Restart Windows by typing **win** and pressing ⏎. The changes you made will now take effect.

Now let's set up Netscape so it will automatically call upon the viewer you've installed whenever it encounters QuickTime files.

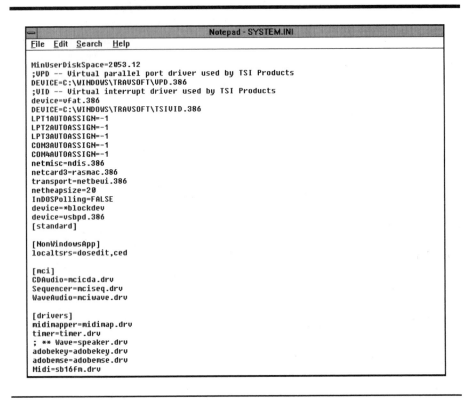

FIGURE 10.4: The Notepad window with the SYSTEM.INI file appearing in it.

Configuring Netscape to Use the QuickTime Viewer

Actually configuring Netscape to use the QuickTime viewer you've installed is quite simple. (Configuring Netscape is strictly a local operation—it affects only your copy of the program, so there is no need to do this while you are connected to the Net.)

1. Start Netscape (but don't bother to start Chameleon Sampler or get connected to the Net). From Netscape's menu bar, select Options ➤ Preferences. The Preferences window will appear.

2. From the list at the top of the Preferences window, select Helper Applications. The Preferences window will update to reflect your choice; it should now look similar to Figure 10.5.

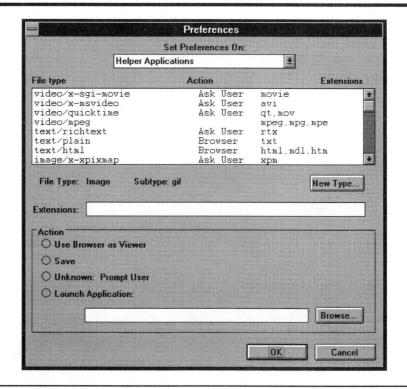

FIGURE 10.5: The Preferences window as it appears after you choose <u>Helper Applications</u>

3. The third entry in the type list (it's the Mime type list in version 1.0, but the File type list in version 1.1) is `video/quicktime` (again, see Figure 10.5). Click once on this entry.

4. In the Action section near the bottom of the window, toggle on the Launch Application: option by clicking on its radio button. Then in the Launch Application: text box, type **c:\windows\mplayer.exe**. (Note that you don't type the period at the end. See Figure 10.6 for an example.)

5. Click on OK to close the Preferences window.

Now you're set—but you're not connected to the Internet at the moment. You'll have to get connected to actually view anything. Start up your Chameleon Sampler connection and launch Netscape, and then you can view

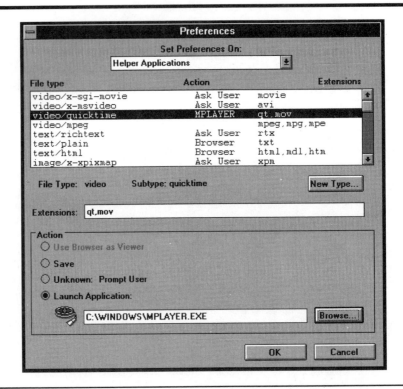

FIGURE 10.6: Type c:\windows\mplayer.exe in the text box, as shown here.

QuickTime movies that are linked to Web pages simply by clicking on their links. Just remember when you do this that QuickTime movies can be many megabytes in length and take lots of time to transfer to your computer.

What's Out There?

Hollywood has premiered on the Web; you can see clips from new movies and celebrity interviews on video by sliding over to the URLs `http://bvp.wdp.com/BVPM` or `http://www.mca.com`.

Getting and Setting Up MPEG Player

MPEG Player, the MPEG viewer we describe in this section, is highly reliable and an excellent choice for viewing MPEG video with Netscape (Figure 10.7).

FIGURE 10.7: A sampling of MPEG video available on the Web

To run this viewer with Windows 3.1 (as opposed to Windows 95), you must have Microsoft's Win32 extension installed. Win32 allows you to run more powerful applications under Windows 3.1; Win 32 is also available for downloading free of charge. For more details about Win32 visit `ftp://ftp.microsoft.com/peropsys/windows/kb/Q120/9/01.TXT`.

Downloading MPEG Player

Of course, before you install and configure MPEG Player, you have to download it. No problem—just follow these steps:

1. Start Chameleon Sampler and then Netscape to get yourself connected to the Net.

2. From the Netscape menu bar, select File ➤ Open Location. The Open Location dialog box will appear.

3. In the Open URL dialog box's URL text box, type **ftp://ftp.ncsa.uiuc.edu/Mosaic/Windows/viewers**. Click on Open. In a few seconds the contents of the viewers directory will be listed in the Netscape window as a series of links.

4. Find the link labeled mpegw32h.zip and click on it. The Unknown File Type dialog box will appear. Click on the Save to Disk button, and the Save As dialog box will appear.

5. In the Save As dialog box's File Name text box, type **c:\mpegw32h.zip**, then click on OK. The file will be transferred to your computer and saved. You'll see the progress of this operation in the status bar at the bottom of the window. When it's all over, you'll be ready to unzip the file and install the software.

6. Close Netscape by selecting File ➤ Exit from the menu bar. The Custom window and the Program Manager window will both appear (at the same time).

7. Disconnect from the Internet by selecting Disconnect from Custom's menu bar and clicking on the Yes button to confirm.

Installing MPEG Player

To install MPEG Player you'll have to first create a directory into which the unzipped files will be saved, then unzip the zipped file.

1. In the Windows Program Manager's Main group, double-click on the MS-DOS icon.

MS-DOS
Prompt

The DOS prompt (C:\WINDOWS) will appear.

2. Type **mkdir \mpeg** to create a directory called MPEG.

3. Type **cd \mpeg** to make your way into the MPEG directory you just created.

4. Now type **unzip \mpeg32h.zip** to unzip the files that make up MPEG Player. As the files are unzipped, they'll be listed along with some details, like their sizes.

5. When all the files are unzipped, type **exit** at the DOS prompt to get back to the Windows Program Manager.

There. The files are unzipped, and stored in the MPEG directory. You're all set to run MPEG Player's setup (installation) program.

6. From the Windows Program Manager's menu bar, select File ➤ Run. The Run dialog box will appear.

7. In the Run dialog box's Command Line text box, type **c:\mpeg\setup**. Click on the OK button. The MPEG Player Setup window will appear (Figure 10.8).

8. In the MPEG Player Setup window you'll encounter some information about the MPEG viewer program. Read it, then click on the Continue button to continue installation. The setup program will copy a number of files from \MPEG into the \WINDOWS\SYSTEM directory, and then a dialog box will appear asking where the program should install the rest of the MPEG Player software.

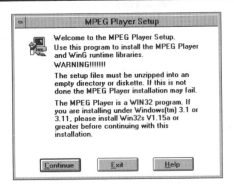

FIGURE 10.8: Read through the MPEG Player Setup window.

9. Accept the default location (\WIN32APP\MPEGPLAY) by clicking on the Continue button.

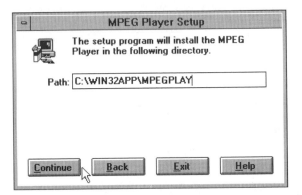

Files will be copied from \MPEG into the \WIN32APP\MPEGPLAY directory, and a dialog box will appear, saying everything is done.

You may (and you should) copy MPEG32H.ZIP to a floppy disk as a backup and then delete the \MPEG directory and its contents after you've successfully installed MPEG Player.

10. Click on OK and the Program Manager will reappear.

Now let's set up Netscape so it will automatically call upon the MPEG Player you've installed whenever it encounters MPEG video files.

Configuring Netscape to Use MPEG Player

Configuring Netscape to use the MPEG Player you've installed is as easy as pie. (Configuring Netscape is strictly a local operation—there is no need to do this while you are connected to the Net.)

1. Start Netscape (without first getting connected) and select Options ➤ Preferences from the menu bar. The Preferences window will appear.

2. Select Helper Applications from the pull-down list at the top of the window. The window's contents will update to reflect your choice.

3. The fourth entry on the type list (it's the Mime type list in version 1.0, but the File Type list in version 1.1) at the top of the screen is video/mpeg. Click once on this entry to highlight it.

4. In the Action section at the bottom of the window, toggle on the Launch Application: option by clicking on its radio button. Then, in the Launch Application: text box type **c:\win32app\mpegplay\mpegply.exe**, as shown in Figure 10.9.

5. Click on the OK button to close the Preferences window.

6. Exit Netscape by selecting File ➤ Exit from the menu bar.

Now, whenever you establish your Internet connection and fire up Netscape, you can view MPEG video that is linked to Web pages simply by clicking on a link. Remember that MPEG video, like QuickTime movies, can be many megabytes in length and take lots of time to transfer to your computer.

What's Out There?

The MPEG movie archive is a collection of clips available for your viewing enjoyment at the URL http://peace.www.wit.com/surrealism/movies.

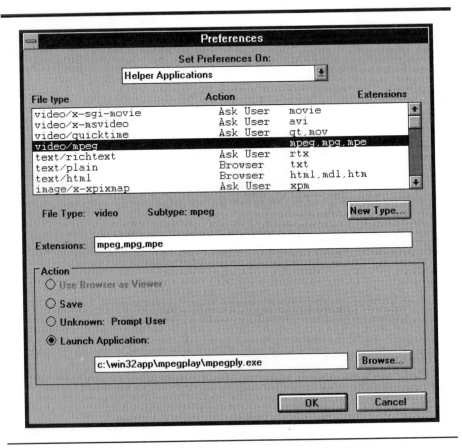

FIGURE 10.9: The Preferences Helper Application window with MPEG Viewer installed

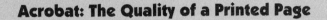

Acrobat: The Quality of a Printed Page

Adobe Acrobat is a product that allows electronic documents to use many of the elements that appear in documents printed on paper: publishers of online documents using Acrobat get to fiddle around with fonts, point-size, formatting, and graphics (even wrap-around graphics) in ways usually unheard of on the Web. You can use the Acrobat Reader—a freely available program that can display Adobe Acrobat files on your computer—as an external viewer for Netscape, which means you can view Acrobat files from within Netscape. Adobe has created a Web page containing all types of information about Acrobat; to find out more, vault on over to `http://www.adobe.com/Acrobat`.

Of course, once you've gone through the hoops of installing Acrobat Reader as an external viewer, you'll want to look at some pages that include Acrobat documents. Adobe maintains a list of such sites at the URL `http://www.adobe.com/Acrobat/PDFsites.html`.

One of the handiest uses of Acrobat on the Net is a complete set of IRS tax forms available at the URL `http://www.ustreas.gov/treasury/bureaus/irs/irs.html`.

Sound and Netscape

Sun Audio (with the extension .AU) is the most common format for sound you'll find on the Net. You'll also find Microsoft Windows sound files (.WAV) and Macintosh sound files (.SND) scattered around. You can play any of these with the sound player WHAM, which you can get from the Net itself.

As mentioned previously, Netscape version 1.1 includes a fully functional player for sound. We include here directions for getting and using sound players for use with Netscape version 1.0.

Some sound cards come with their own sound-playing soft-ware. Check your sound card's documentation to find out if the software that came with it lets you play the file formats mentioned. If this is the case, you may not need to install WHAM.

Downloading WHAM

To use WHAM, you must first get it. Here's how to do that.

To play sound on your PC, you'll need a sound card (the Sound Blaster is good), along with the proper Windows drivers. In this section we're going to assume that you have a sound-ready PC already equipped and configured.

1. Start Custom and connect to the Internet by selecting Connect (from Custom's menu bar). Custom's Connect dialog box will appear; click on OK to continue, and the dialog box will disappear, leaving you with the Custom window and the Program Manager.

2. In the Program Manager, start Netscape by double-clicking on its icon.

3. Select File ➤ Open Location from the menu bar. The Open Location dialog box will appear.

4. In the Open Location dialog box, type **ftp://ftp.ncsa.uiuc.edu/ Mosaic/Windows/viewers**. Click on Open. In a few seconds, the contents of NCSA's FTP server's MOSAIC/WINDOWS/VIEWER directory will be listed in a Web page as a series of links.

5. Use the scroll bars to scroll down the list until you see the link labeled <u>wham131.zip</u>. This is the zipped up file you want.

```
  readme.1st           2 Kb    Wed Dec 28 17:44:00 1994
  speak.exe           20 Kb    Mon Jun 27 00:00:00 1994 Binary executabl
  wham131.zip        134 Kb    Mon Jun 27 00:00:00 1994 compressed file
  wplny09b.zip        18 Kb    Mon Jun 27 00:00:00 1994 compressed file
```

6. Click on <u>wham131.zip</u>. The Save As dialog box will appear.

7. In the Save As dialog box's File Name text box, type **c:\wham131.zip**. Click on the OK button.

The zipped WHAM file will be transferred to your machine. As this happens, you can watch the progress taking place in the status bar along the bottom of the Netscape window. When it's all over,

8. Quit Netscape by selecting File ➤ Exit from the menu bar, and then disconnect from the Internet by selecting Disconnect from Custom's menu bar and clicking on the Yes button to confirm.

Installing WHAM

To install WHAM, the sound player, you'll create a subdirectory of your Windows program and unzip the WHAM files into that.

1. In the Windows Program Manager's Main group, double-click on the MS-DOS icon. The DOS prompt (C:\WINDOWS) will appear.

2. At the DOS prompt, type **md \windows\wham**.

3. Change to that directory by typing **cd\windows\wham**.

4. Now (at the DOS prompt C:\WIDNOWS\WHAM) type **unzip \wham131.zip** to unzip the file. As this happens, the files that are being unzipped will be listed, along with some details, like the sizes of the files.

5. When it's all over, at the DOS prompt, type **exit** to return to Windows.

Now we must set up Netscape so it will automatically call upon WHAM whenever it encounters AU, WAV, or SND sound files.

Configuring Netscape to Use WHAM

Configuring Netscape to use WHAM is no big deal (you don't even have to be connected to the Net to do it, because you're configuring the program itself). Just follow these steps:

1. Start Netscape (and select Options ➤ Preferences from the menu bar. The Preferences window will appear.

2. Select Helper Applications from the pull-down list at the top of the window. The Preferences window will appear.

3. Scroll the large list until you find the audio/basic entry. Click on it once.

4. In the Action section at the bottom of the window, toggle on the Launch Application: option by clicking on its radio button. Then, in the Launch Application: text box, type **c:\windows\wham.exe** (Figure 10.10).

5. Repeat steps 3 and 4 for the selection audio/x-wav.

6. Click on the OK button to close the Configuration dialog box.

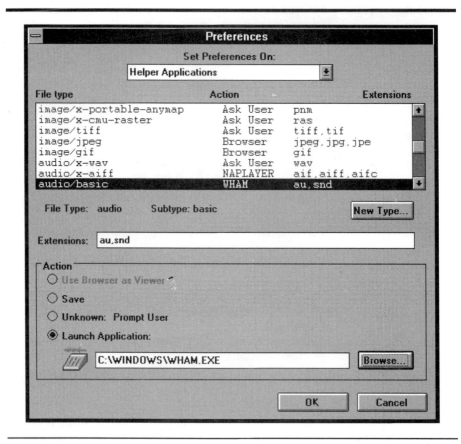

FIGURE 10.10: The Preferences Helper Application Window Configured to use WHAM.

Now, whenever you start your Internet connection and fire up Netscape, if you click on a link to go to a sound file, Netscape will automatically call upon WHAM to play the sound.

What's Out There?

For a quick intro to what's happening in sound (read: *music*) on the Web, drop by the Internet Underground Music Archive (IUMA). IUMA includes digitized sound from many bands at the URL http://www.iuma.com.

You're All Set

So—you're a master Web navigator and burgeoning Web publisher after reading the earlier chapters in this book, and now you even know how to get and use viewers to augment your Netscape experience. You're ready to proceed full steam ahead into your World Wide Web travels using Netscape.

Bon voyage!

What's on the Disk: The Chameleon Sampler

Throughout most of this book, Chameleon Sampler has played a supporting role to Netscape's starring role, but Chameleon has talents above and beyond those we've already discussed. Let's give Chameleon Sampler the spotlight for a while. If you glance around the Chameleon Sampler group in your Windows Program Manager, you'll notice icons other than the now familiar Custom icon. That's because in addition to the SLIP/PPP software that enables you to run Netscape, Chameleon Sampler includes a number of highly useful Internet tools:

◆ Chameleon FTP (File Transfer Protocol)

◆ Chameleon Telnet

◆ Chameleon E-Mail

◆ Ping

In this appendix, we'll go over each of these tools, showing you what they do and how to use them.

In Chapters 1 and 2, we introduce the Internet and describe the purposes of these tools at length. Please turn to Chapter 1 for an overview of the Internet.

Using Chameleon FTP

FTP, or File Transfer Protocol is a popular and useful means of copying files from (and to) other computers on the Internet. Many people, organizations, universities, etc., maintain "FTP sites," which are archives of documents and software—both public domain and shareware files—accessible to anyone on the Internet who has FTP capability.

 As mentioned in Chapter 3, you can access FTP sites using Netscape. Whenever you use an URL in Netscape that begins with `ftp:`, you are really using FTP. Here we are discussing the use of Chameleon Sampler to accomplish the same feats you would if you used Netscape to FTP.

What's Out There?

There are gazillions of FTP sites on the Net, and each offers up something worthwhile or entertaining. You might want to check out the big, comprehensive site at `gatekeeper.dec.com`, the long listings of shareware at `oak.oakland.edu` and `sunsite.unc.edu` (be sure to check out the tarot files there), the music files at `ftp.rock.net`, or even the CIA stuff at `ucselx.sdsu.edu`.

Here's how FTP works: If you have FTP capability and access to the Internet, you can log onto other computers as…shall we say, a *visitor*. This affords you limited access to that machine—you can access those directories and files on that machine that have been made available to you by the machine's owners and operators. If, while looking around, you see a file or files you'd like, you can copy them to the machine on your desk. Similarly, if you have a file or files you'd like to share with others, many sites will accept your contributions—you can upload your files to that site and others will download and use them.

There is a more nitty-gritty level at which this process takes place—it involves sending data packets back and forth using the File Transfer Protocol—but you don't have to know all that to use FTP. Just about everything in the process is taken care of automatically by the FTP software (whether it's Cameleon FTP or Netscape's FTP capability or some other FTP utility) so all that's left for you to do is specify where you'd like to FTP to or from, who you are, and what you'd like copied to where.

When you transfer files using FTP, you have to provide a username and password so you can log onto the server machine. The most common type of FTP interaction is called *anonymous FTP*. Anonymous FTP lets you use "anonymous" as your username and provide your e-mail address as your password, making things simpler for everybody.

An FTP Netiquette Note

Copying files with FTP puts a lot of demand on the server machines offering up FTP sites. These computers, though available for public use, are often simultaneously used by people in business and academia for whatever they do. Too much FTP'ing during the business day has caused many people and companies offering FTP sites to shut down their sites or severely restrict access. To lessen the inconvenience to those who are so generously providing FTP sites for your use, avoid connecting to a site between 9AM and 6PM (and remember to calculate local time for that site).

Downloading Files with Anonymous FTP

Enough yacking. Here's how Chameleon Sampler's FTP utility actually works. We're going to log onto an FTP server to do an *anonymous FTP* download. (Anonymous FTP, remember, lets you log in using "anonymous" as your username and providing your e-mail address as your password.)

1. Connect to your Internet provider by clicking on the Chameleon Sampler Custom icon as you have done to start Netscape, but this time do not start Netscape. This time, we're going to run something else on top of Custom.

2. In the same place the Custom icon resides—the Chameleon Sampler group in your Windows Program Manager—you'll see an FTP icon.

FTP

Double-click on the FTP icon. Chameleon Sampler's FTP window will appear, as shown in Figure A.1.

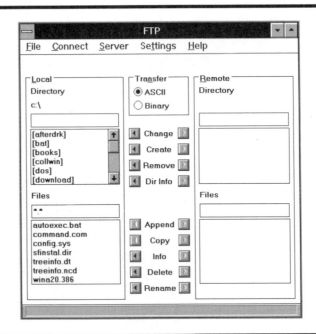

FIGURE A.1: In Chameleon Sampler's FTP window, you'll indicate what's to be

This window is divided into two halves:

◆ The left side—Local—shows you all the directories on your machine in the upper list and all the files contained in *the currently selected directory* on your machine in the lower list.

◆ The right side—Remote—shows nothing when you open it up, but will show the same sort of directory information for the machine you connect to once you get connected to it.

At the top of the window is a menu bar, providing you with the command options you'll use. Down the middle of the window are two columns of buttons. With these buttons, you'll perform the tasks involved in telling Chameleon FTP just what you want to do with which files.

3. To connect to an FTP site, select Connect from the menu bar. The Connect dialog box will appear, as shown in Figure A.2.

4. In the Connect dialog box's Host: text box, type the address of the FTP site to which you want to connect. (No browsing allowed here—you pretty much have to know where you're headed.)

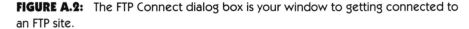

FIGURE A.2: The FTP Connect dialog box is your window to getting connected to an FTP site.

Keep in mind that the address of an FTP site is different from the URLs for Web sites you've seen throughout this book. An FTP address appears in the form of domains separated by periods, like `machine.university.edu` or `hummer.corp.com`. (See Chapter 2 for more on the domain naming system.) If you want a specific example to work along with, try the NASA FTP site at: `spacelink.msfc.nasa.gov`.

5. In the Connect dialog box's User: text box, type **anonymous**. (This is *anonymous* FTP, after all.)

Some sites do not allow for anonymous FTP. These "private" sites require you to provide an actual username and a real password, which of course you do not have. That's no accident.

6. In the Connect dialog box's Password: text box, type your complete e-mail address. (Anonymous FTP lets you fudge the password issue by using your e-mail address.) Note that if you don't type your e-mail address as a password in an anonymous FTP setting, you'll still be able to log on, but this is considered very, very bad form. One should be considerate enough to identify oneself at the very least when one is getting something for nothing.

7. Click on the OK button.

In the best possible world, the FTP window will reappear, and when that happens you'll know that your anonymous login has been successful and you can proceed. If an error message appears instead, it's probably because the site is overused at the moment or access has been limited. If this happens, try again later. Once your login is successful and the FTP window shows up, you'll see in it the contents of the FTP site, as shown in Figure A.3's example.

8. Now you need only to zip around the site's directory structure until you find a file you'd like to copy. To select a given directory and see its contents, double-click on that directory in the Directory list in the FTP window's Remote section.

9. When you find a file you'd like to copy, click on it once to highlight it.

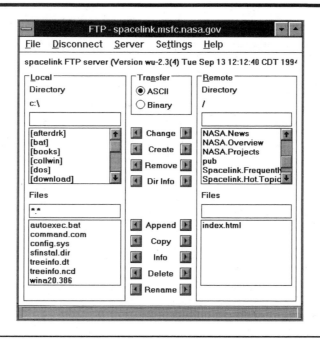

FIGURE A.3: The FTP window now shows the contents of the NASA FTP site we logged in to.

  Some files are very large—they can take a long time to transfer, and they might not fit on your hard drive. If you want to see how big a file is before you copy it, highlight the file's name and then click on the right-arrow button next to Info.

10. In the Connect dialog box's Transfer section, you should click on the Binary button for most transfers.

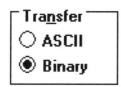

If you are transferring an ASCII file (i.e., a plain text file that, more likely than not, has the extension .TXT), you can select ASCII transfer instead of binary. Selecting Binary is safer, however. Error-checking is built into binary transfers, making them more bullet-proof and less subject to failure than ASCII transfers.

11. The files you are going to copy will arrive in the current directory (the one that's open) on your machine. Which directory is current is indicated in the FTP window's Remote section, under *Directory*. Make sure you've indicated the correct directory here; if you want to change the current directory to another, just click on the one you want. (This is a standard Windows type of operation.)

12. Click the left-arrow button next to Copy, then sit back and watch the file arrive. That's all there is to it.

13. Select Disconnect from the FTP window's menu bar. The Disconnect dialog box will appear.

14. If you want to quit the FTP program, click on the Disconnect dialog box's Exit button. If instead you want to connect to another site and do another FTP download, click on the Disconnect button instead, and then go back to step 3.

FTP is a fantastic tool. Enormous quantities of information and many programs and utilities are available to you via FTP. The CICA Windows FTP archive alone offers almost every Windows freeware or shareware program ever written. Work with it a bit until you get comfortable, take the time to look around (but remember, not during business hours!), and you'll see what we mean.

What's Out There?

A large and quite famous public collection of Windows-related software and files that you can download for your own use can be found at `ftp.cica.indiana.edu`.

Using Chameleon Telnet

Telnet allows you to log into another computer and operate it from your own. It is terrifically useful, for example, for accessing library catalogs and other sources of public information. Given the proliferation of sites and information on the Internet, a lot of stuff is available to you in multiple ways (Web, Gopher, FTP, etc.), and you may find getting to this stuff via the Web or FTP more convenient, but it's good to know how to use all the tools in your Internet tool kit, so let's take a look at telnet.

 Telnet addresses use the same domain-names-connected-by-periods format as FTP addresses; to find out what these domains are all about, see Chapter 2. If you'd like an address to work along with in the upcoming telnet session steps, you can use NASA: `spacelink.msfc.nasa.gov`.

Here are the steps to follow for a typical telnet session.

1. Get connected to your Internet service provider by double-clicking on the Custom icon in the Chameleon Sampler group window. (Don't start Netscape.) The Custom window will appear.

2. Click on Connect in the Custom window's menu bar. A dialog box will appear; in it, click on OK and you'll get connected.

3. In the Windows Program Manager's Chameleon sampler group, double-click on the Telnet icon.

Telnet

The Telnet window will appear. It will be blank, with a menu bar across its top—no big deal to look at.

4. From the Telnet window's menu bar, select Connect. The Connect To dialog box will appear. This is where you'll indicate to which remote system you plan to telnet.

5. In the Connect To dialog box's Host Name text box, type the address of the system to which you plan to connect. (It is assumed by telnet that you know where you want to go in advance of going there.) Leave the Port and Emulate text boxes alone.

6. Click on the OK button.

When you connect to a telnet site, you'll see the site's introductory screen. *Read this screen*; it usually contains instructions for logging in and/or using the available databases (if that's what you've come for). Figure A.4 shows the Welcome to NASA Spacelink screen.

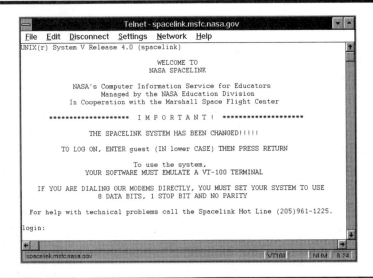

FIGURE A.4: Like the introductory screens at other telnet sites, the Welcome to NASA Spacelink screen provides login instructions.

Every computer system is different—different operating systems, different data structures, etc.—so how you get around once you've connected depends entirely on the machine you're visiting. (Remember, in a telnet session you are actually using your own machine to work on the remote machine.)

7. Follow the directions given by the remote site for how to use the resources located there, and don't be afraid to experiment a little—you can't do any damage to anything on the remote machine.

8. When you're finished at this site, select Disconnect from the Telnet window's menu bar. The Disconnect dialog box will appear.

9. If you want to telnet to another site, click on the Disconnect button and go back to step 3. If you're finished for now, click on the Exit button to quit the telnet program. The Custom window will appear.

10. To disconnect from your Internet service provider, select Disconnect from Custom's menu bar and then click the Yes button to confirm.

That's telnetting in a nutshell. Play around some with telnetting; you'll find it useful for linking into a variety of bulletin board systems and database resources (like the Library of Congress' online card catalog).

Using Chameleon E-Mail

You may already have access to e-mail through a commercial online service like CompuServe or through your work or school computer system. E-mail is one of the most popular aspects of going online. (See Chapter 1 for an introduction to Internet services in general and e-mail in particular.)

When you set up your special SLIP/PPP account to use Netscape, you set up what is perhaps going to turn out to be *another* e-mail account. All you need is the software to access it, and the Chameleon Sampler provides that. If you have and like your existing e-mail service, you may not want to switch at this point.

However, the Chameleon Sampler e-mail software does offer an important advantage: it lets you read and write your e-mail offline, saving you the expense of some connect time. This is called a *POPmail* system—its one that logs on only long enough to *send* what you've written and *retrieve* any new mail you've been sent.

Let's take a look at Chameleon Sampler's e-mail program, how to send and read mail, and how to use an address book.

Setting Up Your E-Mail Account

To get your e-mail system up and running, you're going to have to configure it first. You'll be investing a little time in this, but it's not hard to do. So, roll up your sleeves and follow these steps:

1. Connect to your Internet service provider by double-clicking on the Custom icon in the Chameleon Sampler group window. (Don't start Netscape.) The Custom window will appear.

2. Click on Connect in the Custom window's menu bar. A dialog box will appear; in it, click on OK and you'll get connected.

3. In the Chameleon Sampler group in your Windows Program Manager, double-click on the Mail icon. The small User Login dialog box will appear.

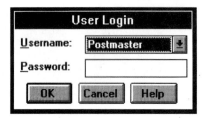

4. Change nothing on the User Login dialog box; just click OK. The Mail–Postmaster window will appear (Figure A.5).

What you've done here is logged in to your Mail program as the Postmaster. This is sort of a personal "mail administrator" function that allows you to configure your e-mail software.

5. From the Mail–Postmaster window's menu bar, select Services ➤ Mailboxes. The blank Mailboxes dialog box will appear.

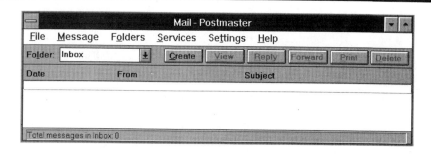

FIGURE A.5: The Mail–Postmaster window as it first appears

6. In the User text box, type a username.

Then click on the Add button. The User Configuration dialog box will appear, with the User: text box already filled in with the name you choose. Note that the same name will appear in the title bar of the dialog box.

*

The name you enter here can be some variation on your real name—its best to use some shorter version of your name, like <u>bkienan</u> for Brenda Kienan—or it can be a "handle" you make up to identify yourself (like <u>whizkid</u>). It also does not have to be identical to the username you established for yourself when you set up your SLIP/PPP account, but it is the name you will use when start up your e-mail software. Rather than keeping track of multiple names (and passwords) for yourself, it is most convenient to stick to one name.

7. In the User Configuration dialog box's Password text box, type in a password.

Like the username you entered back in step 5, the password you enter here does not have to be the one you picked when you established your SLIP/PPP account, but remembering one is a lot easier than remembering two.

8. In the text box labeled *In real life*, type your real, true, full name as you would like it to appear in the headers of e-mail messages you send, where you will be identified by name as well as by your e-mail address.

9. In the text box labeled *Mail Directory*, you can specify the directory on your local machine where you want messages to be saved. You'll find that the program has suggested a subdirectory of the Netmanager directory, which is where the Chameleon Sampler resides. You may choose this by doing nothing or you may type in any other directory you wish instead of the suggested directory.

10. Click on the OK button. If in Step 8 you changed the directory your mail will be stored in to one that does not yet exist, a dialog box will now appear asking you to confirm the creation of the directory. Click on the Yes button to have the Mail program create the directory, and the Mailboxes dialog box will reappear.

11. Now click on the Save button at the top of the Mailboxes dialog box to save the information you just entered. The Mail–Postmaster window will reappear.

12. Select File ➤ Exit from the menu bar. The Mail program will close, leaving you with a familiar view of the Program Manager.

Okay! You're all set up to use your e-mail account to send outgoing mail. To read incoming mail takes a little more setting up, but we'll get to that in a later section of this chapter. In the meantime, let's put your new account to work by sending off some mail.

Sending an E-Mail Message

Let's start by sending a single message—this is what you'll do most often. Once we've gotten the hang of that, we'll go into how to queue a group of messages and send them all at once.

Sending one message is as simple as the steps that follow.

1. If you aren't already connected to your Internet service provider, double-click on the Custom icon in the Chameleon Sampler group window to get connected now. The Custom window will appear.

2. From the Custom window's menu bar, select Connect. In the dialog box that appears, click on OK and you'll get connected.

3. In the Chameleon Sampler group in the Windows Program Manager, double-click on the Mail icon. The small User Login dialog box that you saw when you configured your account will appear, but instead of the word *Postmaster* showing in the Username box, you'll see the user name you selected for yourself when you configured your e-mail account.

4. In the user Login's Password text box, type the password you specified during configuration (this will confirm that you are who you say you are).

5. Click on the OK button. The main Mail window, complete with your username in the title bar, will appear. (You saw this window once before, when you set up your e-mail account.) Now you've logged into your e-mail account for the first time.

6. To start composing a message, click on the Create button in the center of the Mail window. (You can also select Message ➤ Create to do this, but using the Create button is easier). The Message window will appear.

7. To address your message, in the To: section of the Message window, click on the Names... button. The Names dialog box will appear.

8. In the Names dialog box's Address text box, type the e-mail address of the person to whom you'll be sending the message; then click on the OK button.

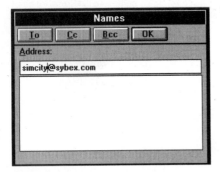

 If you want to send your message to more than one person, just click To instead of OK in step 6, then type in the name of the second person. Do it again for the third, and so on. When you've entered the names of everyone on your list (you'll see all the names you've entered in the Names dialog box), click OK to proceed.

The Message window will reappear with the name of the addressee appearing in the To section of the window.

9. In the Subject text box, type a one or two word subject summary of your message. This will alert your message's recipient to the topic at hand and help him or her to file the thing and find it again if the need arises.

10. In the large blank space that occupies most of the window—the message area—type your message.

11. When you're ready to send the message, click on the Send button. The Message window will close, the Mail program will send the message, and the main Mail window will reappear.

If you want to send another message, start again with step 6. If you're finished with the Mail program, you can close it by selecting File ➤ Exit from the menu bar.

Sending "Courtesy" Copies

Let's say you want to address a message to one person or a group, and you want some other person(s) to know about it. You can send what was once called a carbon copy but is now known more commonly as a *courtesy copy*. To do this, just click on the Cc button in the Names window and type in the names of those you want to be informed. If you want someone to be informed without your message's recipient knowing anything about it, use the Bcc button instead of Cc.

Queuing and Sending Multiple Messages

One of the great things about Chameleon Sampler's e-mail program is that you can do your e-mail work (composing messages and reading them) off-line, saving you the expense of the online time you'd have to pay for to do this with many other e-mail programs. Let's say you want to write a bunch of e-mail messages to your various electronic penpals or business associates, then send them all at once.

Here's how you can do that.

1. Follow steps 3 through 10 in the previous section (*Sending an E-Mail Message*) for each message you want to send, but *do this without connecting to your Internet service provider* (that just means "skip the first two steps").

What we're doing now might seem a bit odd at first glance. How, after all, can you send your messages if you're not connected to the Internet? Well, technically you can't. Remember—we're just writing the messages now, and Chameleon Sampler's e-mail program will store the messages until we're ready to send them off. When you've written all your messages, pick up again here:

2. In the Windows Program Manager's Chameleon Sampler group window, double-click on the Custom icon. The Custom window will appear.

3. Select Connect from Custom's menu bar. A dialog box will appear; in it, click on OK and you'll get connected to your Internet service provider.

4. In the Mail window, select Services ➤ Outbox from the Mail window's menu bar. The Outbox dialog box will appear, as shown in Figure A.6, with a listing of the headers for each message you've composed.

Chameleon's Mail program automatically keeps a copy of every message you send in the "Outbox," even messages you've prepared but have not yet sent off.

5. Highlight the messages you've just composed and now want to send, by clicking on their headers in the Outbox. Then click on the Send button. As the e-mail program actually sends the highlighted messages off to their respective destinations, their headers will be removed from the Outbox.

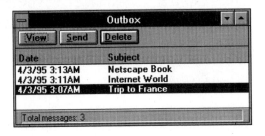

FIGURE A.6: The messages you've prepared but have not sent on their way will appear in the Outbox.

6. Double-click on the Outbox's control box (in the upper-left corner) to close it and keep working in the Mail window.

or

Exit the Mail program by selecting File ➤ Exit from the Mail window's menu bar.

Now you know how to send mail. You'll want to keep your address list up to date and organized, too; Chameleon's e-mail program makes that another simple process.

Tracking E-Mail Addresses with the Address Book

Just like any other capable e-mail program, Chameleon Sampler's provides an address book to save you the trouble of remembering and typing in e-mail addresses every time you write a message.

Compiling and otherwise organizing your address book is probably something you want to do offline; again, this is to save the cost of connect time.

Here's how to put your address book together and use it.

1. In the Chameleon Sampler group in the Windows Program Manager, double-click on the Mail icon. (There's no need to get connected to your Internet service provider or start Netscape, of course.) The User Login dialog box will appear, showing your username.

2. In the User Login dialog box's Password text box, type your password to identify yourself and click on the OK button. The Mail window will appear.

3. Select Services ➤ Address Book from the Mail window's menu bar. The Address Book dialog box will appear.

4. In the Address Book dialog box's Address text box, type any and all e-mail addresses you want to add. (See Figure A.12 later in this appendix for an example.) Then click on the Add button.

When you've added an address, it is immediately visible in the main part of Address Book dialog box, as you can see in Figure A.7. To add more addresses, just repeat step 4 as necessary.

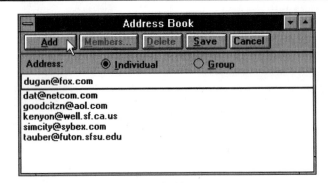

FIGURE A.7: As you add e-mail addresses, they'll appear in the bottom portion of the Address Book dialog box.

5. When you've finished adding all the addresses of interest, click on the Save button, and then close the Address Book dialog box by clicking on its Cancel button. The Mail window will reappear.

Now that you've assembled your address book, sending e-mail is going to be a lot easier. When the time comes to address a message, the addresses you've entered in your address book will automatically appear in the Names dialog box. Instead of typing in the recipient's address, all you'll have to do is highlight the address of interest in the list in the Names dialog box, then click To (or Cc, or Bcc, depending on your intention), and finally on OK. Your message will be addressed as you like, and once you've written the thing, you can just send it off. What could be easier?

Configuring Chameleon Mail for Reading

To get yourself set up to read your e-mail, you must first "tell" the Mail program exactly where it has to look on your Internet service provider's server to find the e-mail addressed to you. This is a simple process you have to do only once (as long as you stay with the same Internet service provider).

Here's how to configure Chameleon Sampler's e-mail program to enable you to read your messages.

1. Connect to your Internet service provider by double-clicking on the Custom icon in the Chameleon group window. (Don't start Netscape.) The Custom window will appear.

2. Click on Connect in the Custom window's menu bar. A dialog box will appear; in it, click on OK and you'll get connected.

3. In the Chameleon Sampler group in the Windows Program Manager, double-click on the Mail icon. The small Login dialog box will appear, showing your username.

4. In the Login dialog box's Password text box, type your password to identify yourself, then click on OK. The main Mail window will appear. (You've done all this before; the new stuff is coming up.)

5. From the Mail window's menu bar, select Setting ➤ Network ➤ Mail Server. The Mail Server dialog box will appear. (You can see this dialog box in its filled-out state in Figure A.8.)

6. In the Mail Server dialog box's Host text box, type the name of your Internet service provider's mail server—this is information you can and should get from your Internet service provider.

 The mail server is the machine on which your Internet service provider stores the messages that are sent to you. Usually the mail server's name will look something like the example `mail.providers.address`. Ask your Internet service provider's technical support people for the correct address.

FIGURE A.8: The Mail Server dialog box will be blank when it first appears; here you can see it all filled out.

7. In the Mail Server dialog box's User and Password text boxes, type the username and password you use to access your Internet service provider. (Remember, *this may not be the same user name and password you chose when you configured the Chameleon e-mail program* as described earlier in this chapter.)

You can usually leave the Mail Server dialog box's Mail dir: text box blank; but some providers will assign a specific directory for your mail storage. If you find you can't retrieve your mail once you've got everything all set up here, you may want to check with your provider's technical support people, and they may tell you something to type into the Mail dir: text box.

8. Click on the OK button. The Mail window will reappear.

Take a look at the option labeled <u>Delete retrieved mail from server</u> in the Mail Server dialog box—it's got an × in it, indicating that it's "on" by default. This means that when Chameleon's e-mail program gets your mail from your provider's server, it deletes the messages rather than leaving a copy of them behind on the server. It's a good idea to leave this option toggled on; that'll prevent messages from piling up on the server.

Reading Your E-Mail

We're all set now to read any e-mail that happens our way. While connected to your Internet service provider and with the main Mail window on your screen (this is where you should be after this last bit of configuring), do the following:

1. If you closed up shop after configuring the e-mail program to receive mail, start your Internet service provider by double-clicking on the Custom icon in the Chameleon group window. (Don't start Netscape.) The Custom window will appear.

2. Click on Connect in the Custom window's menu bar. A dialog box will appear; in it, click on OK and you'll get connected.

3. In the Windows Program Manager's Chameleon Sampler group window, click on the Mail icon. The Mail window will appear.

4. From the Mail window's menu bar, select Message ➤ Retrieve Mail. If you have any waiting mail, the e-mail program will go and grab it from your provider's server and bring it to your local machine. The headers of those messages will appear in the Mail window, as shown in Figure A.9's example.

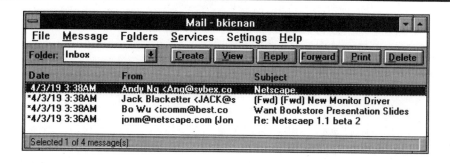

FIGURE A.9: You'll see a listing of headers appear in the Mail window when the e-mail program retrieves your mail.

5. To read any given message, just highlight its header in the list and click on the View button. The message will appear in a Message window, as shown in Figure A.10's example.

6. When you're done reading the message, you can

◆ Click on Next to read the next message in the listing, in which case your message will remain where it is, piling up on *your* machine

◆ Save, delete, print, or reply to your message as described in the upcoming section of this chapter

7. When you've read and otherwise handled all your mail, select File ➤ Exit from the Message window's menu bar.

You're going to want or need to *do* something with the mail you've read; this next section's all about that.

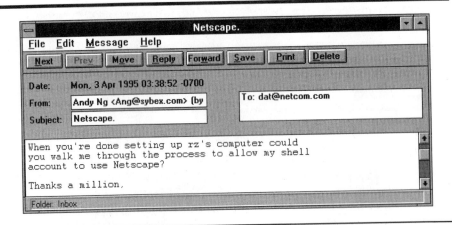

FIGURE A.10: Notice the buttons along the top of the Message window; they provide you with options for handling your mail.

Handling Your E-Mail Messages

Handling your snail mail is a minor chore you probably do daily—you read it, then you throw it away or reply to it or save it as circumstances and the contents of each piece of mail warrant, right? The same process must occur with your e-mail, or message upon message is going to crowd your machine like unrecycled envelopes lying around your office.

Here are some mail-handling options available from the Message window's convenient and alluring button bar:

◆ To save a message in its own file on your hard drive, click on the Save button and enter a filename in the dialog box that appears.

◆ To delete a message, click on the Delete button and—poof!—it will vanish.

◆ To reply to a message, click on the Reply button. A blank Message window will appear, with the original sender's address already appearing in the To: field, and all set up for you to compose an answer. (Once you've sent off your reply, remember to delete (or save) the original message.)

◆ To forward a message to another person, click on the Forward button. A Message window will appear, with the text of the message you're forwarding appearing there along with its subject. Click on the Names... button in the Message window and address the message to the person to whom you want to forward this gem, using the exact same techniques you used when you created a new message earlier in this appendix. (Again, once you've sent this message off, remember to delete or save the original.)

Wasn't all that e-mail talk fun? Seriously, e-mail is a wonderful tool, and this offline writing and reading feature is a great boon to keeping your costs in check. Before we wrap things up, there's one more Chameleon Sampler utility we want to "share" with you.

Ping

Ping does just one thing, and that thing is a lot like its name—Ping sends out an electronic "ping" (a few bytes of data) to see if a given Internet computer is online and running. If the "ping" comes back, the targeted machine is there and running. If there's no response, that machine is obviously unavailable. What's the good of this? you might ask. Well, Ping is a great way to double-check the availability of a Web site when Netscape gives you a persistent *Unable to locate host*. If you ping the Web site's server and get no response, you can give up for the time being, because you know the problem is not on your software's side. Isn't that handy?

Here's how to ping.

1. Connect to your Internet service provider by double-clicking on the Custom icon in the Chameleon group window. (Don't start Netscape.) The Custom window will appear.
2. In the Custom window's menu bar click on Connect. A dialog box will appear; in it, click on OK and you'll get connected.
3. In the Windows Program Manager's Chameleon Sampler group, double-click on the Ping icon.

Ping

The very small and simple Ping dialog box will appear.

4. From the Ping menu bar, select Start. The Host dialog box will appear.

5. In the Host text box, enter the address for the machine you want to ping (Figure A.11). If you're pinging a Web site machine to see why you're not getting access to it in a Netscape session, for example, you can enter the "machine name" part of the URL. (See Chapter 2 for a complete explanation of the domain naming system.)

6. Click on the OK button. If the machine you've pinged is online, Ping will receive data back, as shown in Figure A.12's example. If the machine you ping is not available, a message will tell you so.

7. When you've discovered whether or not the target machine is available, select File ➤ Exit from Ping's menu bar to close up shop. The familiar Program Manager window will appear.

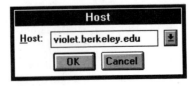

FIGURE A.11: Type in the address of the machine you want to ping.

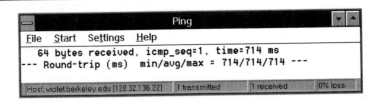

FIGURE A.12: PING! This machine is available—it received and returned the few bytes of data Ping sent its way.

That wraps things up! Chameleon Sampler's Internet tools are a great value; they provide you with a fully functional way to get around the Internet, and in combination with Netscape, you've got a basic tool kit that just can't be beat.

All the best in your Internet travels....

Internet Service Providers

If you need to set up an account with an Internet service provider so you can get started with Netscape, this is the place for you. This appendix lists providers that supply the type of service you need to use Netscape.

Some of the service providers listed here provide their own SLIP/PPP software. Netscape will work with their SLIP/PPP software just as well as it works with Chameleon Sampler.

The list we're providing here is by no means comprehensive. We're concentrating on service providers in the United States, Canada, the United Kingdom, and Australia/New Zealand that offer national or nearly national Internet service. You may prefer to go with a service provider that's local to your area—to minimize your phone bill, it is important to find a service provider that offers a local or toll-free phone number for access.

When you inquire into establishing an account with any of the providers listed in this appendix, tell them that you want a SLIP or PPP account and that you plan to run Netscape. Make these points very clearly—some of the listed providers also offer "shell" accounts, which is not what you want, because shell accounts require you to know Unix commands to use them and (far more important) they do not allow for the running of Netscape.

When you're shopping around for an Internet service provider, the most important questions to ask are (a) "Is this a SLIP or PPP account?" (either one is fine), (b) "What is the nearest local access number?" and (c) "What are the monthly service charges and is there a setup (or registration) fee?"

What's Out There?

Two very good sources of information about Internet service providers are available on the Internet itself. Peter Kaminski's Public Dialup Internet Access list (PDIAL) is at `ftp://ftp.netcom.com/pub/in/info-deli/public-access/pdial`. Yahoo's Internet Access Providers list is at `http://www.yahoo.com/Business/COrporations/Internet_Access_providers/`.

In the United States

In this section we list Internet service providers that provide local access phone numbers in most major American cities. These are the big, national companies. Many areas also have smaller regional Internet providers, which may offer better local access if you're not in a big city. You can find out about these smaller companies by looking in local computer papers like *MicroTimes* or *Computer Currents* or by getting on the Internet via one of these big companies and checking out the Peter Kaminski and Yahoo service provider listings.

Opening an account with any of the providers listed here will get you full access to the World Wide Web, and full-fledged e-mail service (allowing you to send and receive e-mail). You'll also get the ability to read and post articles to Usenet newsgroups.

Netcom Netcom Online Communications Services is a national Internet service provider with local access numbers in most major cities. (As of this writing, they have 100 local access numbers in the United States.) Netcom's NetCruiser software gives you point-and-click access to the Internet. (Netcom also provides a shell account, but stay away from it if you want to run Netscape.) Starting with NetCruiser version 1.6, it is possible to run Netscape on top of NetCruiser, making use of the Chameleon Sampler software that comes with this book unnecessary. Especially for beginning users who want a point-and-click interface and easy setup of Netscape, this may be a good choice.

NetCruiser software is available on disk for free but without documentation at many trade shows and bookstores. It is also available with a very good book (*Access the Internet, Second Edition*; David Peal, Sybex, 1995) that shows you how to use the software. To contact Netcom directly, phone (800) 353-6600.

Performance Systems International Performance Systems International is a national Internet Service Provider with local access numbers in many American cities *and in Japan*. These folks are currently upgrading their modems to 28.8Kbps, which will give you faster access to the Internet.

To contact PSI directly, phone (800) 82P-SI82.

UUNet/AlterNet UUNet Technologies and AlterNet offer Internet service throughout the United States. They run their own national network.

You can contact UUnet and AlterNet (800) 488-6383.

Portal Portal Communications, Inc., an Internet Service Provider located in the San Francisco Bay Area, lets you get connected either by dialing one of their San Francisco Bay Area phone numbers or via the CompuServe

network. (This is not CompuServe Information Services, but rather the network on which CompuServe runs.) The CompuServe network, with over 400 access phone numbers, is a local call from almost anywhere in the United States.

You can contact Portal at (408) 973-9111.

In Canada

Listed here are providers that offer access to Internet service in the areas around large Canadian cities. For information about local access in less populated regions, get connected and check out the Peter Kaminski and Yahoo lists described earlier in this appendix.

 Many Internet service providers in the U.S. also offer service in Canada and in border towns near Canada. If you're interested and you're in Canada, ask some of the big American service providers whether they have a local number near you.

UUNet Canada UUNet Canada is the Canadian division of the United States service provider UUNet/AlterNet, which we described earlier in this chapter. UUNet Canada offers Internet service to large portions of Canada.

You can contact UUNet Canada directly by phoning (416) 368-6621.

Internet Direct Internet Direct offers access to folks in the Toronto and Vancouver areas.

You can contact Internet Direct by phoning (604) 691-1600 or faxing (604) 691-1605

In Great Britain and Ireland

The Internet is, after all, international. Here are some service providers located and offering service in Great Britain and Ireland.

UNet Located in the northwest part of England, with more locations promised, UNet offers access at speeds up to 28.8K along with various Internet tools for your use.

They can be reached by phone at 0925 633 144.

Easynet London-based Easynet provides Internet service throughout England via Pipex, along with a host of Internet tools.

You can reach them by phone at 0171 209 0990.

Ireland On-Line Serving most (if not all) of Ireland, including Belfast, Ireland On-Line offers complete Internet service including ISDN and leased-line connections.

Contact Ireland On-Line by phone at 00 353 (0)1 8551740.

In Australia and New Zealand

Down under in Australia and New Zealand the Internet is as happening as it is in the northern hemisphere; many terrific sites are located in Australia especially. Here are a couple of service providers for that part of the world.

Connect.com.au In wild and woolly Australia, Internet service (SLIP/PPP) is available from Connect.com.au Pty Ltd.

You can contact the people at Connect.com.au by phone at 61 3 528 2239.

Actrix Actrix Information Exchange offers Internet service (PPP accounts) in the Wellington, New Zealand area.

You can reach these folks by phone at 64 4 389 6316.

Get Connected, Get Set, GO!

Selecting an Internet service provider is a matter of personal preference and local access. Shop around, and if you aren't satisfied at any point, change providers.

Glossary

anchors Links, from the other side of the picture—*anchor* is HTML-lingo for a text or image link to any other document.

anonymous FTP A *File Transfer Protocol* that lets *anyone* (regardless of whether he or she has a user name or password) transfer files from the server machine to his or her own.

application A computer program designed to specialize in a specific set of tasks. Word and WordPerfect are word processing applications; Excel and Quattro Pro are spreadsheet applications.

Archie A system that lets you search for files on the Internet that can be downloaded by anonymous FTP.

ARPAnet A now-defunct experimental network of the 1970s on which the theories and systems that became today's Internet were tested. ARPAnet is short for *Advanced Research Project Agency net.*

article A message posted to Usenet and readable with a newsreader.

ASCII The acronym for *American Standard Code for Information Interchange;* a basic text format most computers can read.

authentication A security feature, authentication lets users have access to information if they can provide a user name and password that the security system recognizes.

backbone One of the high-speed networks that form the "backbone" or core of the Internet.

bandwidth The amount of data that can be sent through a communications channel such as a network or a modem.

baud A measurement of the speed at which signals are sent by a modem (more precisely, a measurement of the number of changes per second that occur during transmission). A baud rate of 2400, for example, indicates that 2400 signal changes occur in one second. Baud rate is often confused with *bps* (bits per second), which is defined below.

BBS An online *bulletin board system;* an electronic place provided by kind strangers or misguided entrepreneurs for people with like interests to post (make public) messages in an ongoing conversation, and to upload and download software and files.

binary transfer A transfer of data between computers in which binary data is preserved; often the best type of transfer for software and graphic images.

bitmap An electronic file that represents an image with a collection of bits. (A bit is smaller than a byte.)

bookmark A method for marking and tracking pages for easy retrieval.

bounced message A message that has been returned is known as one that has *bounced.* Usually this happens because the address was incorrect.

bps A measurement—*bits per second*—of the speed at which data is transferred between modems. Higher bps rates indicate faster transfer.

browser Software that enables the user to look at, interact with, and generally "browse" files on the Internet.

BTW Electronic shorthand for *by the way.*

bye A log-off command that means essentially "quit" or "exit."

cd A shorthand version of the commonly used command *change directory.*

cdup A shorthand version of the command *change directory up*, which is used at FTP sites to go from a subdirectory up to its parent directory.

CERN *The Conseil Européen pour la Recherche Nucleaire*—the European particle physics laboratory that was the birthplace of the World Wide Web.

client A computer that *receives;* the computer that connects to a *server.* *See* server.

compressed (a) A term used to describe data that has been *shrunk* or "zipped." This process, performed by utility programs like PKZip, LHArc, and Zip, makes it possible to conserve storage space and to transfer files more quickly; (b) A process of shrinking motion picture files by leaving out some frames, retaining only as many as are necessary to create the perception of action. QuickTime and MPEG are examples of the use of this process.

configure To set up or make programs, applications, and computer systems work together.

CWIS A menu-based system at a university that provides on-line information about the university. CWIS is short for *Campus-Wide Information System*.

dedicated A line, server, or other piece of computer-associated equipment that has only one purpose; a *dedicated line,* for example, might be a phone line that leads *only* to your PC (or modem) and *not* also to a phone.

dial-up A connection to a computer that is accomplished by calling on a phone line with a modem.

dir A shorthand version of the commonly used command *directory.* If at a DOS prompt or an FTP site you type **dir** and press ⏎, you will see the contents of the current directory.

distribution A variation on the original software, usually enhanced, that is being distributed by parties who did not develop the software but who are licensed or permitted to add to and distribute the software. This differs from a *version* in that it does not represent a generation in the development of the software. Air Mosaic is an enhanced distribution of the original Mosaic; Netscape is not a distribution of Mosaic but rather a whole new product.

domain A level in an address, as defined in the Domain Name system (see below). In the address, domains are separated from each other by a period, as in `ed.sybex.com`.

Domain Name system A system for classifying computers into increasingly large groups with names; for example, in `laxness.ed.sybex.com`, *laxness* is a specific machine in a group named *ed*itorial in a company called *sybex* which is in the general category of *com*mercial.

download To transfer files to your machine from another machine.

drive A physical device on which you can store files. Each drive is identified by a letter (A:, B:, C:, etc.).

driver A program that tells your computer what to do with something added to your computer—a printer, mouse, sound board, etc.

e-mail The common way to refer to *electronic mail;* messages that are addressed to an individual at a computer and sent electronically.

emoticon *See* smiley.

encryption Disguising a message (by scrambling it) to prevent intruders from reading it.

FAQ Electronic shorthand for *frequently asked question.*

file transfer The transfer of a file from one computer to another over a network or via a modem.

finger A program that finds and provides information about a user who might be logged in to your network or the Internet.

firewall A security system that creates an electronic barrier protecting an organization's network and PCs from access by outsiders via the Internet.

flame A very unfriendly, often violent, written attack against someone in an electronic forum such as a newsgroup or message area. (A *flame war* occurs when both parties engage in and continue such an exchange, perhaps even inspiring others in the newsgroup or message area to take sides.)

form support To *support* is to allow for, or to be capable of using; Web browser that has form support is one that allows for (is capable of using) on-screen *forms,* which are on-screen versions of the types of forms you'd usually see on paper. Netscape includes form support.

Free-net A network in a community providing free access to the Internet; often the Free-net includes the community's own forums and news.

freeware Programs that are distributed free of charge by those who developed them.

front end The "face" you see on a program, its *interface*, is also often called its *front end.* Sometimes, one program provides a *front end* for other programs or for viewing data or files. Thus, Netscape is a front end for the Internet.

FTP The acronym for *File Transfer Protocol,* a standard, agreed-upon way for electronic interaction to occur in the transferring of files from one computer to another over the Internet.

FYI Electronic shorthand for *for your information.*

gateway A computer system that transfers data or messages between programs or networks that are normally incompatible.

gopher A menu-based system for finding directories on the Internet. Gopher will "go-fer" what you ask it to find.

graphical Represented by pictures or icons.

GUI Short for *graphical user interface;* a gui provides a way for you to interact with your computer by pointing and clicking or otherwise manipulating pictures and icons on the screen.

hack To fiddle around "behind the scenes" in a program or system, presumably to make improvements or to find out how the thing works. (A "hacker" is actually someone who makes furniture with an axe. No kidding.)

header The information at the *head* or top of a page, as in the message header containing the To:, From:, and Time/Date information in an e-mail message.

hit A single access of an Internet resource (example: the Enterzone home page gets over 2,000 *hits* per day).

home page The first page you see when you encounter a World Wide Web resource.

host *See* server.

HTML The acronym for *HyperText Markup Language;* the language used to make ordinary text into Web documents. HTML + and HTML 3.0 include enhancements to HTML.

HTTP The acronym for *HyperText Transfer Protocol;* the agreed-upon standard way for electronic interaction to occur in the transferring of Web documents on the Internet.

hypermedia Hypertext combined with graphics, sound, and even video.

hypertext Text that includes links to other documents.

IMHO Electronic shorthand for *in my humble opinion.*

Infobahn The hip and cool term for the so-called information superhighway.

inline image A graphic *in* a Web page—a graphic that does not have to be downloaded to be viewed.

interface The "face" a program shows you, with which you interact.

Internet A global, interconnected network of networks and single computers that act as if they were networks.

IP The acronym for *Internet Protocol; see* TCP/IP.

ISOC The acronym for *Internet Society;* a group whose purpose is to support and govern the Internet.

knowbot An information-retrieval tool, still experimental but wonderfully named.

LAN The acronym for *local area network;* a lot of machines (well, at least *two*) cabled together so they can share resources like printers and software.

link A connection between Web documents, sometimes called a *hot link.*

local Your local machine is the one on your desk, the one that's nearby. Your local drive is the one on your machine. Local is the opposite of *remote.*

lurker Someone who lurks about on a Usenet newsgroup or other interactive forum without contributing anything to the talk. A silent voyeur. Many people think it best to lurk for a while before you join in; that way you'll get to know the customs and avoid social blunders.

modem The device that connects your computer to a phone line so you can make connections via the phone line to other modems, which are connected to remote machines.

Mosaic Any of a group of programs that lets you browse hypertext pages on the World Wide Web. NCSA was the original. Netscape is a Mosaic-like Web browser, but is not actually a Mosaic.

multimedia The combination and use of *multiple types of media* (graphics, sound, video, and text) in a single document or presentation.

NCSA The acronym for *National Center for Supercomputing Applications;* a federally funded research lab run by the University of Illinois that was the birthplace of the original Mosaic.

Netsite Commerce server A Web server, developed and sold by Netscape Communications, that allows providers to make secure transactions available.

network A lot of (or even just two) computers linked via cables or phone lines so they can share resources, such as software, printers, etc.

network administrator The person who organizes, maintains, troubleshoots, and generally watches over a network.

newsgroups Usenet message areas, each of which is focused on a particular topic.

node A machine on the Internet.

online To be ready or electronically connected.

operating system A program that controls the most basic functions of a computer.

packet Data bundled together—a packet may be thought of as similar to an envelope full of data, with some of the data contained in the envelope actually representing the address or destination information. Packets of data traverse the Internet independently of each other because IP, the internet protocol, is connectionless and orderless.

path The complete description of the location of a file on a specific machine.

Ping A utility that lets you see whether a machine is working and connected to the network by sending out a packet that "pings" (or echoes back) when it encounters a specified remote machine.

point-and-click access An Internet access account that provides you with a Windows-type graphical user interface—one in which you point and click your way around the Internet. *See* GUI, shell account.

point of presence A phone number that gives you (presumably) local access to a specific Internet service provider. Sometimes, unfortunately, there's quite a distance from the nearest point of presence (POP) to you, in which case you may be charged long-distance fees by your phone company for the time you're online.

port (a) One of a machine's input/output plugs; (b) A number that identifies a particular Internet server.

post To make public, as in *posting a message.*

PPP The acronym for *Point-to-Point Protocol;* an agreed-upon way for the interaction to occur on a phone line, which allows packets to be transferred along an Internet connection.

protocol An agreed-upon way for an interaction to occur.

public domain To be in the public domain is to be *not* copyrighted; to be available to the public at large.

real-time The Internet term that means *live,* as in "real-time conversation" (a *chat*).

remote Somewhere else. A *remote machine* is not near you; it is somewhere else.

robot An information gathering tool; a program that wanders the Web gathering data and building a database of resources. Also known as a *spider* or *wanderer.*

router A machine that transfers packets of data between networks.

RTFM Electronic shorthand for *read the f***ing manual.*

searchable A document that contains keywords making it easier to search for the specific information contained in the document.

secure transaction An interaction (which may or may not involve money changing hands), over the Internet, that is *encrypted* to protect against prying "eyes."

self-extracting archive file A compressed file that uncompresses itself. *See* compressed.

server A computer that *serves;* the computer that provides stuff to a *client.* *See* client.

service provider The company or organization that provides a connection to the Internet.

shareware Software that is made available by its developer for people to use on a trial basis and, if they like it, to continue to use in exchange for a one-time fee. *Shareware is not in the public domain.*

shell account A Unix-based Internet access account—one in which you have to type Unix commands to make your way around the Internet. Portal Communications and Netcom offer shell accounts, as do some other service providers and many universities. *See* point-and-click access.

SHTTP A form of HTTP, also known as *Secure HTTP*, that allows secure transactions to take place over the Internet.

SLIP The acronym for *Serial Line Internet Protocol;* an agreed-upon way for the interaction to occur on a phone line allowing packets to be transferred along an Internet connection.

smiley Any of a *lot* of little pictures drawn with keyboard characters to indicate an emotion or to illustrate a sentence. The first one in common use was meant to indicate a smile. :-)

snail-mail What the U.S. Postal Service carries and delivers.

SSL The acronym for *Secure Socket Layer*, which is the protocol developed by Netscape Communications to allow for secure transactions over the Internet.

support To *support* is to allow for the use of; as an example, software that supports hypertext is software that allows you to view or create hypertext.

system administrator *See* network administrator.

TCP The acronym for *Transmission Control Protocol; see* TCP/IP.

TCP/IP The acronym for *Transmission Control Protocol/Internet Protocol;* the agreed-upon way machines on the Internet interact with each other by sending packets across multiple networks until they reach their destinations.

telnet An Internet program with which you can log onto another machine (with permission, of course).

time out What happens when two machines are interacting and one does not respond—the other one times out.

Unix The operating system used to develop the Internet.

upload To transfer files from your machine to another machine.

URL The acronym for *Universal Resource Locator;* an address or location of a document on the World Wide Web.

Usenet An informal, anarchistic network of machines that exchange public messages, also known as *news.* Usenet newsgroups tend to focus on specific topics.

Veronica A system, very similar to Archie, that lets you search gopher sites for menu items.

version A new form of a program, usually with new features and tools; often the version is indicated by a number tacked onto the end of the program's name.

viewer A program that lets you view (or otherwise experience) a certain type of data—for example, a viewer is necessary to view video; another viewer is necessary to "view" sound (which you don't see but rather hear).

WAIS The acronym for *Wide Area Information Service;* a system for searching by keyword for information in databases around the Internet.

Wanderer *See* robot.

Web *See* World Wide Web.

workstation (a) The physical area where you work on your computer; (b) A desktop computer, typically more powerful than a PC, running Unix.

World Wide Web On the Internet, a loose network of documents of different types, connected to each other through hypertext links embedded in the documents themselves.

Worm *See* robot.

zip, zipped *See* compressed.

Index

Note to the Reader: Throughout this index **boldfaced** page numbers indicate primary discussions of a topic. Italicized numbers indicate primary discussions of a topic. *Italicized* page numbers indicate illustrations

GET A FREE CATALOG JUST FOR EXPRESSING YOUR OPINION.

Help us improve our books and get a *FREE* full-color catalog in the bargain. Please complete this form, pull out this page and send it in today. The address is on the reverse side.

Name _____   **Company** _____

Address _____   **City** _____ **State** ___ **Zip** _____

Phone (___) _____

---

1. How would you rate the overall quality of this book?

❑ Excellent
❑ Very Good
❑ Good
❑ Fair
❑ Below Average
❑ Poor

2. What were the things you liked most about the book? (Check all that apply)

❑ Pace
❑ Format
❑ Writing Style
❑ Examples
❑ Table of Contents
❑ Index
❑ Price
❑ Illustrations
❑ Type Style
❑ Cover
❑ Depth of Coverage
❑ Fast Track Notes

3. What were the things you liked *least* about the book? (Check all that apply)

❑ Pace
❑ Format
❑ Writing Style
❑ Examples
❑ Table of Contents
❑ Index
❑ Price
❑ Illustrations
❑ Type Style
❑ Cover
❑ Depth of Coverage
❑ Fast Track Notes

4. Where did you buy this book?

❑ Bookstore chain
❑ Small independent bookstore
❑ Computer store
❑ Wholesale club
❑ College bookstore
❑ Technical bookstore
❑ Other _____

5. How did you decide to buy this particular book?

❑ Recommended by friend
❑ Recommended by store personnel
❑ Author's reputation
❑ Sybex's reputation
❑ Read book review in _____
❑ Other _____

6. How did you pay for this book?

❑ Used own funds
❑ Reimbursed by company
❑ Received book as a gift

7. What is your level of experience with the subject covered in this book?

❑ Beginner
❑ Intermediate
❑ Advanced

8. How long have you been using a computer?

years _____
months _____

9. Where do you most often use your computer?

❑ Home
❑ Work

❑ Both
❑ Other _____

10. What kind of computer equipment do you have? (Check all that apply)

❑ PC Compatible Desktop Computer
❑ PC Compatible Laptop Computer
❑ Apple/Mac Computer
❑ Apple/Mac Laptop Computer
❑ CD ROM
❑ Fax Modem
❑ Data Modem
❑ Scanner
❑ Sound Card
❑ Other _____

11. What other kinds of software packages do you ordinarily use?

❑ Accounting
❑ Databases
❑ Networks
❑ Apple/Mac
❑ Desktop Publishing
❑ Spreadsheets
❑ CAD
❑ Games
❑ Word Processing
❑ Communications
❑ Money Management
❑ Other _____

12. What operating systems do you ordinarily use?

❑ DOS
❑ OS/2
❑ Windows
❑ Apple/Mac
❑ Windows NT
❑ Other _____

13. On what computer-related subject(s) would you like to see more books?

_____

_____

_____

_____

14. Do you have any other comments about this book? (Please feel free to use a separate piece of paper if you need more room)

_____

_____

_____

_____

- - - - - - - - - - - - - PLEASE FOLD, SEAL, AND MAIL TO SYBEX - - - - - - - - - - - -

SYBEX INC.
Department M
2021 Challenger Drive
Alameda, CA
94501

Let us hear from you.

 **T**alk to SYBEX authors, editors and fellow forum members.

 **G**et tips, hints and advice online.

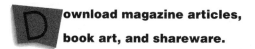 **D**ownload magazine articles, book art, and shareware.

Join the SYBEX Forum on 🖥 **CompuServe**®

If you're already a CompuServe user, just type **GO SYBEX** to join the SYBEX Forum. If not, try CompuServe for free by calling 1-800-848-8199 and ask for Representative 560. You'll get one free month of basic service and a $15 credit for CompuServe extended services—a $23.95 value. Your personal ID number and password will be activated when you sign up.

 Join us online today. Type **GO SYBEX** on CompuServe. If you're not a CompuServe member, call Representative 560 at **1-800-848-8199**.

SYBEX (outside U.S./Canada call 614-457-0802)

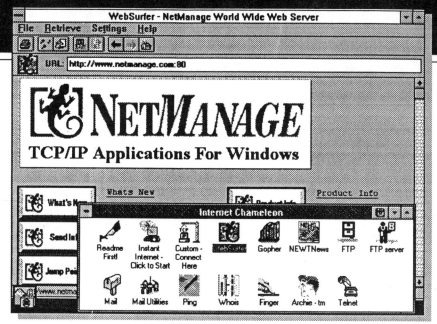

Chameleon Sampler Gets You on the Internet and Gets You Netscape

To get Netscape from the Internet and use it, you need special SLIP/PPP software that "introduces" your Internet service provider to Netscape. Chameleon Sampler from NetManage, Inc. provides you with a fully functional SLIP/PPP connection to the Internet, allowing you to establish the high-speed connection that lets you download and use Netscape, the Web browser of choice today.

This software includes a powerful set of tools you can use to maximize your Internet experience:

◆ TCP/IP software and Winsock capability for the vital SLIP/PPP connection

◆ E-mail for communicating with colleagues and friends all over the world

◆ Telnet for logging on to remote machines on the Internet

◆ FTP for transferring files across the Internet to and from your machine

◆ Ping for determining whether a remote machine is available on the Internet

See Chapter 8 for instructions on installing Chameleon Sampler and getting Netscape from the Internet; see Appendix A for information about using all the tools Chameleon Sampler has to offer.

Customer Service and Support

For Chameleon Sampler technical support, call (408) 973-7171.

For Netscape technical support, call (800) NET-SITE.

SYBEX®

© 1995 SYBEX Inc.